D1074728

Sales Automation

DONE RIGHT

Sales Automation

DONE RIGHT

LEVERAGING TECHNOLOGY
FOR COMPETITIVE ADVANTAGE
IN SALES

Keith Thompson Ph.D

SalesWays Press
Toronto

SalesWays published books are available at special discounts for bulk purchases by corporations, institutions and other organizations. For more information please contact us through the SalesWays Web Site.

All companies, people, products and situations referenced in examples and case studies throughout this book are totally ficticious and are not intended in any way to relate to real life business situations.

SalesWays Press
P.O. Box 142
Malton, Ontario L4T4C2
905 673 2085
www.SalesWays.com

Library and Archives Canada Cataloguing in Publication
Thompson, Keith T. (Keith Thomas), 1943-
Sales automation done right : selling in the digital age / Keith T. Thompson.
Includes index.
Also available in electronic format.
ISBN 0-9737247-0-6 (bound).--ISBN 0-9737247-1-4 (pbk.)
I. Selling--Data processing. I. Title.
HF5438.35.T48 2005   658.8'00285   C2005-901969

Printed in Canada
10 9 8 7 6 5 4 3 2

Cover by William Ng

CONTENTS

Part 2   The Core Competencies

Part 3   Understanding the Sales Opportunity

Part 4   The Technology of Sales Automation

ILLUSTRATIONS

ACKNOWLEDGEMENTS

This book only happened because of the dedication of a few remarkable individuals who helped carve out the sales method that plays such an important part of the story. From the start, Chris Fales and Chris Hamoen chose CRM and SFA technology as their lifetime career path because they developed an early passion for the possibilities of this exciting business. Darka Migus, the head of a very successful sales team, kept us all on track, so we didn't stray from the guiding principles of the sales process, until she tragically passed away in 2001. This was a dream team, and I thank them all for making it possible.

Throughout the lengthy history of getting this book together I was fortunate to have two wonderful editors. Ted Frankel guided me in the onerous task of crafting my raw material into the beginnings of a respectable book. Leo Law took the mostly complete manuscript and challenged every nook and cranny of it until it met his very high expectations. Without either of them I could not have got this project finished. Jeffrey Barrie, I thank, for his enthusiasm and his efforts to speed up the schedule!

Many other people contributed, and I'm sorry that I can't mention them all by name. But special acknowledgement is due to all those very successful salespeople who lived and breathed the ideas of *sales automation done right*, and put them into practice. After all, they were the ones exposed to the most risk as their livelihood depended on maintaining high sales. But the new technology didn't let them down, and now they are the most ardent proponents of it. Thank you again.

PREFACE

In my early years I was not sure what to do with my life, and I think that this may have eventually given me the credentials to write a book about sales automation. Let me explain.

I studied as a physicist. When I look back, I took the easy way out. Doing physics was the easy way out because I was reasonably good at it—good enough to get a PhD. Unfortunately being good at something doesn't always mean you like it. Some aspects of research physics imposed disciplines that I thought were good for me. I liked the logic and the questioning. I was taught to question everything: Why? Why not? What does this mean? Why does that happen? A physicist never writes anything down unless it is understandable and defensible before their peers.

But at last I realized that physics didn't really excite me—but selling did. Even though I wasn't selling professionally, I was doing my best to persuade everyone I knew that my way was the best, whether it was which car to buy, or which book would make the best read. I wondered about a career in sales, maybe selling the very complicated instrumentation that I used everyday in my research. After all, I had some strong feelings about that too! So eventually, I escaped academia to start a career in high technology sales. Nine years of learning and practicing physics left me with skills I might not otherwise have had. The same skills helped me in my effort to find the best way of using the computer in the sales process.

That's why this book looks at sales automation through a magnifying glass. It examines the process of selling in a way that the technology would want to see it—clearly, with no ambiguity. The origin of the earth in a "big bang" can be described in the few lines of an equation. Why can't an accurate sales forecast depend on a nine-point Probability Matrix and the Priority Cube? In fact, it can, because logic and mathematics are the easiest languages for computers to understand. Existing sales methods need to be rethought so they fit better with the computer. This is what I've tried to do, and I think all those years in physics helped me get it right.

The Beginnings

In the early eighties, a few visionary companies introduced the personal computer, and although it was tagged "personal," it was quickly adopted for business use, and driven by new spreadsheet and database applications that were designed specifically for it. Around that time, I started a distribution company specializing in the sales and service of high technology instrumentation. From the start, I was hooked on the way PCs could assist in all facets of business, even if it had very limited power by today's standards.

Business first adopted the PC in the financial and accounting departments (the Back Office). This is understandable, as the pure number crunching environment of the Back Office suits the computer best. But soon, other high value uses were found. Graphics and Desktop Publishing applications transformed the effectiveness of the marketing department. Networking and electronic mail made it possible for everyone to get *connected*. Also everyone quickly realized that networked PCs provided an excellent solution for the storage and dissemination of information. In large organizations, the PC was a genuine alternative to the mainframe; in small companies it was the first engaging taste of the possible impact of technology on business success.

Sales teams became interested. They are in the Front Office and their concerns were different to their Back Office comrades. While they do deal with numbers, much of their vital information was stored in the form of *text*. If a salesperson engineered a last minute tactic that saved a sale, the details could be recorded, and the information could be reused to secure future deals. To do this, technology was needed that could store *all* the significant events in a company's history with its customers, and then to make that information universally accessible to anyone who might need it. Previously the Mainframe could do it, but, now the PC could too. Technology's promise of connected work teams combined with easy and low cost access to an abundant store of customer information was Nirvana to the early champions of automation in the Front Office.

The technology that first enabled true electronic collaboration between members of the sales team was Ray Ozzie's brainchild, Lotus Notes. Notes brought the essential pieces of the puzzle together in a gloriously unified and easy-to-use package: messaging, synchronization, security, collaboration, databases, and on top of all that, fast application development. In 1993, I realized that our company had to move to Notes if we really wanted a culture in which customer knowledge was created and shared by everyone, no matter where they might be, or what time of day it was.

We took the data from the endless files that resided in the marketing, sales and service departments. Files from paper, computers and people's heads were all put into *one* Notes database. Then we wrote the applications that allowed everyone to put information in, and take information out. When we finished, we had developed our own Customer Relationship Management (CRM) software. But, going forward from the progress we had made, we were fascinated by another important question. Given that the computer had so much capability to store information and analyze it in a million different ways, should it not also have the potential to help win a sale? I don't mean in the sense of being a glorified secretary, but actually getting involved in the sales process itself. The hopeful result would be that the salesperson would *win* more sales.

SFA and CRM

The term "Customer Relationship Management" or CRM, describes the vision and effort used by a company to develop close bonds with its customers. In the last ten years, software applications have been developed that are indispensable in making CRM objectives happen. CRM is predominantly focused on Front Office (customer facing) processes, and sales is a very important part of the Front Office.

The sales department is only one (albeit very important) element of the Front Office. Processes that happen in the sales department contribute to the overall CRM effort. Sales Force Automation (SFA) is about using computers to make sales teams perform better, and part of that mission is tightly integrated with CRM process, but part of it is not. This is why the understanding of CRM and SFA has too many businesses and salespeople confused.

The terms SFA and CRM are often confused and wrongfully equated. Sales Force Automation should focus on increasing the *effectiveness* of the salesperson, that is, to make them more competitive in the sale itself. This is a little outside of the scope of CRM, which is more focused on the *efficiency* of the salesperson in handling the customer transaction. As you can see, SFA and CRM are closely intertwined and even though some readers might think this book should be called "Customer Relationship Management done right," that would not be correct. *Sales automation done right* strives to demystify the separate identities of CRM and SFA by focusing on the impact of technology on *sales effectiveness*.

My company's early work in using technology in the business had given us a CRM tool in which we could embed our sales automation. After all, we had a company to run and our business was selling. Our primary objective was to give a computer to every salesperson and let them run with it. When we looked at existing sales methods, we realized they were designed in an earlier time—before computers were so easily accessible. We now had to devise a method to fit the computer.

Developed and Tested in Real Life

Over a ten year period, we crafted the ideas and methods that form the bulk of *sales automation done right*. The design team was a wonderful mix of seasoned (but open-minded) sales veterans and enthusiastic young computer programmers. The ideas presented here evolved through debate, argument, and acres of diagrams scrawled over whiteboards and the backs of napkins. As we developed the ideas, we rolled them out through the software to the sales force. We had a dozen salespeople, so we quickly got feedback on whether our stuff worked, and in many cases we had to do some fine tuning.

The reason that I am a zealot for automation in sales is that I have first hand experience of the dramatic benefits it can bring to the success of the company. Our CRM and SFA infrastructure enabled our business to sustain double digit growth over many years, with very little increase in administrative and support overhead. Our salespeople were able to win more sales by being more competitive and more efficient. The thing is, any company can do it, but sadly, most don't. Large enterprises have rushed to embrace sales automation (through CRM), but small business is lagging way behind. It's a pity, because the payback can be very high and the returns come quickly. There's no doubt that managers and executives who have the ability to make the changes are thinking about it, but with this kind of business change, it's easy to deliberate on the issue for far too long. I hope that some of the ideas presented here will provide the catalyst to hasten more budding projects into reality.

How to Read It

If I pick up a new book, I always skim it. I gravitate to books that lend themselves to be read that way, so it's no surprise that *sales automation done right* is just like that. For that reason, there are a lot of diagrams. The chapters tend to be short, and are divided into five Parts. Essential points are summarized at the end of each chapter. In Parts 2, 3 and 4 there is an underlying thread which is important for the reader to understand.

Part 1 talks generally about SFA, what it is and how it relates to CRM. It discusses the impact of CRM and SFA on the company and the people within it, and how it affects and changes company culture. There is also an illustration of the natural steps that organizations follow in adopting technology to solve operational and process pains, and how to short track the final solution.

Part 2 shows how the day-to-day selling activity evolves around four core competencies of selling management. It shows how sales automation can have a positive impact on the administration, organization and management challenges associated with those competencies.

Part 3 is the heart of the book and centers on the *meaning* of "selling" and the need to describe it in a language that the computer can understand. It shows how customer interactions fall into two distinct categories, one of which leads to the framework of the sales process. A picture of the sales cycle evolves with fundamental selling skills used in the appropriate way as the sale develops. A generic way to gain consistency in forecasting is presented, and a link is drawn between the judged value of a sale at a specific point in the sales cycle to the priority that the sale has in a portfolio of opportunities.

Part 4 homes in on technology and the different ways it impacts the goals of sales automation. There is discussion of how a model of the sale can be derived, which can then be stored in the computer and used to measure progress in an actual sale. The importance of good interface design is explored, along with the advances in hardware and connectivity that make the application useable.

Part 5 briefly discusses the issues that are important to make sure the sales automation project works, warns of potential pitfalls, and reflects on the importance of technology as applied to improving sales effectiveness.

A few words about the layout: Propositions are scattered liberally in most of the chapters, and are meant to be thought-provoking. Bolding stamps out **big** words that are essential to the concept and italicizing reinforces the *power* of the word in its context.

A number of definitions appear in the text, where appropriate, mainly in discussion of the sales method. A more complete collection of definitions is included in the glossary.

Even though the content of *sales automation done right* was conceived in the working business environment of a company that was at the smaller end of the SME (Small to Mid Enterprise) designation, I think that the material is of value to anyone in sales, from the executive heading up the global sales operation, to the manager of a small sales team, to the solo salesperson working it out on their own. The wonderful thing about the sales process is that it is simple, elegant and universal.

Whether you have the stamina to plough through it all, or you just catch a piece that makes your sales effort stronger, I hope *sales automation done right* makes an enjoyable read.

Technology and Sales

CHAPTER I

Blending Technology with Techniques

To do it right—you can't have one without the other

Technology is dramatically transforming the way people do things. Acutely aware of this, business is scrambling to reinvent itself. Companies are striving to profit from any way that technology can streamline and enhance all their business processes. Technology is revolutionizing and redefining every corner of the organization.

There's no excuse to remain in the dark ages. The best technology is *affordable* to any business, and the last ones to find this out will be left in the dust. Even solo entrepreneurs working in basement offices are using technology that was previously the domain of the large enterprise: global communication, accounting, finance, graphic design, electronic marketing, and more.

The way technology is used is also changing. Until recently, companies focused on using technology **inwardly**: making more product and cutting expenses. Now they are turning **outwardly** towards the customer. Technology can play a pivotal role in fostering closeness with the customer, which is something that every organization wants and can use to differentiate itself from the competition.

Every CEO voices the mantra of "Know your customers and serve them well," but how do they make it happen? The whole company has to get involved and focused—especially marketing, sales and customer service. These are the three functional groups, known collectively as the Front Office, that are first in line to interface with the customer. The way to move the company closer to the customer is to apply technology to the Front Office, and the best place to start is in the sales department.

Automating the Sales Department

Part I is an overview of the positive changes that techology can impart to the sales team. The team is an important concept because modern field salespeople rely heavily on the support organization around them.

Sales automation is a **tool** which has the potential to produce a significant increase in sales for the salesperson together with the company, organization, or enterprise. Actually, the word *significant* is not strong enough; good sales automation solutions produce *dramatic* increases in sales. But there are caveats. Sales automation products differ a lot in capability, and a successful roll-out of automation across the company takes a lot of commitment from everyone.

Automation for the sales team is inevitable. Every company will eventually get there. It's as certain as the adoption of the network, the notebook computer, and the word processor. Companies have started to realize this, and have decided that if they don't provide their salespeople with computers, they will buy their own (maybe with dangerous consequences). But the toughest issue is how to do automation right, since it is so easy to do it wrong.

Proposition
Sales automation done right blends technology with techniques.

The overall premise is that to harness technology for the selling process, the traditional established techniques of selling need to be translated to a form that can be understood and utilized by the computer.

Technology

The technology that propels sales automation is based on computers, networks, and the application software that makes it all tick.

After the personal computer established itself in business, PC networks followed closely behind. Networks assist people to work in teams, no matter how far apart they may be. Sales teams can be scattered across thousands of miles and different time zones; some are on the move and others are tied to the office. In the past few years, a new type of software dependent on networks has enabled teams to communicate and collaborate freely. Sales automation comes alive when it runs on this kind of technology. The ability to exchange ideas, information, and strategies in real-time, makes the sales team more efficient and competitive. Add the potential of the largest network of all—the Internet—and we throw a whole new light on the possibilities of automation. The Internet's capacity to reduce communication costs and to provide universal accessibility is now well entrenched in business.

Application software is the "stuff" that makes the hardware come alive. We see later that there are two ways to sell better. One is by freeing up more time to sell, and the other is by becoming more skilful. Only with the right application software will we achieve the compound benefits of **efficiency** and **effectiveness**.

This book describes exactly what to look for as you embark on your search—features, frills, and ideas that determine if the sales automation solution is done right.

Techniques

The thread that weaves throughout *sales automation done right* is that technology alone is not enough. Sales automation should incorporate established techniques that are rooted in the process of selling.

Techniques (*selling* techniques) are the time-tested maneuvers, strategies and tactics that ensure the best chance of winning the sale from the competition. We are not talking about fancy new sales systems, but rather the traditional *proven* rules of selling. However, there's a twist. We need to adapt, refine, and tune "tried and true" selling techniques to leverage the enormous benefits of technology in assisting the sales process.

Salespeople must know *unambiguously*, "Is this a lead or an opportunity?" "Am I starting to prove too early?" "Where am I in the sales cycle?" "Should I try to close this sale before the competition gets in ahead of me?" True sales automation integrates an appropriate sales method directly into the software that makes the answers to these issues clear.

A Foundation Built on Sales Methodology

There are two compelling reasons for sales automation to be built from the ground up using a strong sales method.

The first is to immerse the sales force in a "best practice" selling culture by embedding that culture in the productivity tool that they are all craving for—the computer. Regular sales training is not practiced as much as it should be. Every so often, sales managers will put their teams through a sales course. Then what happens? Everyone forgets to practice what they've learned. The methodology has to be *in-their-face* every day. What better way of achieving this than to have the sales methodology infused within the software? The software plays out the method and the method is in sympathy with the software. This way, salespeople get *constant reinforcement* of the basic skills of selling.

The second reason is to provide potential for the computer to *proactively* assist salespeople in their everyday selling, meaning their use of true selling skills. Unless the computer *understands* the sales process, this kind of functionality is impossible. This idea is explored in great detail in later chapters, in a way that is new to the arena of sales automation. It will be controversial, especially with salespeople set in the old ways because there will be a large focus on the absolute fundamentals of selling, which they will claim to be thoroughly familiar with. Unfortunately, most people learn sales by being totally immersed in the process before they are ready. Sure, they pick up the essentials, but usually in a fairly haphazard way. Then they move on to more complex instruction on tactical sales which they are required to layer over this imperfect foundation.

Sales automation done right restates the fundamentals of selling in order to build a sales method that's totally compatible with the computer. This is a method that will unleash the extraordinary power of the computer to provide a better way to sell.

Sales Automation—A Definition

Everyone has a different idea of what sales automation really is. That's because just about any software that's been given to salespeople has been tagged with the "automation" label. To some, it is the ability to provide a multimedia presentation on their notebook computer. To others, it is a way to send customers birthday congratulations by e-mail. A manager may see it as the best way to get a consolidated roll-up of the forecast each month. For each definition there are twenty others. However, there is a common thread based on the beneficial use of technology in everyday selling. Sales automation is a catchall phrase that pulls together all sorts of ways that technology can make the sales team sell better. But it helps to have the definition tightened up a bit.

Sales automation: The application of technology to assist in the efforts of selling, indirectly and directly. Indirectly, by improving the salesperson's **efficiency**, and directly, by improving the salesperson's **effectiveness**.

Well-designed sales automation always brings improvements in efficiency to the sales department. But automation must take account of many differing requirements ranging from workflow processes to building a library of knowledge about interactions with customers. All too often, attempts to automate are shoe-horned into place using inadequate tools. Once the process is started, there is often reluctance to go back and start again. The end result can be chaotic and counter-productive.

Sales automation *creates efficiency* by moving away from the traditional paperbound methods of doing things. You can't share information quickly using paper. The only answer is to get rid of filing cabinets and move strategic information onto a digital storage medium. Critical customer information becomes easily accessible to all interested parties in the organization. Going digital makes all business processes electronic, providing easier, cheaper and more accurate customer transactions. These are the *indirect* benefits of automation, and they create efficiency.

But there is another important angle to explore. Can technology make the salesperson more effective? Can there be a fundamental improvement in the true skills of selling, measured by the all-important won/lost ratio? Yes, technology does have the potential to deliver, but, everything has to align for this to happen, and if it works, the rewards are beyond belief. To get it right, salespeople should have confidence in the technology and they must believe in the underlying sales method that drives the automation. Every time it's used, the computer reinforces and teaches the best practices of selling—it *understands* the sales process! Seems far-fetched? But this is exactly what *direct* benefits of sales automation are all about.

Points to Remember

1. Automate your sales force *now*. The competition is already doing it!

2. Build on a strong sales methodology platform using proven principles of selling.

3. Don't just settle for the *indirect* benefits from increased efficiency. Find a solution that also brings *direct* benefits.

CHAPTER 2

Direct and Indirect Benefits

The split personality of sales automation

The terms **direct** and **indirect** benefits have been coined to describe two quite different but equally important aspects of how sales automation impacts the sales team. Indirect benefits have as much influence as direct benefits; you have to have both. Indirect benefits are discussed first, as they are the ones that most good sales automation solutions offer. The same is not true of direct benefits—that's why most of this book is about technology that improves sales effectiveness.

Benefits are indirect if they don't *directly* assist the salespeople to make better use of selling skills. Instead, they work by freeing up more *time* to sell, and providing more support for the selling process. Indirect benefits reduce two major distractions that preoccupy salespeople and defocus them from face-to-face selling: **communications** and **administration**. If these background support processes are reduced, more time can be made available for direct contact with the customer.

Unfettered communication across the entire organization is essential for a competitive sales team. If communication is difficult, selling strategies have less chance of getting implemented properly. There can't be excuses like, "I thought you knew," or "Didn't you get that message yet?" Getting the message through quickly and accurately makes the sales team more nimble and keeps them ahead of the competition. Today, e-mail is the communication tool of choice for customers. Seamless electronic communication should be viewed as a core indirect benefit of successful sales automation because it moves knowledge easily to any part of the company. Successful sales teams need to share information quickly.

Sales administration can get overwhelmed with the management of **lists**: customers, accounts, appointments, products and prices. The early use of computers in business focused on management of lists using database technology. The first successful list-management software application for both personal and business use was Contact Management. Contact Management software provides the ability to store important details about people (contacts) and the interactions that have occurred. In business, important contacts are *customers*. Contact Management applications were the forerunners of today's Customer Relationship Management and Sales Force Automation technology.

Moving lists to the computer creates efficiency, but only if it is done right. Cutting down the number of disparate lists and putting the information in *one place* where everyone has access to it makes life easier. Unfortunately, Contact Management software has been so universally adopted in early attempts at automating sales that users have stretched its capabilities.

Getting work done by moving it through specialized workstations is called **workflow**. Tasks are broken down into manageable pieces, each of which can be handled at one desk. Once completed, it's passed over to the next desk, until the task has been finished. A simple example is processing a sales proposal. The *salesperson* prepares a rough draft of what's needed and sends it to an *inside sales assistant* to work up a formal proposal. The proposal is passed over to *sales administration* who produce the final document, attach product literature, and send the package to the customer. This requires effort by three people in three departments. If one person gets bogged down, the process freezes. The old way of doing workflow is to move paper around the company. Paper is a *nuisance*. It proliferates quickly, is slow to move (because *people* have to move it), and no one knows what to do with it. Sales automation gets rid of paper by moving information electronically. If the electronic process slows to a snail's pace because of a people problem, the computer flags the crisis and demands a change.

Aside from eliminating paper, electronic workflow also gets the job done faster and more accurately. It's best to apply rules to the workflow, such as "You can't do that until you have done this." Instituting rules ensures customer information is up to date and complete. For example, "You can't make a proposal for this customer unless their key information is in the database, and if it isn't, then you must put it in!" If workflow is electronic, this rule is easy to implement. *Sales automation done right* provides many examples where devising sensible rules and sticking to them ensures accurate information, which is something that the customer respects and demands.

The Essential Indirect Benefits

Here's a list of what's needed to apply all the indirect benefits:

- There must be a network. Layered over the network should be effective messaging within the company. Messaging makes communication and collaboration happen. Communication is either "one to one" (send a message to one person only) or "one to many" (send the same message to more than one person). This is easily accomplished by regular e-mail. Collaboration is "many to many" communication; information is put where people can view, add or edit if they need to. This happens through a **shared database**. Examples are sales discussion groups, including the latest news on the activity of the competition, the latest industry gossip or personal stories from the front line on how to win the sale.

- The network solution must remove the constraints of geography (distance) and time. Access to information has to be available for the whole team. When Head Office has gone home for the day on the East Coast, the West Coast salesperson is logging in today's events on the computer. This information can then be accessed at Head Office in the morning. The Internet has revolutionized twenty-four hour accessibility to information.

- Salespeople on the move should have the capability to disconnect from the network and work with their data offline. Later they can reconnect to home base, pick up new material and send back anything they have contributed since being disconnected. The technical name for this mutual exchange of data is **synchronization**. Good synchronization technology also resolves conflict issues when two people may unknowingly edit information at the same time.

- Every time someone in the company interacts with the customer, the essence of the interaction must be recorded in a central database accessible by the sales team.

- Workflow should be automated. Business processes must be made electronic with the goal of streamlining and the *elimination of paper*.

These challenges are focused on improving the salesperson's ability to work efficiently, especially gathering, storing, and disseminating information. The impact of indirect benefits can be huge. If they can be made to work, one part of the equation of sales automation is solved. The other part—how sales automation directly benefits the sales team—is next.

Direct Benefits of Sales Automation

Sales automation has been around for a long time, but without much emphasis on using technology to make the *sales process* come alive. Maybe there's been too much focus on indirect benefits. After all, that's the easiest place to start. **Direct** benefits of sales automation exploit the computer's potential to understand how salespeople sell. When this happens, the computer can provide *proactive* assistance in the sale, dramatically improving *sales effectiveness*.

Sales methodology is central to the vision of the direct benefit. All too often, established sales methods invented in the days before the PC have been translated directly into digital space, which is not much better than using paper forms to manage the sales process. There needs to be a fundamental rethink on how to bring sales methods into line with modern technology. The computer is intensely logical—it is happier crunching billions of numbers in a fraction of a second than trying to figure out why a salesperson is having a tough time in a sale. But if the sales method recognizes the computer's natural disposition towards numbers, it's much easier to derive the direct benefits of automation.

In fact, salespeople are embroiled in numbers much more than they realize. At any time they may have fifty to one-hundred open sales opportunities each at a different point in the sale. Each position in the sales cycle calls for appropriate selling skills. Opportunities differ in their *value*, which determines the attention they get. Value depends on many issues. With the right sales method, it's possible to assign *numeric* value to factors that make up the parameters of the sale. Invariably, the salesperson works it out in their head and uses their gut feel to determine the way to proceed. Sometimes it works, and sometimes it doesn't. It's much better to let the computer do it.

Sales methods crafted for the computer impart some **intelligence** to the technology; the computer takes on an *understanding* of the sales process. The seasoned salesperson will say, "The computer can't teach me how to sell!" This is certainly true if we consider the "Art of Selling," but in the case of the "Science of Selling," things are quite different.

Proposition
Selling is both an art and a science. To be successful, the
salesperson has to master both.

Yes, there are two quite different facets of sales success—one, salespeople are born with, and the other, salespeople (and the computer) can learn.

The Art of Selling

Successful selling depends heavily on interpersonal skills. Salespeople who find it tough to relate to customers will find it very difficult to sell. A large part of the art of selling depends on the *individual* salesperson and what makes them tick. But the art of selling also involves the ability to build talent from experience. It takes years to become consistently successful at sales. There's nothing better than losing a few orders to teach vigilance for the future.

The art of selling is built upon the mostly inherited, but partially learned skills of relating well with people, coupled with wisdom developed through the many trials and errors that occur over a sales career—technology can't help much here. The art of selling gives the salesperson the ability to "read" the customer and to know what they are thinking during discussion. Salespeople who have this flair definitely have an edge, even before their true *selling skills* are put into play.

Although technology hasn't yet developed to the point where it can improve the salesperson's art of selling, in the case of the science of selling, it definitely has.

The Science of Selling

The science of selling is a virtual rulebook that describes how to handle a sale, specifically, where certain skills and strategies should be employed, and to what degree they should be used. These rules have been compiled and refined over many years by sales professionals. They are applicable across a wide range of selling situations and have been tested exhaustively to prove that they work.

Here are a few examples of the rules:

- Every sale has a defined start and finish that together define the sales cycle.

- Each phase of the sales cycle needs emphasis on a particular selling skill.

- Effective sales strategies need an understanding of the competition, even when the *only* competition is the situation of the customer doing nothing.

- Don't try to prove the worth of your solution to the customer until you have established that they may need it.

- Don't try to *close* a sale until the customers have been given enough information to allow them to comfortably make a decision.

There are many more of these rules. Notice that they are of the type, "This is what you *should* or *should not* do at this point." Also notice that the rules need not be exact—that's OK, they are still rules. Some of the rules are industry-specific, but most are general enough that they can be applied to all types of selling. Mastering the rules can only be accomplished by gaining experience with them.

The most successful salespeople master both the art and the science of selling. If the computer helps with the science, the salesperson has more time to devote to the art.

E²—Compounding Direct and Indirect Benefits

Why E squared? Because **efficiency** and **effectiveness** work together as a potent combination to drive sales up. Take a simple example:

The sales automation project is well under way, and after a diligent effort to get the *indirect* benefits in place, there is a 20% improvement in *efficiency*. This means that a salesperson who could previously handle 100 sales opportunities per year comfortably, can now deal with 120. If this team is good, they can turn one out of two opportunities into booked business (their won/lost ratio is 50%). Before automation they achieved 50 sales. After automation they win 60 sales because of the increase in efficiency.

But, what if there is also a 30% improvement in effectiveness? There are 30% more sales that are won. The won/lost ratio goes from 50% to 65%. Out of the newly increased available 120 opportunities, the team now wins 78.

Summary:

Before automation	50 sales
With 20% increase in efficiency	60 sales
With 30% increase in effectiveness	78 sales

Sales have improved by 56%!

This example, although presented simply, shows exactly what can happen in practice. The only barrier is getting the *sales automation done right*. There are many examples of companies that have seen this kind of improvement and even better. However, they are not too eager to divulge all the details to the competition, and that's why there is more news about failed projects.

Be assured that the ideas presented in this book have evolved from direct experience of running a company over a ten year period of intense growth, which was made possible only by the remarkable results of E squared.

Proposition
Effectiveness on top of efficiency produces dramatic increases
in sales. It's the same as compound interest in the bank account.

But that's not all. Believe it or not, streamlining processes and removing paper result in a *decrease in costs*! It takes someone's time to move paper around from desk to desk, and to file the stuff when the job's done. Consolidating random communications into a streamlined electronic workflow also dramatically reduces costs previously incurred by old style methods of mail, courier, fax and phone calls. The same can be achieved with less. Not only is there a reduction in wasted effort, but the same team will be able to handle the extra work brought about through growth in the business.

Points to Remember

1. Interpersonal skills of selling are primarily inherited rather than taught.

2. There is no substitute for experience when it comes to strategizing a sale.

3. There are well-defined rules that can be applied to the selling process *and* which can be understood by a computer.

4. Finding time to work on more sales opportunities *while* improving your chances to win them is a potent combination.

5. Costs go down when a good sales automation product is successfully implemented into the sales organization. Increased sales coupled with decreasing costs make a compelling reason to automate

CHAPTER 3

Sales Methodology

What's the point of definitions?

Sales automation done right is a blend of technology and techniques. By techniques, we mean selling techniques which are part of an overall **sales method**. A method is a *prescribed way* of doing something in accordance with a particular theory. The method involves a set of rules that everyone uses.

A sales method is a recipe for conducting the sales process. It is well defined, and can be written down. For example, "Here is a set of criteria you must use when you convert a lead to an opportunity." Teaching a sales method means teaching the rulebook on the science of selling. The science of selling *can* be taught. In fact, every rookie salesperson will, at some time, be taught the basics of selling either in a formal sales training course, or directly on the job from the experienced sales professional.

A way to ensure that the sales team is up to speed on the essential skills of selling is to make the sales automation and the sales method so intertwined that they become inseparable. Actually, *if* sales automation is done right, there won't be a choice, because the sales method must be there to get the direct benefits. This is a win-win for the sales team. They use the computer to make them efficient, and at the same time, the computer constantly reinforces the sales method that makes them more effective.

Implementing a sales method across the entire sales organization drives a degree of consistency that benefits the company as a whole. It's good to know that customers are getting the same view of the company from all of the front line sales team. Salespeople analyze their sales opportunities in exactly the same way and use the same set of proven selling skills. If everyone grades their sales opportunities using identical criteria, the job of forecasting gets easier and the forecast becomes much more accurate.

Definitions

The rules discussed in the previous chapter, under The Science of Selling, are an important component of a sound sales method, but there is also one other.

> Proposition
> A successful sales method relies on a series of well-understood
> *definitions* that can be used to describe all aspects of the sale.

A definition is the precise meaning of a word or phrase. Direct benefits of sales automation hinge on teaching the computer about the sale, which cannot be done if issues concerning the sale are poorly defined. The computer and the salesperson have to work hand-in-hand; a well understood method with a set of clear definitions can make this happen.

Definitions are part of the theoretical framework of the sales method. For example, differentiating between the terms **lead** and **opportunity** is critical for consistent lead qualification, yet salespeople often use these terms interchangeably. The problem gets worse if the computer is expected to assist with the qualification. There has to be unambiguous definitions of all stages, activities and conditions surrounding the sales process.

A good example of ambiguity is the word *customer*, which has universal usage in sales. The sales team sometimes refers to an organization as a customer, or a person as a customer. In sales automation, this is too vague. Either the computer is not expected to understand the term, or the term is made completely unambiguous through a much tighter definition.

Definitions will crop up repeatedly as we get into the description of a proposed sales method. The reader should put them into the context of their personal selling experiences. As an example, here are three important definitions that occur later in the book.

Sales cycle: The time between the customer contact starting the buying process and the time a decision is made to purchase.

Lead: An interest expressed in a product or service by the customer contact.

Opportunity: The chance that the customer contact gives a salesperson to sell a product or service.

Points to Remember

1. Keep the sales team tuned into the skills of selling by providing them with sales automation that is built from the ground up with a solid sales method.
2. Determine the underlying definitions of your sales method and ensure that both the computer and sales force thoroughly understand them.

CHAPTER 4

SFA and CRM

Not the same thing

A book on Sales Force Automation (SFA) would not be complete without a discussion of Customer Relationship Management (CRM). Unfortunately these two terms are often confused and sometimes used interchangeably— even by the experts. SFA and CRM are closely intertwined, but are *not* the same thing.

Chapter 2 defined SFA as using technology to make the salesperson more efficient and effective. Technology is an essential part of the definition of SFA. However, CRM was originally a *vision* of how businesses should develop a new closeness to their customers. Throughout the extraordinary growth of the CRM industry in the past ten years, the defining vision of CRM has become entangled with the issue of the technology needed to realize it. This is purely a matter of definition, but it is important for anyone in business who is considering a CRM project to clarify before they go ahead.

CRM is not exclusive to the sales department because it applies to *every* part of the organization. It involves a process that works toward a perfect partnership between the supplier and the customer, one that is founded on *collaboration* and *trust*. Achieving the goal of CRM only happens if the maintenance of this relationship is a lifelong mission.

We'll see that SFA and CRM share some important components, but the central thesis behind SFA, which is increasing sales effectiveness, reaches outside of the meaning of CRM.

CRM—A Vision of Doing Business

CRM is a **philosophy** which attempts to ignite everyone within the company to focus their efforts toward the goal of customer intimacy. Someone in the company should be evangelical about the benefits that CRM can bring, and must have authority and determination to force the belief of CRM into every corner of the organization.

Proposition
The two defining elements of a successful CRM strategy are process and knowledge.

Building relationships with customers can't happen unless the customer likes and wants your product. Product doesn't just mean the goods or services in the price-book—it also encapsulates the way business is conducted *before* and *after* the sale is made, that is, the entire **customer transaction.**

The customer transaction encompasses finding the customer, satisfying their needs, and building lifetime loyalty and commitment. Successful Customer Relationship Management demands that all the processes in the company that move the customer transaction within and between departments are seamless, efficient and effective.

The more companies understand the people they do business with, the more they can customize their approach of doing business. How often does the customer buy something? What are their preferences or tastes? Does the customer take time to evaluate competitive products, or do they prefer to deal with a well-tried and proven vendor even though the cost might be higher? The only way to answer these questions is to collect information over time about all that happens between anyone in the company and the customer. That word *anyone* is important as it means that all groups or departments in the company share in the responsibility of reaching the CRM goal.

Therefore, an indispensable byproduct of the CRM philosophy is a complete history of all of the *interactions* between the company and the customer; a complete store of knowledge that defines what has happened in the past (good or bad), and one that sets the benchmark as to what should happen in the future. We call this bank of information the **Customer Knowledge Store.** The Knowledge Store must be regularly reviewed, updated and renewed to reinforce the CRM vision. It is only useful if people have access to it, which means that its information must be freely available across the whole organization. If this happens, the exact needs of the customer can be *predicted* and the product can be *customized* to match, which is one of the core objectives of CRM. The idea is to be sufficiently close to the customer to know what's important to them. Once this happens, supplier and customer can enjoy a much more rewarding business experience.

CRM Technology

The basic idea behind managing customer relationships is as old as the hills, but the term CRM is relatively new. Today, CRM is almost universally understood as meaning the **technology solution** that helps achieve the customer relationship vision. Why? Because technology can really make that vision come true, especially when it comes to process and knowledge.

Networked computer systems are the best enablers of process. They also provide the platform for communication and collaboration so that everyone knows what the other is doing. But managing the Customer Knowledge Store is where technology really shines. Information Technology and Knowledge Management are technology tools that pull information from far and wide within the organization—information that holds the knowledge about the customer. Technology not only makes it possible to store vast amounts of data efficiently, but also to break it down into data subsets that aid in customizing services and products to better fit client needs.

Front Office and Back Office

Front Office is a term used for the functional groups of a company that have the most direct contact with customers, most obviously marketing, sales, and after-sales service. The people outside of the Front Office are in the Back Office. Back Office groups are those that process the customer's transaction inside the company. They include manufacturing, inventory control, shipping/receiving, or support teams such as finance or IT. Associating CRM technology with just the Front Office is misleading, but that's the way the CRM industry has evolved. It doesn't matter how well marketing can find a new customer, or how well sales can persuade the customer, or how well service can care for the customer if manufacturing cannot make the product in a reasonable amount of time. *Everyone* is responsible for meeting the demands of CRM.

The Back Office teams have had technology to help them for years. The benefits of making the Back Office more efficient are much more visible—costs go down, product gets out quicker, and profits can be easily tracked directly to action taken. For this reason, business has found it easier to spend money on the Back Office than the Front Office. Now that the Back Office has been computerized, many companies are looking to see if it is possible to harness technology to serve the Front Office. However, the problem is different; you need another kind of technology for Back Office than for Front Office. The Back Office is concerned with directly processing the transaction between the company and the customer. We are dealing with number crunching here—numbers that show lead times, inventory levels, profit, losses and much more. However, the Front Office deals with textual rather than numerical data. This is information on our relationship with the customer. What was the last conversation that the salesperson had with the customer concerning the proposal for their latest project? What went wrong on the last preventative maintenance visit by the service department? Is the customer prepared to act as a reference for the support that has been provided? What is the content of the last mail-piece that the customer received on our newest product, and did the customer send in the return slip?

A good example of the unique requirements of Front and Back Office is the way accounts are allocated. The accounting department almost always sets up accounts according to the customer's payment locations. This account designation may have nothing to do with the way the sales department needs the accounts to be set up. The sales department is more interested in breaking down customer organizations into convenient groups that they can market and sell to. For small customer organizations, the account designations for Front Office and Back Office may be the same, but for large customers they are typically quite different. Customer contacts also tend to be different; the Front Office talks to buyers and users, whereas the Back Office talks to the administrative structure of the customer's organization.

So, we really do need two different technology solutions for Front and Back Office, although that does not mean that the two systems should not talk to one another. The premise of CRM, as we said, is to drive everyone from both Front and Back Offices to be customer focused. For this reason, there has to be sharing of information between the two. It is not within the scope of this book to explain how this can be done, but suffice to say, it is best to find the "best of breed" solution for each domain, and make the job of connecting the two systems a separate project. Does all information have to be shared? Of course not. There is such a thing as "information overload." The Customer Knowledge Store needs sufficient information for everyone to make the CRM vision work. Each group—sales, accounting, or manufacturing will have their own Knowledge Store needed to complete their part of the customer transaction. The Knowledge Store will have a subset of this data for everyone to share, enough to piece together the full story of the current relationship with the customer.

If we take a close look at how the customer's transaction is processed between the Front Office departments, we will begin to see the how CRM and SFA are related.

The Front Office CRM Process

Finding customers, selling them product, and maintaining the quality of the product after the sale is made, are responsibilities of the Front Office organization. Ideally, there is a smooth process flow between the three core departments of marketing, sales and service. Figure 4-1 is a diagram showing the essential steps.

Note the words that define the Front Office CRM process: POTENTIAL—**Identify**—TARGET—**Market**—LEAD—**Qualify** —SALES OPPORTUNITY—**Win**—NEW CUSTOMER—**Nurture**.

For the product or service that we are selling, there is a POTENTIAL number of customers out there that could buy it. From that potential, we **identify** a TARGET group of customers to whom we focus our **marketing** efforts. Through our marketing, we produce LEADS—indications that we have contacts who might be interested in buying from us. Leads must be **qualified**, and if the interest from the contact is genuine, we have discovered a SALES OPPORTUNITY.

Everything in the CRM process to this point comes under the mandate of the marketing department. That is, marketing scours the available market, promotes the product and service and finds real opportunities for the sales department. Whether or not your company is big enough to have a separate marketing department doesn't matter; whoever is fulfilling the process above is wearing a marketing hat.

Figure 4-1: The Front Office CRM process

Marketing then hands over the sales opportunity to the sales department, whose job it is to convince the customer that the product is best suited to their needs. The goal is to **win** the order and create a NEW CUSTOMER.

Notice that we show only one step in the CRM process that is devoted to sales. Even so, this step is the most important one in creating success for the company. This is the part of the process that is driven by sales automation technology.

Proposition
Sales automation is at the core of the CRM technology tool
and has the potential to provide the most business reward.

CRM doesn't work unless you have customers. CRM alone won't ensure a steady flow of customers, so we need the sales department to contribute their special skills to make this happen.

Once the sales department has signed up a new customer, the service team must **nurture** the customer throughout the lifetime of the product or service that was purchased. What comes after the sale is made is as important as what goes before it. The customer must be happy with the buying decision in order to come back again when the need for a replacement or new product arises. When this happens, they are considered a POTENTIAL purchaser for new product. If they buy again, they become a repeat customer. One of the foremost benefits of a well-implemented CRM process is being able to keep existing customers, as well as create new ones. That is why we refer to the Front Office process diagram using the long-winded title of **customer acquisition and retention loop**. It costs a lot for the company to find a new customer, but it costs much less to retain an existing one, and this is why CRM technology is enjoying so much attention.

Where SFA Fits In

The whole CRM process loop can be automated with computer technology. Indeed, there are products that focus on just the automation of marketing, or sales, or service, but most automation vendors offer products that focus on the complete customer acquisition and retention loop. Here we have to be careful when we evaluate the part that focuses on sales. Sales automation delivers on two distinct fronts: one of which is CRM related, and one that really isn't. When you choose a product, you may have to decide which is of greatest importance to you: winning the sale or enabling your CRM vision. Unfortunately, it's all too easy to pick something that does one or the other well, but not both.

> Proposition
> The expectations of SFA are twofold: (1) To contribute to the development of knowledge about the customer's relationship with the company and (2) To bolster the critical CRM process step of winning the sale.

The key to understanding this is recognizing that some people think if you know your customers well enough and are zealous in preserving your relationship with them, you will always get the sale. That's not necessarily the case because we are overlooking the issue of "How well can you sell?" (we're back to the familiar territory of the direct benefits of sales automation). An overriding objective of sales automation software should be to assist in closing more sales through directly improving the ability to sell.

Yes, one important focus of sales automation is to record information that is needed for the Customer Knowledge Store. Salespeople have to be one of the best sources of this information as they are on the front line when it comes to customer contact. But sales automation was first introduced as a way for salespeople to close more sales rather than as just a building block of the overall CRM vision. Then sales automation got drowned in a frenzy of big business adopting the "customer intimacy" theme. The original idea, centered on making the salesperson more *effective* took a backseat. Fortunately, there is now a swing back to the core objective of SFA. Sales teams everywhere are demanding tools that offer the promise of sales improvement in the most defining sense; bringing in more sales because of superior selling skills.

Good SFA delivers on both counts. It is a major contributor to the company's CRM initiative and a driving force in building sales effectiveness, which leads to a recurring theme.

Relationship or Opportunity Focused?

Companies that believe that good customer relations are all that's needed to produce sales organize their sales teams accordingly. Their salespeople become account managers, nurturing people and organizations in a well-structured way. We refer to this style of selling as being **relationship focused**. Other companies however, home in on the sales opportunity, emphasizing the importance of discovering it early and using carefully planned strategic approaches to stay ahead of the competition. Here, the emphasis is on using true selling skills. This style of selling is **opportunity focused**. Which way is right? They both can be, but *sales automation done right* encourages a mix of the two. Some might say that the ability to work well and relate with the customer is a selling skill, but in fact, it is a distinctly different skill than the one required for competitive selling. The best salespeople have the ability to use both relationship oriented skills and raw selling skills; they adjust the blend of skills according to the need.

Interactions between the salesperson and the customer are important in building the substance of the Customer Knowledge Store. In any interaction with the customer, salespeople can show different degrees of relationship and opportunity focus, and according to the time and the place, one focus will win over the other. When that happens, we must be sure to recognize that the intrinsic nature of the interaction has dramatically changed. Interactions that predominantly involve relationship focused selling are called **relationship focused interactions**. Ones that heavily depend on the opportunity focused style are referred to as **opportunity focused interactions**.

Later on, Chapter 14 shows how *characterizing* customer interactions according to the relative use of relationship building skills or basic selling skills is essential to *sales automation done right*. You can't separate the idea of CRM from the skills of selling, but the salesperson's job is made that much easier if the customer respects their company and product. A good sales automation product will be mindful of one central tenet of the CRM philosophy, and that is to monitor the company's success or lack of it in serving the customer. Opportunity focused interactions are the heart of SFA, and relationship focused interactions are central to CRM. In fact, without the idea of the opportunity focused interaction, *sales automation done right* would be hard-pressed to define the sales process (more on this in Chapter 14). The definition of CRM in terms of *process and knowledge* applies equally well to SFA, but process takes on a much more significant meaning in the context of sales process. What goes on in the sales process occupies over fifty percent of this book.

The Sales Team

High customer expectations combined with more complex products makes it impossible for the salesperson to carry out the sale alone. Companies are now seeing that selling is a **team** effort, and that nothing beats the strategy of *sending out the team* to win customers' confidence in the product. The heart of the team is the salesperson and their manager, but at some point, we need *specialists*, the product experts, and the people who understand the myriad of customer requirements that may necessitate customized configurations. The customer service team may also be needed in some pre-sales strategies. Inevitably, the team, and not the sales representative alone, forge and implement the strategy of winning the sale.

Proposition
Sales automation reinforces and assists team selling.

Why is that? Because sales automation empowers and encourages discussion with every member of every team. Developing and tuning sales strategies on-the-fly is much easier if everyone has up-to-the-minute information on the dynamics of the sale. Moving faster than the competition makes the difference between winning and losing. The automated sales department will be way ahead of the pack.

Politics

Even though companies have flattened their organization structures, **hierarchies** are still there, especially in the sales organization. But salespeople are getting less nervous about managers looking over their shoulder. Soon, the idea of the sales force (**Us**) and sales management (**Them**) being at odds with each other will be obsolete. Both parties are striving to sell as much as possible.

Proposition
Sales automation breaks down hierarchical structures by making information available to everyone in the company.

Bear in mind, customers are oblivious to the internal politics of companies courting their business. They are inclined to give their business to the sales teams who act with *shared enthusiasm*. Sharing information across the company is not optional, it's mandatory. Today's technology makes it impossible to be selfish with information, thereby breaking down the barriers between us and them.

The Culture of Sharing

Part of the redesigning process that a company goes through in adopting CRM is an introspective evaluation of its own internal culture of sharing. The unassuming little word **share** plays a big role in CRM, and by default, sales automation. Making information freely accessible across the organization is one of the major indirect benefits. Sharing is something that many people find difficult to do, and often, a major shift has to occur to make it happen in business. Sharing is OK when we need to use material that someone else has contributed, but what if we have to share our own hard-earned knowledge around the team? The answer is, "Get used to it," because without the sharing of information, the sales *team* can't function. The central theme of this new technology is that *sharing is in*. There's no reason to hide stuff anymore—it's all there for the team to share and use. Everyone must adapt and reap the rewards.

Salespeople still get a bad rap for protecting their territorial rights and the information they uncover. It's taking a long time to dismantle the adage, "Information is power." The sales team has to understand that information is only powerful *if it is shared*. Salespeople regard the idea of sharing with trepidation. After all, they are encouraged to run their own show with their own territory and accounts. They maintain their own sphere of influence, and, if the *numbers* are OK at the end of the quarter, everything is fine. Salespeople develop a protective stance about anything belonging to their "turf" and won't share any more than is necessary about what's happening. This is one of the most common reasons that sales automation projects fail. Previously, *not sharing* has been easy to do because the technology that makes it easy and transparent to do so simply was not there. Now, things are different.

New ideas about creating closeness to the customer (CRM) make it a requirement that all customer interactions are kept, and the knowledge be made accessible to everyone across the organization. This is the way to provide exactly what the customer wants. Marketing can tailor its campaigns to customers with similar interests. Field Service can measure their success (or failure) with ensuring the customer's long-term commitment to the product. This is only possible if the database can tell us about the customer, what they want most and how they feel about us.

Salespeople are in the enviable position of being nearest to the customer, and they must be the mouthpiece of the customer. If this information is not collected, warehoused, and studied, there will be serious holes in the company's understanding of the customer—something that can't be tolerated given that the company is committed to the vision of CRM.

Successful organizations get close to their customers and are passionate about it. Technology can be used effectively in this mission, but technology is only the enabler. There must also to be a culture of sharing built on everyone's understanding that *they* can contribute an important "piece of the pie."

Points to Remember

1. CRM and SFA are not the same. SFA is a technology tool that automates the sales department with the principle goal of increasing sales effectiveness. CRM is a philosophy that stretches outside the scope of sales into all other parts of the organization.

2. Beware of the distinction between SFA and CRM when you are putting technology to work in the Front Office. Don't neglect the enormous potential of SFA to improve the sales team's closing rate. This can happen if you select a CRM product that has an inadequate sales component.

3. If your company is moving into team selling, sales automation will provide a tool to energize your team and coordinate their efforts.

4. Sales automation breaks down cultural and hierarchical barriers by supporting and encouraging sharing of information.

CHAPTER 5

Customer Knowledge Store

Reaping the benefits of past efforts

The previous chapter stressed the need to record information on every aspect of the way business is conducted with the customer. When this information becomes suspect—inaccurate, dispersed or difficult to retrieve, we have the first signs of trouble, and there is no hope of pushing the CRM vision forward. The lack of a Customer Knowledge Store, or a Store that is not trusted, is the first call to arms to institute CRM technology. There comes a point in a company's growth when the need to consolidate the storage of strategic information becomes evident. The warning signs are the proliferation of inadequate, duplicated data and the inevitable frustration of the people having to deal with it.

Disconnected Databases

An unavoidable result of the way in which companies evolve is that important information gets scattered and strewn around the organization. Growth is always accompanied by the formation of functional groups, each with its specific expertise in getting a part of the operational process accomplished. It is natural that a certain degree of autonomy develops in these departments. They are jealous of the information they have accumulated and sometimes reluctant to share it. They start to *hoard* data about their dealings with the customer, and the result is **multiple disconnected databases.**

Usually, an individual group decides how and where they will store the information. Accounting may use their Back Office computer system, marketing may use a separate relational database, sales may rely on paper in file cabinets, and service may use a spreadsheet. It sounds like a mess, and often it is. It's obvious that this process leads to uncontrolled duplication, and unfortunately, the first thing to suffer is the accuracy of the knowledge about the customer.

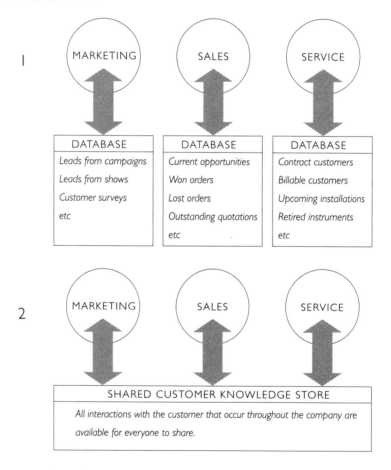

Figure 5-1: Reducing multiple knowledge stores to just one

Consider an example of a small company in this dilemma. The marketing department has a central list of potential customers stored for use in generating leads. The sales department also has a list of active customers in the process of buying a product—the all-important "opportunity" list that drives the forecasting process. Moving on to after-sales service, this group should be keeping information on customers who own the company's products. In addition, there are lists of support requests, warranty commitments, or service contract customers. The company has at least a half-dozen different places where information on customers or potential customers is stored. The left hand does not know what the right hand is doing. Inevitably, the customer suffers! Figure 5-1 shows the problem.

Figure 5-1 (1) shows the situation just described, where marketing, sales and service keep their own store of information about the customer and there is no direct sharing of knowledge. To get information, you walk from one department to another and ask for it—if you know that it exists there. As the organization matures, these disparate pockets of information grow out of proportion, and it becomes more and more difficult to dig down for historical data that could assist in making current dealings with customers more effective.

When a company is at this point, they are in a lot of pain. The problem becomes obvious to everyone who needs access to *complete* information to help them service the customer transaction. Waste and inefficiency creep in, but also a recognition that something needs to be done about it.

Things change in Figure 5-1 (2) of the diagram, after the implementation of CRM technology. Information is gathered from all over the organization and stored in one place for everyone to share. First, all the critical data is taken out of the filing cabinets and put into a standard electronic format, with no exceptions company-wide. If necessary, information is downloaded on a regular basis from other departments' databases into the common shared database. Everyone who needs the information has the means to access it whenever and wherever they want.

There are "out of the box" technology solutions that make this process straightforward and cost effective. There is no excuse, not even, "We can't afford it." The truth is, you can't afford not to. Even the smallest of companies have to quickly recognize when they are in the multiple disconnected database mode, and get out of it as quickly as possible. Not doing this will mean waste, frustration, and cost.

What Information Do We Keep?

What information is of such strategic importance that we need to keep it? This is an important question to get to grips with before implementing a CRM system. The answer is to keep all the information about any interaction between the company and the customer which contributes toward fulfillment of the **customer transaction**, an idea first discussed in the previous chapter.

The customer transaction is driven by the process at the center of the customer acquisition and retention loop. How did marketing find the customer? How was the customer qualified? How did the sales process progress? How long did it take to deliver on our promises? Does the customer like our product? Would the customer buy from us again? Each question needs a host of information to qualify its answer. In addition, notice that we need to assemble data from both Front and Back Office. To gauge how effectively we delivered on our promises, we need to know things like, Did the customer's order get held up by a credit check? Did manufacturing run out of a critical part which slowed down delivery? We also need to know the answers to other issues that impact our future business, such as, did the customer pay the invoice on time?

Even though the Customer Knowledge Store has to be filled with data from all parts of the organization, the heart and soul of the Store should reside in the Front Office. Part of the reason is that if you look at the CRM process as linear, the start of it resides with the marketing and sales departments. These are the people who first find the customer and log the essential information: name, address, organization, business likes/dislikes, account, sales territory, and much more. This is the start of a lifetime effort to store the data on that customer. The marketing and sales departments also have to review and maintain customer information, and they are best qualified to do it.

Information can be put into the Knowledge Store directly, or can be downloaded from an external source (be careful here, it first has to be "cleaned;" someone should review it for accuracy before it goes in). The field salesperson will directly enter the core information on an important visit with the customer. Statistics on accounts or individual contacts can be entered automatically at set time intervals. Remember, the idea is that anyone in the company who needs the "big picture" should have the relevant data at their fingertips. Some data will be confidential and only available to a certain few, so security is an issue with the chosen technology.

Making the Information Accessible

The Knowledge Store is not useful if people can't use it. Everyone can get access to it by employing technology. Perhaps the greatest mark that technology has made on business over the last ten years is to provide effortless access to information without constraints of any kind.

The Knowledge Store is located in one place (a server computer) under the control of whatever technology infrastructure exists—the IT department or whoever has been "put in charge"of technology. People can work directly off of the central database, or they can remotely connect to it and view only the information they need. The key here is that the information is stored and secured in *one* place, and everyone uses it there, or they *copy* off the piece that they need for their contribution, later to restore it with any additions or subtractions they have made to it. This process is **synchronization**, where any changes made on the same piece of data by more than one source are automatically reconciled by the software.

The Customer Knowledge Store has to be viewed by the company as one of its most critical assets, and one that should be jealously protected. In multiple disconnected databases, strategic company information is insecure. Nowhere is this truer than in the sales department.

If we are in *multiple disconnected database* mode, each one of those disconnected databases is sitting on the hard drive of an individual salesperson, so be warned. If the salesperson moves on to a different company, your information goes too. Why? Because the salesperson thinks of your information as their own! This happens all the time, but companies are still slow to wake up to the fact that if they leave the information storage decision to individual team members, they are at great risk when someone breaks away from the team. The only thing to do is to make sure that if the information is taken, you have a copy of it. If the information is shared, then the only risk is that a part will be lost. Make sure that it is not the only copy.

The problem gets compounded if there's no universal format to store the data. One salesperson uses ACT!, another uses their own design in Access, another uses Outlook, another uses their DayTimer; this is a recipe for disaster! If the sales team allows an individual member to do their own thing, the potential risk is that they lose all customer interactions over the work history of the salesperson in question—ouch!

There is no other answer than a common database, a common format and a mandate of sharing. That word "sharing" has come up before, because it is essential in establishing the CRM vision through technology. Let a user copy or replicate the information that they need. If they later decide to leave the company, it's difficult to stop them from taking their copy, but nothing is lost; it still resides safely in its central location.

The Information Has To Be Accurate

Information that cannot be relied upon is worse than no information at all. It is surprising how companies put a lot of energy and resources into creating a central library of information, only to have it populated with bad data. Once bad habits set in, it's tough to turn things around. The only way to roll out CRM is with clean data. Yet most people are so anxious to get going that they flood the new database with a rushed import of information from the old system. Once the database is clean, conscious effort should be put into ensuring data integrity.

The easiest way to move large amounts of existing data into a new database is through an automatic download. Unfortunately, this taints the new information store with the sins of the past. There has to be some manual cleansing before the moving process. This is achieved by putting the new data into quarantine, in a separate database, and then letting someone check it for validity before allowing it into the Knowledge Store.

The whole concept of customer knowledge is founded on building *accurate* information. It's an insult to the customer to record their personal details incorrectly. The worst examples involve names being misspelled, or getting genders wrong. Nothing will turn off a customer quicker than referring to them as Mr. instead of Ms. Limit the number of data entry points and use rules for inputting data. For instance, important information such as organization name, telephone number, address, etc. should be entered by a select few. There will be resistance from those who think that their liberty is being threatened, but after a while, when everyone sees the benefits of clean data, the issue will go away.

When the company gets big enough, it's best to bite the bullet and get a dedicated database manager. It's more of a question of reallocation of efforts than extra expense. A good custodian of the database will ease the pain for everyone. The thing about good data is that it is *reusable* and eventually becomes trusted. If you capture correct data once, the software will make it available over and over again with the click of a mouse.

Don't forget the other wonderful benefit of automation—process. Institute automated processes and you reduce the risk of a contaminated database. How? *Sales automation done right* makes the electronic processes mandatory and won't let anyone circumvent them through the back door. If a salesperson wants to send a proposal to a new customer, the rules won't allow the process to go forward unless the detailed contact information has been put into the database. Automation will ensure that the rules are enforced, while passing the process through human hands is not so certain.

Points to Remember

1. The Customer Knowledge Store is a strategic asset of the company and it should be guarded with appropriate security.

2. At the start-up of a new CRM project, take steps to avoid inheriting bad information from previous years.

3. Sound database management and effective processes are needed to keep the Customer Knowledge Store clean.

CHAPTER 6

The Four Waves

Which wave are you on?

Hopefully, Part I has made a strong case for automating the sales force and has persuaded the reader that SFA is a worthwhile business investment. But before embarking on the project, let's see how the trailblazers and early adopters fared, and learn from their experience.

Most companies that have functioning sales automation systems got there the hard way, a natural evolutionary route that follows the same pattern. Looking back, they would probably agree that there are faster and more effective ways to achieve the same end. This route to automation is invariably driven by **reaction** to business pain, felt because of frustration from inadequate or non-existent processes. When a pain develops, the tendency is to quickly throw something at it to achieve a quick fix.

The process of reacting to perceived barriers leads to four distinct phases of growth toward a technology solution. We call these phases the **Four Waves**. In this chapter, we see that progressing logically through the Four Waves is not the way to go. It's best to take some shortcuts, but to do this, it is essential to recognize what the Four Waves are, and on which wave you are currently riding.

From Paper to Power

What are the start and end points in the drive to embrace technology into SFA and CRM processes? The *start* is no technology at all, in other words, paper. This is Wave One. The *end* is everything that is described in *sales automation done right*, and is Wave Four. In Wave Four, technology drives all the customer facing processes, *and* contributes to a real effort for skills improvement in the sales force. The Four Waves run the gamut from "Paper to Power," from antiquated paper-based record keeping to efficient and effective sales automation based on a solid CRM platform.

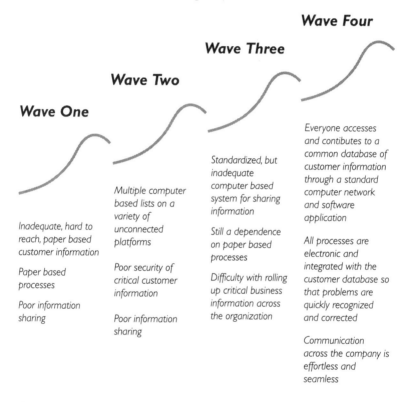

Wave One

Inadequate, hard to reach, paper based customer information

Paper based processes

Poor information sharing

Wave Two

Multiple computer based lists on a variety of unconnected platforms

Poor security of critical customer information

Poor information sharing

Wave Three

Standardized, but inadequate computer based system for sharing information

Still a dependence on paper based processes

Difficulty with rolling up critical business information across the organization

Wave Four

Everyone accesses and contibutes to a common database of customer information through a standard computer network and software application

All processes are electronic and integrated with the customer database so that problems are quickly recognized and corrected

Communication across the company is effortless and seamless

Figure 6-1: The Four Waves—moving technology into the sales department

Only in Wave Four does the company achieve the full benefits offered by diffusing technology throughout the sales organization. This doesn't happen overnight. Even so, it's best not to be deterred by the seemingly long road ahead. It is possible to jump one or more waves at once and the faster we can get to Wave Four, the better.

We've discussed the importance of rallying the entire organization behind the goal of customer satisfaction, and the role technology can play in bringing the team together. Each of the Four Waves is a reflection of how successful the company has been at integrating technology into the daily life of all employees.

Technology is a major theme of the Four Waves, but technology alone doesn't get us to Nirvana. The Four Waves model takes into consideration the importance of sales methodology, which is the blueprint for the sales business. After all, some of today's best sales methods were developed before computers became available. Technology and methodology go hand-in-hand as you move through the Four Waves. The methodology must evolve alongside the technology, and they must complement each other well.

Wave One—Buried in Paper

The first attempts at SFA and CRM focused on paper to manage *lists*. This had to be the case because at that time, computers were not available. Unfortunately, some companies still rely on paper lists, but hopefully not too many. The lists are ubiquitous; lists of customers, opportunities, quotations, service calls, so on and so forth. Very few people know where all the lists are. They are certainly on paper, but the paper could be anywhere in the building. It becomes a real chore to get good information out of the lists, and even more difficult to share the information throughout the company. Inevitably, this system leads to gridlock and everyone gets buried in paper and file cabinets. The result is less efficient service for the customer, making the company less competitive.

Proposition
If you are making custom boots for a client list of twenty-five,
paper is OK. Unless you plan to expand, stay in Wave One and
relax.

Otherwise, you could not be in a worse condition; you are living in the dark ages. Wave One is a dreadful place to be, and it can bring down good businesses that now have to compete with companies that have progressed into Waves Two, Three, and Four. The best advice to those in Wave One is to move out now, and hop two steps while you are at it!

Wave Two—Move Lists to Computers

Salespeople start using computers in Wave Two, most often using Contact Management which is low-cost and serves their immediate and personal needs. All too often, individuals make their own decision on which software to use.

The first thing that happens is that customer information lists are moved from paper onto the computer. Each salesperson keeps their own customer list and there is little sharing of information with the company. As the salesperson can configure the software any way they like, it's impossible for the company to impose rules on data validation or cleanliness. It is also tough for the company to enforce expectations on *which* information it needs to be recorded. The more successful the salesperson, the more they are able to do it *their* way, which goes counter to any company's long range plan to build a Knowledge Store of all its involvement with the customer. Wave Two inevitably results in the accumulation of *bad* customer data.

Companies in Wave Two don't yet have their departments talking to each other electronically. When someone else in the company needs the information, they have to rely on paper, fax, or phone to obtain it. Obviously, this isn't the most efficient way to get things done. It's especially problematic for remote employees who are working directly with customers. When front line staff can't get customer information back to Head Office quickly, the customer suffers.

In Wave Two, when a salesperson leaves the company, they take all the knowledge stored on their computer with them. Any information they've taken will have to be manually reconstructed from old paper records, which have hopefully been left behind. That's no way to run a business in the 21st century.

> Proposition
> Wave Two is treacherous; precious customer information is neither safe nor under your control. Who knows where that information is? It's dispersed, duplicated and probably inaccurate.

Make sure that if you have made it to Wave Two, you skip Wave Three and go directly to Wave Four. If you are thinking of going from Wave One to Wave Two, forget it. In many ways it could be worse.

Wave Three—Share Files

In Wave Three, the company takes steps to remove some of the pain that they experienced in Wave Two. First is an effort to standardize the software that salespeople are using on their computers. Often, the company goes with the flow and chooses the software that is most preferred by the sales team. Here the loudest, most persuasive user will get their preference chosen, and this is not the best way to implement a mission-critical piece of technology. The Third Wave company will probably go forward with the technical tool that has been used in Wave Two, which will lead to awful compromises.

The next step in the right direction is to try to synchronize the information generated by the sales team into one central file. At least that way, if someone leaves, a copy of their data resides at head office. This roll-up process is usually a headache. Many issues involve timing. Who edited the information last? Is it up to date? Who is acting as referee on which version is correct? And the information is not usually delivered in real time because the roll-up process is not effortless. Hopefully the company in Wave Three has a network with e-mail and Internet connection, which will make the file synchronization process easier.

Wave Three companies are making solid efforts to share their information and keep it secure. However, they are not yet automating their processes. Workflow still happens through the movement of files from one desk to another, and there is no linkage from Front Office to Back Office.

Proposition
In Wave Three, people share the same database, but making changes to it across the organization is difficult. Wave Three is dangerous, and companies can languish here before realizing that it will never work.

In many cases, it has taken a lot of sweat to get to Wave Three, and because of that, there is little incentive to go further. That's a shame because the technology infrastructure could already be sufficient to support Wave Four. There is no point in delaying.

Wave Four—Nirvana

In this wave, the company reaps all the benefits of technology. At the heart of the system is a Customer Knowledge Store of strategic customer information which is secure from theft. The Knowledge Store provides an accurate picture because everyone contributes to it and it is carefully maintained. There is a sharing culture within the company; people recognize that they can't go it alone, and that they need the team. Information is freely shared, and no one hoards.

Characteristics of Wave Four are tightly integrated *electronic* communication and collaboration capabilities. No matter where or when, salespeople can retrieve or contribute information on the customer. They have the means to easily share their experiences.

Backing up the effort is a workflow process that does not rely on paper. Because it is electronic, it is easy and self-regulating. If the workflow gets bogged down, flags are raised. The customer's transaction flows through faster and with fewer mistakes and this makes people happier about what they are doing. The result for the salesperson is that there is more time to spend with the customer.

Wave Four companies have also implemented the *direct* benefits of sales automation. Their salespeople are better than the competition because they sell to an agreed-upon and respected sales method, backed up with assistance from their computer.

Proposition
Once you are here, you will wonder how life was possible in earlier Waves.

The only place to be is in Wave Four. All good companies are trying to get here and recognize why they must do it. But it isn't easy and many get stuck along the way. How fast is business moving through the Waves? That's difficult to say, but generally, slower than expected.

Fighting the Waves

After evaluating which wave your company may be following, you may wonder what everyone else is doing. In 2001, we conducted a survey on a sampling of over one thousand companies in North America within the small to mid-market segment. The total number of companies in this target group was estimated to be 220,000. Executives were surprisingly open in their expression of the pains that they were encountering in the sales organization. This study reinforced the validity of the Four Wave model in its representation of the effort to solve the fundamental issues within the Front Office under the challenges of growth. Here are the results:

Within the target group, 10% of companies were in Wave One, 60% were in Wave Two, 13% were in Wave Three, and 17% were in Wave Four.

The 10% figure for Wave One represents 22,000 companies that still manage their sales teams through paper processes. Since 2001, one would hope there has been a massive exodus out of Wave One, but that's probably not the case. Small and mid-sized businesses are missing out on one of the most powerful and cost effective ways to boost bottom line profitabiliy.

Points to Remember

1. Take stock of where you are now and choose the shortest path to reaching Wave Four.

The Core Competencies

CHAPTER 7

The Challenge of Managing Sales

Breaking it into chunks

Part 2 explores how sales methods can be adapted to sales automation, starting with the outer "shell," a framework that follows the established fundamentals of selling, on which can be built the details of the method. In *sales automation done right*, this framework is based on the core competencies of selling.

Sales automation systems can often become bloated and complicated simply because of the massive functionality that can be put into them. The software is expected to store every scrap of information about the customer, but also to provide the workflow and administrative infrastructure that keeps the selling process humming. Yet, it also has to be easy and intuitive to use.

Proposition
The usability and acceptance of a sales automation system
depends on how well its structure follows the real life
challenges that face the sales team.

After all, what goes on in the computer should follow the sales method, and the organization of "how we sell" has a lot to do with the method. Salespeople shouldn't need to fumble through a maze of menus and screens figuring out how to get their selling job done because the layout of the software should make that obvious.

So, what challenges do salespeople face daily? Knowing the answer makes it easier to design a sales automation system that encourages and supports more productive selling.

The Salesperson's Responsibilities

A salesperson must be a strategist, a communicator, an HR expert, a psychologist, a mind reader, a statistician, and above all an excellent manager and organizer of his or her own personal resources. The number one personal resource is time. Salespeople must organize themselves to create as much selling time as possible.

The dilemma is always, "What is the best way to use my time?" Is it making new contacts? Visiting my best accounts? Developing new accounts? Traveling my territory looking for new business? And, the biggest concern of all, "Which sales opportunity should I be working on first?" Not surprisingly, salespeople have faced all of these issues before, and some well-proven management principles have evolved to make things easier to handle. These principles need to be included in the automation software. This exercise is the first attempt at making the sales method mesh with the technology.

Chunk It!

A common way to deal with what seems to be an unsurmountable task is to "Chunk it!" Break down the "whole" into manageable pieces, or chunks. How to chunk the salesperson's management challenges is revealed in a snapshot of what he or she does from day to day.

They visit customers and potential customers because salespeople don't exist without customers. Customers are people, or *contacts*, and occupy the top level of importance in the sales profession. With their customers, they discuss opportunities to do new business—*sales opportunities* with associated *sales cycles*.

The salesperson normally doesn't just call on a single contact; rather, the visit will be to an *account*, where there will be many like-minded contacts all of whom represent potential business. If the account is large, it may be all or part of an organization. Focusing on accounts is an efficient way for salespeople to utilize their selling time.

Salespeople must be conscious of where their accounts are located within their *territory*. The territory is their area (mostly geographical) of responsibility, and within it, it's up to the salesperson to make things happen.

We now have a structure on which we can chunk:

- The chunk that relates to the geographical scope of the salesperson's responsibilities is called *Territory* Management.

- The chunk that relates to groups of customers within organizations is *Account* Management.

- The chunk that relates to sales opportunities is called *Sales Cycle* Management.

- The chunk that relates to people is called *Contact* Management.

A competency is a skill that must be mastered to be successful. We've identified four *management* competencies that apply to salespeople. These competencies are about the management of *selling* (not *sales* management, because that has developed to mean something quite different), and every salesperson has to first understand their significance, and then go on to master them.

Proposition
To sell successfully, salespeople need to master only a few core
competencies, specifically four.

Each of our four competencies addresses a well defined segment of sales activity, and each confronts salespeople with a different test of their skills.

The Relationship Between the Competencies

There is a relationship between the four competencies that we can use to advantage in the sales automation system.

The Territory contains all the Accounts for which the salesperson is responsible. Each individual Account contains a number of people, or Contacts, who could be potential customers. When it comes to sales opportunities, we get very precise. The sales opportunity (with its associated Sales Cycle) is given to the salesperson by the customer contact. This is the way it works in reality. Even if a team is in charge of the purchase, there is always one contact that is the central point of focus in the sale. This contact is in charge of the sales opportunity. In some businesses, it is possible that the salesperson may be working on more than one opportunity from the same contact, and *sales automation done right* accommodates this.

Notice that this discussion is within the realm of *definitions* discussed in Part I. The precision of definitions is needed to develop a convenient relationship model of the competencies that reflects reality, and one that ultimately, the computer can understand. Remember, the computer (technology) will be reinforcing definitions to the salesperson through the method (technique).

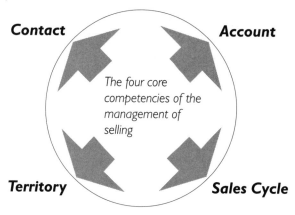

Figure 7-1: The four core competencies (TASC)

Hierarchy Rules!

Figure 7-2 shows the relationship between the competencies in the form of a **hierarchy**. The structure of the hierarchy flows directly from real life experience.

- The Territory is at the top, and has one or more Accounts. In some sales organizations, the territory may be only one account, but it is usually more.

- The Account is at the second level, and each account can have one or more Contacts within it.

- Contacts are the third level down, and as we said earlier, contacts can each own one or more sales opportunities with individual Sales Cycles (the fourth level).

- Although the Sales Cycle is shown as the lowest level, the hierarchy can go one step lower. As we shall see later, a special type of customer contact interaction is linked specifically to the sales opportunity.

Another way to describe these relationships is to say that the Territory **owns** the Account, which in turn owns the Contact, who in turn owns the opportunity with its related Sales Cycle. This is going further into language that the computer understands.

Proposition
The relationships linking the four core competencies can be expressed in a hierarchical structure that can be duplicated on the computer.

This hierarchy makes it easy to drill down through the Customer Knowledge Store to get information that links directly to the four core competencies. An additional benefit of this structure is that information becomes more accurate. The software is designed such that a new opportunity can't be added unless all the information above it in the hierarchy is already in the Knowledge Store. If it isn't, then it must be put in.

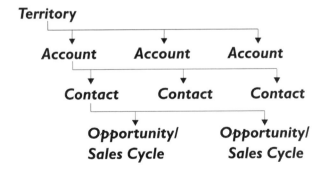

Figure 7-2: The T, A, S, and C relationship

The core competency hierarchy imposes a sense of order into the information system. Many SFA programs allow critical information to be entered without rules, and lets any piece of information be linked to another. This is dangerous from several points of view. If anyone can enter information in their own style, inconsistency creeps in. This makes it difficult for team members to understand what their colleagues are doing, and even tougher to collaborate on an agreed strategy. The other issue is method—having a structure (hierarchy) entwined with the Knowledge Store makes it much easier to overlay a sales method. Sticking to a defined method involves discipline, and it takes less effort to enforce the discipline if the data is entered in a structured way.

In the next four chapters, we look at the four core competencies one by one. This is not meant to be an exhaustive review, but just an inkling of where automation can excel. After all, the bulk of this book is about just one competency—Sales Cycle Management.

Points to Remember

1. The four core competencies of selling are Territory Management, Account Management, Sales Cycle Management and Contact Management.

2. Sales automation software should be designed to provide easy access to areas that are specific to each core competency.

3. The four core competencies follow a convenient hierarchical relationship which can easily be modeled on the computer.

CHAPTER 8

Territory Management
Where do I operate?

Jealously guarded, the territory is highly prized by salespeople, which is not surprising, since the size and quality of the territory directly impacts the salesperson's income. Throughout the course of history, disputes over territorial dividing lines have led nations to wars, and in the sales department, it is not much different. Emotions can run high if sales territories are ambiguously defined or unfairly adjusted because of changes in the business.

The last chapter made Territory the top of the hierarchy of core competencies, but not because it is the most important. Rather, the Territory sets the *boundary limits* within which salespeople are given responsibility. It tightly defines the accounts that are assigned to the salesperson, and Account falls directly under Territory in the hierarchy.

The Territory

Territory is usually thought of in terms of geography—for instance, consider the following examples: "West of Highway 11 and North of Highway 7," "Southwest Ontario," "Midwest US," "New York City," "Asia." These could be the territories of a random selection of salespeople from different organizations. Someone selling aircraft might have the whole of Asia as a territory, and a copier salesperson could have just New York City. The geographical size of the territory varies largely depending on the type of business and the product. For the most part, territory definitions are determined by how accounts are distributed, and how easily a salesperson can service the business by traveling from one account to another.

Geography may be a determining factor in defining the territory, but it is usually not the only one. Territories can be geographically disjointed, especially in larger sales teams that are responsible for diverse product lines. For instance, John's territory could include the entire state of New York for the Industrial Copier product line but he may also have special responsibilities to sell the High Speed Printer line only in the city of New York. So a more appropriate way to define territory is in terms of accounts.

> *Territory*: The list of accounts over which a salesperson has been given the responsibility to sell their products.

This list could in fact be defined by "every account in the state of Arizona," in which case we are back to geography, but often it is not so simple. The definition has some interesting ramifications. A territory may have hundreds of accounts in it or maybe just one. It's not uncommon for a salesperson to be responsible for just one account if the level of business and attention to customer satisfaction warrants it.

Territories can also overlap. The same account may be handled by two different salespeople from the same company, each having a different product line to sell (more on this later).

Territory Management

Salespeople face quite different problems than sales managers when it comes to Territory Management. The sales manager is interested in setting up and administering territories and making the necessary changes with business growth or turnover in the sales force. Salespeople are more focused on managing travel in their territories to make better use of time when it comes to developing, sustaining and harvesting business.

Salespeople can't be in two places at the same time. With accounts scattered all over the territory, the question is "Where do I go next?" The challenge of Territory Management is overwhelmingly driven by consideration of location and geography.

Proposition
The essence of Territory Management for the salesperson is
"Where?"

Where do I go next month to close out year-end business? Where do I go to develop new business? Where do I go to put out the fires? Where are my top ten accounts located? All responsibilities of the salesperson have a *where* component about them. The key to good Territory Management is devising travel schedules and routes to efficiently work as many sales opportunities as possible. Problems get more profound as the territory gets larger.

Sales automation can really help the salesperson in deciding where to go next. All they need to do is open up their computer and view any part of their business according to geography: globe, continent, state, city, street and building if necessary. There should be a complete history of the past business, current business and future potential, tagged by *where* it is—sales administration has made sure that everything that goes into the Customer Knowledge Store, from leads to proposals to purchase orders, is tagged with exact addresses and locations.

The objective for the salesperson must be to intelligently devise travel plans that provide regular contact with accounts in the territory, while having due concern for the logistics and personal resources. If the accounts are confined to one large city, problems in determining routes won't be so bad, and if necessary, quick adjustments can be made whenever emergencies crop up. Problems arise with very large territories in which accounts may be hours away by plane or car. Expenses mount up and travel time is often wasteful. If the question is, "I'll be in New York the week after next, let's see what's going on there," then the computer can help.

Sales managers, although they also have a keen interest in seeing their salespeople working their territories effectively, have an additional problem—how to create and administer territory structures. Managers initially set territories at a size that is manageable by the salesperson, with sufficient sales potential to compensate fairly. As a company grows, the sales force grows with it. Territory definitions then need constant tweaking and may sometimes have to be completely rechartered. Conversely, for companies facing bad times, sales teams may downsize and territories can get larger. When salespeople come and go, as they inevitably do, territory performance has to be maintained through the changes.

Once a territory exists and is producing, its revenue performance must be measured and monitored. Is it yielding business comparable to expectations and to other territories? What does the sales manager do when he sees that Rick is extracting $3 million per year from his territory when everyone else is doing $1 million? Taking accounts from Rick to give to someone else will make him unhappy, but the playing field may have to be leveled to make it fair for everyone. It's time for the territory to be divided.

Whether you are the sales manager or the salesperson, sales automation makes management of the territory much, much easier. We'll review a few important cases of how this is so in the next few sections.

Organizing Territories—Territory Groups

Adjusting and administering territory definitions along with the associated chore of reallocating salespeople's responsibilities can be a huge headache. *Sales automation done right* introduces the concept of Territory Groups, which makes the job a lot easier.

As an example, let's take a company working on creating territories from the many accounts in a metropolitan area, shown diagrammatically in Figure 8-1. The problem is compounded by the fact that the company has two distinct product lines: High Speed Printers (HSP), and Industrial Copiers (IC). The accounts for each product are quite different. Copiers are sold to large print facilities, and the HSP line is sold directly to end users, typically smaller institutions. Each product line needs its own team of specialist salespeople.

The HSP team has enough accounts in the city to warrant four sales-people, so they conveniently create four territories: Northwest, Northeast, Southeast and Southwest, as shown in Figure 8-1 (1). The territories are allocated respectively to Bob, Rick, Sue and John.

Figure 8-1 (2) shows that the IC team has only enough accounts within the city for two salespeople, and it decides to make two territories, West and East—West includes the Northwest and Southwest territories of the printer team, and East includes the Northeast and Southeast territories. The West is given to Glen and the East is given to Steve.

The Technical Support team does the post-sales training, maintenance and support on both the High Speed Printer and the Industrial Copier lines, and in addition, it does pre-sales assistance for both teams. Ralph is a technical specialist and his territory, seen in Figure 8-1 (3), comprises all of the accounts for the two product lines in the entire metropolitan area.

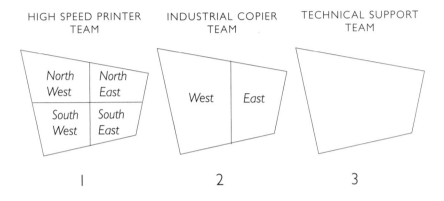

Figure 8-1: Territories for High Speed Printer sales team, Industrial Copier sales team and Technical Support team

So within the city there are three distinct sets of territories. *Sales automation done right* refers to these sets of territories as Territory Groups.

The Territory Group: The administrative structure of the territories belonging to a sales team.

A company may have just one Territory Group where each salesperson sells all of the products. There could be many Territory Groups depending on product lines or other sales related functional groups such as technical support. The example shows Territory Groups that overlap, which is very common. A Territory Group can consist of just one territory, such as Ralph's in our example.

Administering Territory Groups

What happens if Steve decides to leave the company? His manager decides that, at this time, he won't be replaced. Instead, Sue, having worked in the IC group before, will take Steve's territory in addition to her own for a period of six months. Sue's territory now straddles two territory groups. If you asked Sue what her sales territory was, she would reply: "Well, it's the whole eastern part of the city for copiers, and just the southeast for printers." Her territory description still fits within our definition of territory. She is really telling us the accounts for which she is responsible for both printers and copiers. Overlapping of responsibilities across territory groups happens a lot, especially as the company moves more toward team selling. For instance, in the example above, Ralph is an essential part of the selling effort for both product lines because his responsibilities span six territories and two territory groups.

Figure 8-2 shows the structure of Territory Groups within the company, and notice again that it is a hierarchy. When territory information is organized this way on the computer, it becomes easy to roll-up territory information. For example, the territory's sales are obtained by a summary from the accounts in the territory. Just one step further takes the roll-up to the level of the Territory Group, and the manager of the HSP division, for instance, can easily see the group's performance and its breakdown by territory.

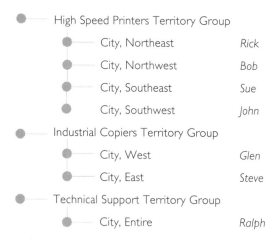

Figure 8-2: A sales department's territories structured as Territory Groups

The Territory Group is created after first creating the accounts. The next step is to define the territories within the group by allocating the accounts. Only then are the salespeople assigned to the territories. When Territory

Groups and territories have been determined, it will be up to sales administration to ensure that the system is maintained and updated. When a new account is added, for instance GDPN Boston, it may belong to the Northeast territory for printers and the East territory for copiers. It will be allocated to each territory automatically by referencing its Zip Code. Salespeople have already been assigned to their respective territories and are therefore automatically tagged by the computer to the account.

Administering even a small sales team can be challenging. When the team numbers go from ten to fifty to one hundred, the problem gets intimidating, and a sales automation system is the only way of avoiding this potential nightmare. This is another example of the how the computer creates efficiency for the sales team, which ultimately translates into a win-win for both the company and the customer.

Points to Remember

1. A good sales automation tool makes it much easier to see where potential business, current business and past business exists in the territory. Personal resources (most importantly, time) can then be better allocated.

2. Administering territories as the sales force grows to more than one can be tough. If the sales force is over fifty, it can be a nightmare. Make sure that your sales automation solution has all the features that make adding, changing or consolidating salespeople into territories that much easier.

3. Organize territories for different sales teams into Territory Groups.

CHAPTER 9

Account Management
Efficient selling

The *account* can be a fixation with salespeople. Salespeople want to "own" accounts. Owning an account means that the competition is so convinced it's yours, they won't give it much time. This can only happen if the salesperson has built a reputation for delivering a solution that works. Solutions are not just sold; there has to be ongoing support, laying down the foundation for more business. It takes a long time to develop an account to the point where there is trust of one vendor's product over another. That loyalty can easily be lost through mismanagement by the salesperson or the sales team.

In the four competencies hierarchy, the Account falls directly below Territory. As we move down the hierarchy we are getting closer to the two most important competencies. Contact is the first of these, and the importance of accounts stems from the fact that the Account is a group of contacts, each of whom could be a customer.

The Account

Accounts are related directly to *organizations*, and organizations can range in scope from gargantuan to tiny. The word "related" is chosen carefully—accounts don't have to be organizations—they can be *small* parts of large organizations.

Within the account are *contacts*, who fuel business for the salesperson. The contacts are focused on a common goal, simply because they work for the same organization. They require similar products or services and represent the chance for multiple sales opportunities and ongoing business within the account.

> *Account:* A group of like-minded people (contacts), in one location that can be conveniently targeted by the sales team using a common sales strategy.

Accounts can be companies, governments, universities, hospitals, factories, doctor's offices, private residences—in fact, almost anything, depending on what's being sold. *Sales automation done right* takes the view that the account provides a piece of business that can be managed and developed by an *individual* salesperson. Viewed from the corporate or enterprise level, an account could be global, but the salesperson only worries about the account that he or she sees—typically local.

Take the example of a large multinational pharmaceutical company that has plants and offices scattered throughout the world. If you make drug manufacturing equipment, you might view the pharmaceutical company as just one account. But, it's a different story if you are a manufacturer of office equipment, in which case, your product has universal application and can be used anywhere. In this case, the pharmaceutical company would constitute hundreds of potential accounts worldwide.

Account Management

The idea of the account being a group of contacts with similar goals and interests suggests that there may be an opportunity for efficient selling.

Proposition
The essence of Account Management is *efficiency.*

The efficiency comes from serving a group of similar customers at the same location, which means efficient marketing, sales effort, service, logistics, and therefore, reduced selling costs. The benefits are huge to the sales team that sets out a sensible account structure with an active and ongoing Account Management strategy. Sales automation plays a significant role in making this happen.

The best kinds of accounts are the ones that have the possibility of providing a salesperson with multiple selling opportunities, where each opportunity has a different contact "owner." Here, there is a real chance of building loyalty in the account through long term attention to relationships and service. The reputation that the salesperson gains with certain customers can be used to win others over within the same account.

Efficient *marketing* has already been mentioned, and indeed, the marketing department has a lot to gain from account driven strategies, and the benefits will, of course, trickle through to the sales department. Contacts within the account think on the same wavelength, and short, low cost, focused marketing campaigns usually generate lots of willing listeners.

Multi-level Account Structures

As with Territory Management, administering accounts can present headaches to the sales department. In the case of large multinational or global accounts, assigning and maintaining them is definitely challenging. Sales automation helps, but only if some work has been done up-front in breaking down complex organizational structures into conveniently-sized sales accounts. Some pause for careful planning in setting up account structures pays off in spades later on.

Let's look at an example: Smith Print Corporation (Smith PC) is a manufacturer of high quality digital printing equipment and they have just implemented a new CRM/SFA system. Their sales administrator is setting up the account structure for their largest customer, Global Digital Printer Network or GDPN. GDPN is a company specializing in all types of printing, from mass produced to publish-on-demand, and has offices worldwide. Smith PC sells equipment to them in every country in which they are located.

Smith PC has two distinct product lines that address both the low-end and high-end market for digital printing equipment. Each product line has its own specialist sales force. GDPN is large and diversified, and it uses both of the Smith PC products. GDPN manufacturing plants use the sophisticated Industrial Copier that costs hundreds of thousands of dollars per installation. Decisions for this product are made within the Head Offices of GDPN, in conjunction with the manufacturing locations. GDPN Research

Centers use Smith's low-end High Speed Printer product, and as this product is much cheaper, buying decisions are made directly at the location.

The Smith PC sales administrator breaks down the global GDPN organization into accounts that fit the efforts of the two sales teams, recognizing their different selling processes, revenue volumes and sales staff in each territory. She determines that each Research Center represents enough business to warrant it being an individual account handled by an individual HSP salesperson. The Branch Offices and Training Centers carry a lot of weight in the purchasing decisions at the Research Centers, so she also breaks those out into accounts and hands them off to the salesperson covering the Research Center.

GDPN Manufacturing Plants each buy their own equipment with heavy input from the Head Offices in each country. Accounts are created accordingly and divided up amongst the IC sales team. Her initial list of accounts for the GDPN groups in the United Kingdom, Germany and US is represented by Figure 9-1. Each account represents a separate physical location. All the informational details such as address, contacts, and organization structure are linked to this one line account description.

The list looks a little intimidating to anyone wanting to find information about specific GDPN accounts, especially when only three countries are shown—what would the entire global GDPN structure look like? The reason it looks challenging is that the sales administrator is working with just a one level account structure. She has to somehow accommodate a complex organization chart within a single line description. It's easy to see that this is restrictive for handling large organizations. Data is difficult to enter and even more difficult to retrieve. If someone wants to find the Research Center in London they can't use any kind of easy "type ahead" feature. They would have to type "GDPN, UK, London, R.. ," before they got to it, and no one has the patience for that. The way to overcome this problem is to add more account levels.

Figure 9-2 shows what happens if the software provides a three level account structure. Again, this is a *hierarchy* which seems well suited to the computer. The sales administrator has set up a top level of "Country," then a second level of "City," and a third level of "Facility." If account information is set up this way, data is more easily accessible. To locate details of the same

GDPN UK Research Center in London, first go to GDPN—UK, then to London, then Research Center. This is much easier than looking through a huge list of similar sounding possibilities.

- GDPN, UK, London, European Headquarters
- GDPN, UK, London, Research Center
- GDPN, UK, Glasgow, Branch Office
- GDPN, UK, Glasgow, Training Center
- GDPN, Germany, Hamburg, Head Office
- GDPN, Germany, Hamburg, Training Center
- GDPN, Germany, Hamburg, Ink Research Group
- GDPN, Germany, Frankfurt, Manufacturing Plant
- GDPN, US, Boston, North American Headquarters
- GDPN, US, Boston, Research Center
- GDPN, US, Boston, Training Center
- GDPN, US, New York City, Manufacturing Plant

Figure 9-1: Single level account structure

In the same way as Territory Groups in Chapter 12, information can easily be rolled-up with this kind of account structure. The manager for IC sales in Europe can see the total sales for Germany by consolidating the sales for Hamburg and Frankfurt.

The Designated Account

Be careful not to confuse account with organization. The example shows that the GDPN organization stretches far and wide, and must be subdivided to fit the needs of the Smith PC products and sales teams. Smith only has one salesperson in Germany for their high value Industrial Copier, their account is GDPN—Germany. The High Speed Printer group has two salespeople covering the country, and a different salesperson handles each of the GDPN accounts in Hamburg and Frankfurt. The term *designated account* is useful to describe which part of the account organization has been given as a specific salesperson's responsibility. In our example, therefore, GDPN—Germany is a designated account for the lone Smith Industrial Copier salesperson in Germany. Other subordinate levels in the GDPN account structure are designated accounts for salespeople belonging to the HSP team.

Figure 9-2: Three level account structure

The more the number of specialist sales teams and the larger the customer's organization, the more complicated the structure of accounts becomes. This is not a problem with a sales automation system that easily handles a multi-level account structure.

Front Office Accounts or Back Office Accounts?

The Account is not an idea that is exclusive to the Front Office. Actually, the very word *account* rings up images of finance—yes, the Back Office has its accounts too. It seems tempting to have just one list of accounts across the entire company, but this may not be such a good idea.

The principal focus in the Back Office finance group is that invoices get sent to the right addresses and that bills get paid. Their list of accounts is set up accordingly. If the customers are small organizations, the accounts may be the same as those set up by the sales department, but as the customers get larger, this is usually not the case. The account that pays for the product could be in different city than the account that originally purchased it. The product may also get shipped to a different address than the one that the salesperson sold it to.

As we said earlier in Chapter 4, the sales department sets up accounts totally differently. They concentrate more on breaking down customer organizations into convenient groups that they can market and sell to. Customer contacts also are different; the Front Office talks to buyers and users, whereas the Back Office talks to the administrative people in the customer's purchasing and receiving departments.

The answer is to maintain two completely independent lists of accounts, but to have them linked together through the CRM technology—information sharing between Front and Back Office is expected anyway. Let each side set up their accounts how they want to, and bring them together in the information sharing process.

Points to Remember

1. Dividing large customer organizations into accounts that are suitable for your product range and sales team can be a challenge. Make sure that your CRM/SFA system provides the flexibility of a multi-level account structure to make the job easier.

2. Watch out—the accounts that belong to finance can be quite different from those that belong to sales.

CHAPTER 10

Contact Management

The relationship reigns

Everyone in sales has heard of Contact Management. If salespeople don't have a corporate sponsored CRM system, you can bet that they administer their valuable customer information through one of the popular brands of Contact Management software.

Contact Management is the forerunner of all SFA and CRM applications. It's easy to understand why—the salesperson depends on a foundation of a strong rapport with the customer, and Contact Management software is a powerful tool to help build that rapport and maintain it.

In the core competency hierarchy, the Contact falls beneath Account. We have seen that accounts consist of groups of people (contacts) that are working together with a common purpose.

The Contact

Generally a contact is anyone that we communicate or associate with. In sales automation, the scope gets narrowed down to include just the people who directly affect the salesperson's business, or have the capability to influence it. Contacts may have needs which at some point, will turn into sales opportunities, and they have to be treated with the importance that they richly deserve. Without the contact, there is no business.

Contact: Someone who has the potential to purchase your product or who may have the power to influence its purchase.

The contact is a person; a real live human being. The contact is the customer, or someone very close to the customer. At the end of the day, the contact controls or impacts the sale.

Contact Management

Originally Contact Management software was introduced as a specialized database application to log information about people we know and our ongoing dialogue with them. Business quickly adopted this tool, and salespeople, especially, flocked to it. When this happened, features were added to include more of the sales process, which led to *Sales Force Automation*. Expansion of functionality outside of the sphere of the sales department led to the humble Contact Management application ultimately morphing into *Customer Relationship Management*.

Proposition
The essence of Contact Management is the *relationship*.

Relationships are very important—between people and between companies; after all, organizations are just groups of people working together. When those people are doing business according to the traditional buyer-seller model, the relationship that exists between them becomes very meaningful.

There are good relationships and bad relationships, and of course, the salesperson strives to create customer relationships which will hopefully assist in the effort to win the sale. Good relations are based on trust, co-operation, shared feelings, and a mutual need. Relationship building is largely dependent on the art of selling, but is also partly based on the care with which the salesperson manages the knowledge formed from previous dialogue with the customer. As far as the customer is concerned, the salesperson should only be focused on *them*—it's of no interest that there may be ninety-nine other contacts vying for some attention. So, the information on any one customer should be recorded and *known*. The average salesperson has hundreds of contacts, and to manage all of that information, there is a need for notebooks, rolodexes, and the computer.

The best way to manage contact information is by using a two-pronged approach. First, the core information about the contact has to be recorded, both personal and business related, and then the history of the relationship must be logged. Many people are guarded about their personal information, and salespeople should be sensitive to this. Only the information that the customer is comfortable with providing should be recorded. Some customers may like getting birthday cards from salespeople, but not all of them will, and the salesperson has to judge whether it is appropriate or not. Some customizable fields may be needed in the database for salespeople to store their own favorite pieces of information about their contacts. Relationship building is much easier if salesperson and customer share common interests outside of business. Business related information will consist of the routine phone, fax and e-mail data, but also the position and responsibilities of the contact within their organization, and whether they are customers or influencers.

One thing is certain, people like any kind of information stored about them to be totally accurate. Unfortunately, it's easy to build sloppy databases where information is incomplete or just not correct. A lot of damage can be done to the relationship if contacts think that they are not important enough to even get their name spelled correctly. If contact data is being collected within a CRM system, quality becomes more important to watch out for, because a number of different people may be entering information on the customer. A good automation tool will have features that encourage the collection of quality data.

Relationships depend on an ongoing conversation with the customer. Here, we are using the word *conversation* in the greater sense, meaning the historical exchange of information between buyer and seller that will determine the quality and the sustainability of the relationship. The way this exchange happens is through an interaction with the customer, and what happens in that interaction is of vital importance.

Interacting with the Customer

Salespeople should spend as much time in front of their customers as possible, because relationships are built and developed best through personal contact—face-to-face is better, but if that's not possible, the phone is next best. The essential results of these interactions with the customer should be recorded. In this way, a history of the relationship is always available for review. In business, relationships last a lifetime, but sales teams change, and current strategies can only be honed from knowledge of what has happened in the past.

Customer interactions are so important in sales automation that two chapters are devoted to them in Part 3. Interactions feed the information that is used to build the relationship. Direct personal contact is not the only kind of interaction that is important. Any event involving communication between the salesperson, or (in the case of CRM) the salesperson's organization, is a customer interaction and must be recorded. This will include marketing promotions, purchase orders, invoices, service requests or any other component of the business transaction. If a customer phones, it should be possible to quickly review their interaction history to see when the last contact was made, and to get a broad picture of what has been happening (or maybe not happening) in the relationship. Customers are impressed when you know what was discussed the last time you both spoke, even though that may have been six months ago.

One particular customer interaction is very important, and that is the one that occurs during the period of time where the salesperson is making an active effort to win a sale against competition. Later, we delve into why it is important to be able to record this type of interaction in the context of the particular sales opportunity that it applies to. This lets us see a summary of the current state of the *sales process* and its effectiveness in winning the sale.

In closing off this chapter on the contact, we need to reinforce that good relationships are essential for successful sales, but be careful. This contact is also a customer with interests driven by higher forces within their own organization. They may turn away from you if the competition can offer a solution that might suit their situation better. Relationships are put aside when greater allegiances or other agendas prevail. Salespeople cannot rely on relationships alone; the requirement to actually *sell* can never be relinquished.

Good salespeople balance their skills of bonding or rapport against pure selling skills, which will lead us, at the end of Part 2, into a valuable discussion of which core competency is Number One. But, before that comes the sales cycle.

Points to Remember

1. The most successful way to build relationships with people is to know and understand as much about them as possible. The Contact Management section of your SFA or CRM software can make this happen.

2. If you collect and store information about contacts, make sure it is correct. People get upset if they see their personal data badly mangled through careless record keeping.

3. Relationships are ongoing and dependent on the results of interactions over time. The essential results of all interactions with the contact have to be stored to form the true description of the relationship.

CHAPTER 11

Sales Cycle Management
It's time to sell

Salespeople don't sell all the time because they have to do many other things to support their selling efforts. True selling skills are reserved for a time frame that is special—one that *encapsulates* the customer's buying process. This period in time is called the **sales cycle**. The sales cycle plays a central role in describing the **sales opportunity**. In fact, this chapter could easily have been called "Sales Opportunity Management," but for reasons that will become clearer in later chapters, we prefer to use the term "Sales Cycle Management."

In the hierarchy of the core competencies, the sales opportunity is linked directly to a contact, and s*ales automation done right* is very specific about this. A customer contact (a person) *owns* a sales opportunity with its associated sales cycle. Some might argue that the sales opportunity comes from a committee, a company, an account, or a group of contacts, but in nearly all cases, there will be a central figure that spearheads the effort to buy. It is up to the salesperson to identify that individual as the owner of the sales opportunity.

Associating an opportunity with a single contact makes it much easier to navigate through a large list of opportunities. Often, other contacts will affect or influence the buying decision, and the salesperson must include them in sales strategies. But the individual who is logged as the owner of the opportunity will usually be the customer who has the most to gain from the purchase, or who is a principle advocate of the need to buy.

The Sales Cycle

The sales cycle is so closely associated with the sales opportunity that both terms need to be discussed together. A sales opportunity is aptly named because it is a chance for the salesperson to show their stuff and go win a sale. An alternative word for opportunity is "break," as in, "Give me a break." A salesperson might say, "I've had a two month spell with nothing happening—something has to *break* soon," meaning, "I need someone (a customer) to give me an opportunity to *sell*."

> *Sales opportunity*: A well-defined situation in which the salesperson is given a chance to sell their product or service against an alternative competitive solution.

This element of competition is important—selling always involves competition. A sale involves two parties; one tries to *influence* the other in making a specific choice from a number of options (minimum two). There are "competing" alternatives—the customer makes a choice, and one possible response is to buy nothing at all. Competition offers the customer the widest view of available options, and also offers a prospect of negotiating the best value.

> *The sales cycle*: Measured in units of time (days, weeks, months, years), it is the lifespan of the sales opportunity. It also represents the *only* available time to get the sales job done.

The sales cycle has a *start* and an *end*. Once the start date is identified, the length of the sales cycle can be established by estimating when the customer will make a final decision on what to buy—then the sales process has to be made to fit. This is why the sales cycle is so important, and why the salesperson should always be conscious of how much time is left within the sales cycle to complete the sale.

Fortunately, sales automation can help by keeping a list of open opportunities along with their *current* sales cycles. We say current, because a sales cycle can quickly and unexpectedly take on a life of its own and compress or expand, becoming shorter or longer. Because the date the sale started is fixed, the only way for the sales cycle to change is if the projected end date moves closer or further away.

It is the sales opportunity that represents business value to the salesperson. An opportunity is characterized in a number of important ways, some of which are: the monetary value of the deal, the ease with which the deal can be won, and the point in the future that it can be won. The sales cycle is the arena in which competitive selling skills occur to make the sale happen for one salesperson over another. Managing the sales cycle involves the appropriate use of true selling skills—*which* skills to use and *when* to use them. The salesperson that gets this right has the best chance of winning the sale. The logical flow of the sales process within the sales cycle leads to a better understanding of the value of one sales opportunity over another, and helps the salesperson manage their resources to best benefit the overall sales effort.

Figure 11-1: A sales opportunity has an associated sales cycle

Two Sales Cycles?

When a customer decides to buy something, they follow a *process* to ensure that the final purchase is the right one. All options are researched and an appropriate period of negotiation is set aside to make sure that the best deal is struck with the winning supplier. This *buying* process takes time, and the amount of time taken is the sales cycle. As soon as the customer brings in potential suppliers for consultation, the sales cycle has begun—this is the customer's sales cycle. The sales cycle *as seen by the customer* exactly mirrors the buying process.

The customer's sales cycle: The time that elapses between the customer initiating the buying process to making the final decision to purchase.

But for the salesperson, the start of the sales cycle is literally the day that they *find* the sales opportunity. If this is the day that a purchasing agent calls the office to say a competitive proposal is needed for a customer's requisition, it is too late—the sales cycle, as far as the customer is aware, started a long time ago. The competitor has been working the sale for a while, and you knew nothing about it. Now, it's uphill all the way; cross your fingers and hope that something can be salvaged at the last minute.

The actual sales cycle: The time that elapses between the salesperson *discovering* the sales opportunity and the customer making the final decision to purchase.

The actual sales cycle is the only one that the salesperson needs to worry about. Those smart (or lucky) enough to be working with the customer from the start of the buying process have an actual sales cycle that is equal to the customer's sales cycle. This is a situation that all salespeople should strive to achieve. Later, other vendors might stumble on the situation and get a chance to participate, but they have some time to make up. Their actual sales cycle is *less* than the customer's sales cycle. Figure 11-2 shows the two sales cycles.

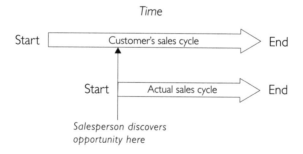

Figure 11-2: The sales cycle as seen by the customer and the salesperson

Since the actual sales cycle begins only when the salesperson becomes *aware* of the customer's intention to buy, it is almost always shorter than the customer's sales cycle, and in many cases too short. If the customer waited two months before contacting the salesperson about a product with a six-month sales cycle, the "actual" sales cycle will be six months, whereas the customer's sales cycle would be eight months. A shortened sales cycle means that there is less time to sell, and makes the sale much more difficult. This is why continual interactions with the potential customer base are necessary to discover new opportunities *early* in the customer's sales cycle.

Sales Cycle Management

One of the most important issues about managing the sales cycle is recognizing that a sales opportunity exists and the sales cycle has started. Salespeople must be continuously on the lookout for new opportunities during their regular conversations with customers or potential customers. Once the opportunity is identified, it should be recorded, preferably in the sales automation system and not just in the salesperson's head. This way, it won't be forgotten.

Sales cycles vary from days to years, depending on the complexity of what is being sold.

Proposition
The essence of Sales Cycle Management is *time*.

An integral part of recording an opportunity is to enter the date that the sale is *expected* to conclude (the date the opportunity is logged is taken to be the start date). With these two dates, the computer calculates the duration of the sales cycle in units of time. Sometimes the date of conclusion of the sale is referred to as the *close date*.

As each opportunity gets recorded, a list of *potential* business is built up. When the opportunity is won or lost, the record is closed (but still saved in the Customer Knowledge Store), and removed from the list. A description of each opportunity should include basic information such as customer name, account, product, and price, but most importantly, an estimation of the date that the sales cycle will *end*.

As mentioned earlier, it's possible, even likely, that the close date will be revised a number of times. So not only must the details of the opportunity be logged initially, they must be *updated* as the sales cycle assumes its normal flow. A good sales automation system can monitor the sales cycle on a daily basis and keep track of what should be happening at that point, but this only works if the salesperson provides up-to-date information on when the sale is expected to end.

Keeping an eye on the time left to sell is important, but so is *timing* of events within the sales cycle. In the sales cycle, the salesperson interacts with the customer through meetings, phone calls, proposals, e-mail and a variety of other ways. These *interactions* together form the process for executing strategies and tactics that the sales team thinks have the best chance to secure the sale. The substance of the interactions is important, but so too is their timing. When do they happen in the sales cycle and how do they happen in relationship to one another? Successful selling depends on mastering specific skills and knowing how and when to use them at different times within the sales cycle. Using the wrong skill at the wrong time can cause a setback in the sale. Planning customer interactions would not be too bad if there were just one sales opportunity, but that is never the case. A busy salesperson could be working on scores of opportunities at any one time. These sales cycles will be running on totally different time schedules. Keeping track of what to do and when to do it is very difficult. Sales automation can make the job much easier, as the computer has no problems at all in keeping an eye on time and determining when things need to get done.

Predicting the Future

Pinning down the start of the sales cycle is a singular event—it happens once, and that's it. However, the predicted end-date of the sale will more than likely change many times in the sales cycle. There are lots of reasons for this, but the principle one is that customers invariably take longer than they think to make decisions. Expectations set down early in the sales cycle are often proven wrong. This means that salespeople have to be on their toes to watch for signs that the projected purchase date has been moved, either forward or back. Managing the sales cycle means staying on top of the "best guess" of when it will end. It is the only parameter that tells the salesperson (and the computer) how much time there is left to sell.

Predicting when the customer will make a final decision can be straight-forward in some cases, but difficult in others. It may be necessary to look months, or even years into the future. If the customer is rushed to meet a deadline for the purchase, they may be prepared to share that information with the salesperson. If there is no urgency on the part of the customer to make a decision, the sales cycle can drag on. If the sales cycle is long, perhaps a year or more, it's very difficult to forecast within a few months when the purchase date will be, especially in the early stages. Obviously, the job gets easier closer to the end, when most of the work has been done in the evaluation and the customer can go ahead and make a decision.

But no matter where we are in the sales cycle, the beginning, toward the end, or somewhere in the middle, it is extremely important for the salesperson to be cognizant of when the sale will *end*, and to update that information as best they can, whenever it changes. All too often this is forgotten, and there is danger of losing track of how business is progressing and when it is going to happen. This problem is compounded when many opportunities are being worked at one time.

Predicting close dates is important because all salespeople are required to forecast. Forecasting is one of the sales team's most important and fundamental responsibilities. There is always pressure on business, from enterprise level down, to predict performance into the future, quarter-by-quarter and year-by-year. The top-line driver to business performance is revenue, which is derived directly from the sales team's bookings. There are all sorts of ways that sales managers grapple with forecasting. Historical results, economic climates and seasonal considerations are a few factors that influence forecasting, but when it comes down to it, going to the salespeople and asking them what they are going to book next month or next quarter is the best way to do it. There's no option for the salesperson other than to open up the list of opportunities and review each sales cycle to judge when it will close, and this becomes the basis for the forecast.

But, salespeople should have their own personal reasons for knowing the end of the sales cycle. Without having a good idea of how much time there is left in the sales cycle, it turns out that it is very difficult to manage the list of current opportunities. The challenge becomes tougher as the list swells—so tough that if the salesperson is not careful, opportunities will start to fall through the cracks. That means wasted business and lost revenue. In today's increasingly competitive business environment, salespeople have larger territories, more accounts and consequently, more opportunities to handle. The list of opportunities must be organized, characterized and managed so that the salesperson's resources are used to best effect.

Salespeople should regularly review their open opportunities and update the close date for each one. We'll see later that the smart ones review their opportunities after each important interaction with the customer. It makes most sense to log any change in the close date at this time.

Managing Many Sales Cycles

On any day, a salesperson will be working a number of sales opportunities. They have to, because they are not going to win all of them—competition is fierce. It's important to review the opportunity list regularly to make sure nothing is getting overlooked. The problem is compounded by the fact that there will usually be a large spread of sales cycle lengths within the list. Some reasons for this have been discussed already; different products will have their own sales cycles, and the average sales cycle varies anyway, because of unusual influences within the sale. There is also another factor that causes widely varying sales cycles, and that is the issue of the salesperson discovering the opportunity later in the customer's sales cycle (this effect is so important that it will be discussed in greater detail in Chapter 19).

The salesperson will be faced with managing situations with sales cycles that range from early (the sales opportunity has just been found) to late (the customer is about to buy, and the salesperson needs to close), and inevitably, cases of everything in between. This is a tough proposition to manage, and the salesperson is tugged into many different directions at once. A decision has to be made on which order to work the opportunities. It's not good enough to take the common approach of simply concentrating on the opportunities that are about to end. This tactic often leads to neglect of opportunities which are early in their sales cycle, meaning not enough work will have been done to ensure that a successful closing is possible later. In fact, the entire sales cycle should be worked with the same intensity throughout. A consistent selling effort is needed all the way through the entire sales cycle, but this kind of discipline is rarely practiced by salespeople.

Fortunately, the computer can do a great job of maintaining a long list of opportunities and making sure that they are all treated with the right degree of importance. Here is an example of where *sales automation done right* can really make the salesperson's responsibilities much more painless, and this is the story that unfolds throughout the whole of Part 3.

Influencing the Length of the Sales Cycle?

There has been much written about how CRM and SFA offer the potential to shorten the sales cycle, which will theoretically lead to more sales. A shortened sales cycle implies that the customer needs less time to carry out the buying process. There's no doubt that companies who faithfully execute the principles of CRM will win respect from customers, and that will mean reduced competitive influences in the business relationship. This not only results in "easy" deals, where competition is given just a token invitation to participate, but sometimes in exclusive deals where the customer feels comfortable enough not to invite alternative proposals.

The realities of tougher economic times have made customers more tuned to the increased value that alternative bidding brings to the table, and it's difficult to remove all elements of competition entirely in dealings with the customer. However, there are some situations where the sales cycle can be shortened. A solution may be unique and stand head and shoulders above the competition, or there could be some single differentiator that cannot be matched, in which case the customer may be prepared to stop the normal procurement process and quickly make the decision to buy your product.

In most cases, it is not possible to have a significant impact on when the sales cycle will finish. The competitive sales process plays out in its own time: proposals have to be reviewed, products evaluated and careful buying procedures followed. The process takes its natural course, and salespeople can rarely hasten it up.

Sales automation done right is a little different and suggests that the salesperson should try to *lengthen* the sales cycle. We're not suggesting for one moment to try to delay the close date—rather, learn about the opportunity sooner, and lengthen the actual sales cycle. This, more than anything else, will ensure that there is plenty of time to sell, with no pressure from trying to force important sales strategies into inadequate sales cycles. If, for whatever reason, the sales cycle gets compressed, the salesperson could be faced with a stiff uphill battle. The objective must be to do all that is possible to ensure that the sales cycle has enough room in it to execute the sales process in the best way possible.

Points to Remember

1. The essence of selling includes competition, and competitive sales environments deliver sales opportunities.

2. Every sales opportunity has a measurable sales cycle.

3. Getting the sales team to recognize the start of the sales cycle as early as possible is the first important step to moving them from reactive to proactive selling.

4. Log and update! Log the opportunity and, at the same time, make the best guess at the close date. Watch out for issues in the sale that will modify the close date.

5. The only sales cycle that the salesperson should focus on is the actual sales cycle. For better or for worse, this represents the only time there is to sell.

6. It's tough to manage multiple sales cycles in different stages of development. There must be some way to place a value on the sales opportunity, one to another. This happens through a conscious analysis of the sales cycle.

CHAPTER 12

T, A, S and C

Where do we go first?

We've broken down a salesperson's responsibilities into four categories that we call the core competencies, and we've shown how each competency can be positively impacted by sales automation. There is nothing new here—this way of looking at the daily challenges facing salespeople has evolved through many years of trials and experience. But we have viewed the problem with a strict focus on technology and sales, and when you do this, the logical division into Territory, Account, Contact and Sales Cycle seems to jump out at you.

Even though the management of selling has been reduced to just four competencies, there will always be the question of, "If I had to pick just one competency to master, which would it be?" The strict answer is that the competencies are interdependent, and salespeople should work to master them all. The best salespeople combine their attention to the competencies so as to provide a harmonized approach to their selling activities.

But, against better judgment, we will now attempt to rate the competencies, and this is not such an easy job. We'll start at the bottom and work our way up.

Number Four—Territory

Territory Management: Sound *organizational* skills are all that's needed to manage the territory properly. Even people who sell poorly can still concoct ways to travel around their accounts in a way that makes sense. This is not to undermine the importance of knowing where to find the business in the territory, and being able to get to it regularly and effectively. Salespeople have to constantly allocate their time appropriately to creating new accounts, closing current business and taking care of established customers. They have to fit these activities into their schedules in a way that guarantees not only this year's revenue goals, but also those of years to come.

Number Three—Account

Account Management: There is a lot about Account Management that has to do with marketing. After all, a typical account has many contacts, each of whom could be a customer, and mostly, there is a commonality across their needs. This represents an opportunity to project a message to a narrow subset of highly interested listeners. Accounts have to be managed using a consistent targeted approach and with a view to revenue development, revenue renewal, and revenue maintenance. Part of the account management process is a regular review of all account activity, including the business generated and interactions made with all the contacts. This is only possible using a good SFA or CRM application with robust Account Management features.

Numbers Two and One

Out of the two remaining competencies, it's very difficult to choose a winner—they are almost in a dead heat. On first thought, that might not seem to be the case, after all, without contacts there would be no sales opportunity. We know that's the case because the business transaction between a buyer and a seller doesn't make sense if you remove one of the participants. This strongly suggests that Contact Management should come first in the list of competencies.

But it's not so simple. In Contact Management, we've seen that strengthening relations is key. However, salespeople can't rely on relationship building alone to survive, and at some point selling skills are needed to compete, and this is where Sales Cycle Management comes into play. Earlier in Chapter 4, we talked about two distinct styles of selling. The "relationship focused" style relies on building customer rapport to win the sale, whereas the "opportunity focused" style depends fair and square on using sales skills. The best salespeople have both skills and can blend them with varying degrees to fit the current need. There are two quite different situations that the salesperson needs to contend with, in which the blending of relationship building and true selling skills is sharply different. The boundary between these two states is governed by whether a customer is in a current buying process or not. In mid sales cycle, the salesperson will be heavily opportunity focused, but if the customer is between purchases (sales opportunities), the salesperson must be in relationship focus mode, well-positioned for when the next sales opportunity comes along.

What's obvious is that the two distinct selling styles depend heavily on the mastery of the top two competencies, as we see in Figure 12-1.

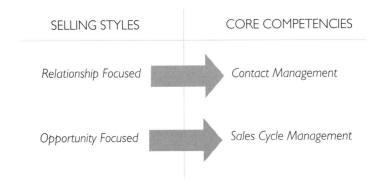

SELLING STYLES   CORE COMPETENCIES

Relationship Focused   Contact Management

Opportunity Focused   Sales Cycle Management

Figure 12-1: The top two core competencies are related to selling styles

Contact Management is the competency that is all about relationships—how to develop them, and, just as important, how to maintain them. This is the part of selling that is the art, but the art has to be controlled and used at the right time and place. That is where Contact Management comes in.

Proposition
The *relationship focused* selling style depends on mastering the competency of *Contact Management.*

Relationship building relies on the salesperson's personal traits, but other resources are needed too. For successful rapport with many contacts, a huge amount of personal and work-related information needs to be known and recorded. The only way to do this is by practicing good Contact Management, and using the technology tools that support it.

Sales Cycle Management defines what selling is all about. Within this special time domain that represents the sales opportunity, the salesperson exercises special selling skills with just one goal in mind—to convince the customer that their solution is the one to choose. This is the time for opportunity focused selling.

Proposition
The *opportunity focused* selling style depends on mastering the competency of *Sales Cycle Management*.

There should be a total awareness of the sales cycle, the position in the sales cycle, and what is happening—which skills should be used, how the process is moving along, and whether the strategy is playing out as planned. This is the science of selling, and for maximum effectiveness, the salesperson leans on Sales Cycle Management for assistance.

The perfect salesperson has the ability to sell effectively with both styles, but for best results, *blends* relationship and opportunity focus to suit a particular customer interaction. The corollary is that *both* the competencies of Contact and Sales Cycle Management need be mastered to help to make this happen.

Balancing Opportunity and Relationship Focus

The perfect salesperson can switch at will from one selling style to the other. Individual salespeople will feel more comfortable with just one style. Some will be gregarious, and love socializing with people; they will lean toward a relationship focused style of selling. Those who like the strategy of the sale and the calculated execution of a well defined sales process will be more inclined to be opportunity focused. Salespeople who naturally graduate towards one style will try to offset this inclination if it's inappropriate for the moment. For instance, if at the close of an important sale, the salesperson relies entirely on their strength with people but totally ignores basic closing skills, there won't be much chance of winning. Some opportunity focused activity has to occur even if it goes against the grain. The natural balance of the two basic selling skills within the individual leads to four *types* of salespeople. Figure 12-2 shows how this happens.

The diagram shows four distinct situations dependent on whether the salesperson shows a high or low *natural* degree of relationship or opportunity focus. "Natural" means the usual day-to-day practice that is most comfortable for them. There will be many instances where they are fighting against this comfort zone.

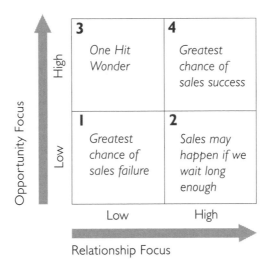

Figure 12-2: Four different types of salespeople

Quadrant One: Salespeople in this quadrant shy away from the personal touch, and to compound matters, they are not that good at seeking or closing deals either. Fortunately, there are not too many Quadrant One salespeople in the profession—they left long ago.

Quadrant Two: Here, salespeople exhibit a high level of success in winning over customers on a personal level, but have poor skills when it comes to competitive selling. With some luck, they will net some sales, but more determined and able competitors will give them a hard time.

Quadrant Three: Salespeople in this quadrant are aggressive sellers, but show little attention to establishing trust or rapport. They may win some sales, but have little chance of creating a revenue stream from repeat orders. The contact simply has no confidence in the salesperson. If there are many accounts in the territory, the salesperson can move on and get more business, but at some point, they will run out of customers. Business will be unsustainable because customers won't trust the salesperson.

Quadrant Four: This is where all salespeople should strive to be. These salespeople have developed trust and loyalty with their customers through ongoing attention to the relationship. But at the same time, they are always searching for the sales opportunity, and when it happens, their sales skills are sufficiently developed and tuned to win the sale. This salesperson has the unique talent to use both relationship building and selling skills in complete harmony and to vary the mix of these skills as required by the *immediate* moment in the selling discussion. In Chapter 14 we'll show how this idea helps out immensely when we try to classify the customer interactions that are most important for *sales automation done right*.

But If We Could Pick Just One

Even though Contact and Sales Cycle Management are rated as the top two competencies, when we are really pinned down, Sales Cycle Management must come out on top. That's because *sales automation done right* is about the technology and sales—Sales Cycle Management is where this coupling produces the best return. Sure, technology can help manage contacts, accounts and the territory, but that is just glorified database management.

Not so with the Sales Cycle—the computer can do much more than file and sort a list of sales opportunities. It can be made to understand and assist with all that goes on in these precious moments of time that determine the possibility of doing business. It can suggest the proper skill to use at specific times in the sale, it can judge the true value of an opportunity, and warn the salesperson that it needs more attention. What's more, it can fill the role of a friendly sales coach in the analysis of an ongoing sale.

More than in any other area of SFA or CRM, the positive impact of technology is the greatest when it comes to managing the sales opportunity and the sales cycle. If all sales teams could be convinced of this fact, they would start looking at their computers as being a great way to move toward the coveted Quadrant Four.

Figure 12-3 is a simple diagram of what we are trying to express. The Sales Cycle is the central competency and the other three are peripheral, but important. In fact, the competencies of Contact, Account and Territory Management are just three different ways to tackle the real job, which is mobilizing all the best efforts of the salesperson to work the prized opportunity list in ways that will generate most revenue.

Now we move on to Part 3, the meat of *sales automation done right*, and an explanation of how automating the major processes in Sales Cycle Management can be realized in practice.

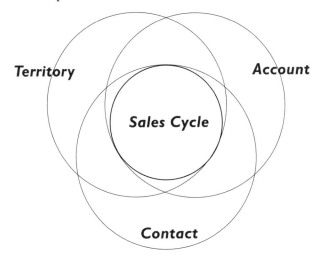

Figure 12-3: Sales Cycle Management is the central competency

Points to Remember

1. Mastering all the four competencies is the way to go, but the enormous importance of relationships and sales opportunities make Contact Management and Sales Cycle Management stand out as the top two to work on.

2. Sales Cycle Management is the competency that benefits most from applying technology to sales.

PART 3

Understanding the Sales Opportunity

CHAPTER 13

Finding Sales Opportunities

They don't just grow on trees!

Some companies say that they don't have sales opportunities; their sales-people sell by *servicing* customers. The idea is that if you are good to your customers, they will keep buying from you (this is a central theme of Customer Relationship Management). But at some point in the past, the customer had to consider your solution over another—and, you had to *sell*. An integral part of the sales opportunity is competition. No sale is given away free. When we sell, we are using our skills against a competitive alternative, and sometimes, the alternative is that the customer does nothing.

The real danger is assuming that the sales opportunity will *come to you*, rather than you actively seeking it out. This philosophy usually results in a shortened sales cycle, coupled with the reaction of, "We were in too late." The earlier the sales opportunity is identified and recorded, the sooner a strategy can be put together to win it.

There's one important issue that has to be taken care of first. Where do we find the sales opportunity?

Leads—The Origin of The Opportunity

A sales opportunity starts life as a **lead**. The sales lead is the first indication from a contact that there could be some business ahead. As soon as there is a need for a product or service, the contact will approach potential suppliers. The approach can happen in many different ways: a phone call, a response to an advertisement, or a casual visit to a trade show booth, or within a regular meeting with the salesperson. This first approach is an *inquiry*.

> *Lead*: An indication, expressed by a contact, of interest in the salesperson's product or service.

Note the difference—with a lead, we don't yet know if the customer has started the buying process, and with an opportunity, the buying process is under way. The method of determining if the buying process has started is called "qualifying."

Qualifying The Lead—Is This The Real Thing?

The lead is a potential sales opportunity; to establish if this is the case, it must first be **qualified**.

> *Qualifying*: The questioning process used by marketing to establish if someone who has expressed interest in our product is, indeed, a potential buyer (we say qualification is done by marketing, more on that later).

The process of qualifying involves talking with the contact who is the subject of the lead. A lead may be qualified as positive or negative. If the contact is found to have no intention to buy, the lead is qualified as *negative*, but a record of the lead is kept for future marketing efforts. On the other hand, if the inquiry is serious, and there is a strong expression of a future purchase, the lead is qualified as *positive*, and a new sales opportunity is logged.

It's important to try to achieve consistency; each lead should be qualified using the same rules and standards. This applies not only to the leads of the individual salesperson, but also to those of the entire sales team—each lead must be treated the same way. Inconsistency creeps in when salespeople handle their own leads, rather than trusting it to the marketing department.

With the introduction of sales automation, processes become more standardized—including lead qualification. Qualification becomes routine.

Has this customer started the buying process? Answering *yes* determines that the lead has been qualified positive—the lead becomes an opportunity. Answering *no* determines that the lead has been qualified negative—the lead is stored in the marketing database for future campaigns. Answering *don't know* keeps the lead open for future clarification. These are the *essential* questions that must be answered to establish if a lead is a possible opportunity.

The Identified Business Opportunity

Once a lead has been qualified and it has been established that the customer has started the buying process, the sales cycle has begun and you now start the selling process. In *sales automation done right* the sales opportunity is called an **IBO**, short for **Identified Business Opportunity**. This term reinforces the fact that the sales opportunity comes from a *rigid qualification process*, and there is a good chance that this customer intends to buy.

Although it may seem trivial, it's a good idea to have an acronym for something so important in the salesperson's daily life. Each opportunity is unique, and it should be stored on the computer with its own identification number. Usually, a specific IBO will be labeled as IBO #1234, or something similar. This makes it easy to track events and activity that occur through the sales cycle, and to tie them to the IBO in question. Within the sales team, a heavily worked IBO soon develops its own persona, and people will start to refer to it using its numeric identifier. This makes life a lot easier for the team who is reviewing progress in dozens, or even hundreds of opportunities at forecasting time.

Long-Term Lead

There is an important case in lead qualification where neither a positive nor a negative qualification can be made, and this is called a **long-term lead**.

> *Long-Term Lead*: A situation that sits between an opportunity and a closed lead. It is established that although the contact has not initiated the buying process, they will likely be in the market for a solution in the distant future.

A good example of this is when a customer takes a lease on a new car, perhaps for three years. The salesperson knows that at the end of three years, the customer will definitely be in the market for another car, but for now, an immediate sales opportunity does not exist. This is a good case for creating a long-term lead. A good sales automation system will be able to recognize this type of lead and remind the salesperson to make regular interactions with the customer in the future with a view to making another sale.

Marketing and Sales

Part I talked about CRM and showed the processes that flow between the three prominent customer-facing groups of marketing, sales, and service. In fact, the transition of a lead to an opportunity occurs at the boundary line of responsibilities between the marketing department and the sales department.

Marketing Department: The functional group that finds prospective customers, qualifies them and hands over positively qualified leads (IBOs) to the sales department.

Sales Department: The functional group that has the responsibility of winning as many IBOs as possible!

For CRM to be successfully implemented, it's important to take account of these clear distinctions when setting up the work processes between marketing and sales, and to ensure that the boundaries are enforced. Sales automation deals only with the sales opportunity. Marketing automation takes care of finding leads and qualifying them.

In many companies, salespeople are asked to qualify their own leads. In this case, they are wearing marketing hats, and as soon as the lead is qualified as an opportunity, it's time to switch to the sales hat and get on with the job of selling.

Opportunity Driven or Not?

It's not uncommon to hear sales managers state that their business doesn't lend itself to a well-defined sales opportunity—rather, their salespeople service the accounts and wait for the orders (they are relationship focused). Yet when those same managers are asked if they experience competition, the answer is always yes. If there is a competitive battle going on, there will always be a sales opportunity underneath it, and the salesperson who discovered the opportunity first and started a well-planned strategy to win it is most likely to be successful. The point is that you can't really develop a strategy for something that you don't recognize is there.

It's possible to stumble on a sales opportunity, only to find it's too late to do a decent selling job. If this happens frequently in a sales team, the manager will usually recognize that the team's sales cycles are far too short—maybe one month instead of nine months. This puts the team under a lot of pressure, as the selling has to take place over an inadequate time period. If a sales opportunity first gets logged when the bidding documents are delivered to the door, three-quarters of the customer's buying process has probably passed. Ideally, a salesperson should be present throughout the entire buying process to get the sales job done properly.

In competitive selling (is there any other kind?) there is no substitute for discovering an opportunity before your competition does, and beating them to the punch. This can only happen if the sales team has a culture of opportunity focus. This team is constantly on the hunt for the signs of developing needs from their customers—needs that will ultimately lead to a move to buy, and the opportunity to sell.

Points to Remember

1. A structured questioning process that everyone understands will ensure consistency in qualifying leads.

2. Make sure that the sales and marketing teams clearly understand the difference between a lead and an opportunity.

3. The unqualified lead belongs to marketing; the Identified Business Opportunity (IBO) belongs to sales.

4. The earlier a sales opportunity is discovered, the more time there is to do a thorough selling job.

CHAPTER 14

Customer Interactions

Building the sales process

Chapter 4 showed us how technology plays an important role in making the vision of Customer Relationship Management possible with the introduction of the Customer Knowledge Store. This is the database that acts as an archive of all dealings with the customer. Using information from the Knowledge Store, a company can tailor its services to fit the customer's needs, thereby creating loyalty and a more substantial and sustainable business relationship.

What kind of information goes into the Knowledge Store? Any *interaction* that occurs between the customer and anyone in the company that can impact the business transaction. In *sales automation done right* some interactions take on special significance. This chapter and the next delve deeply into the idea of interactions, or more specifically, **customer interactions**.

The Customer Interaction

A check in the thesaurus for the word "interact" turns up **relate**. Here is the connection between customer *interactions* and customer *relationships*—you can't have a relationship without interactions.

> *Customer Interaction*: Any event in which the company touches (relates with) the customer with regard to securing a mutual business relationship.

Customer interactions come in all descriptions, but the most important are those that involve people, and most significantly, *people in discussion.* Every customer interaction has the power to impact, positively or negatively, the company's relationship with the customer. Interactions don't necessarily involve people communicating directly—in our context, an interaction may be an event involving a marketing piece, a purchase order, a proposal, a service request and more. But these are still touch points, and must be recorded to preserve the record of an ongoing conversation with the customer.

Proposition
Customer interactions are the essential knowledge bytes that combine to form the CRM Customer Knowledge Store.

The only way to properly populate the Customer Knowledge Store is to keep *all* customer interactions, good and bad. This means *anyone* within the company should be sensitive to the fact that their interactions with the customer should be recorded. This must be done to ensure a complete picture of the customer relationship. If anyone decides to opt out of this responsibility, the interaction history will be incomplete, and an inaccurate representation will be worse than none at all. In working through this chapter, you may think that there is an obsession with customer interactions, but be patient. Many of the ideas presented on interactions are new, and provide ways to get much more value from the Knowledge Store. One certain type of customer interaction takes on a special level of importance in the way it impacts the sales process, and having a well-defined sales process is core to the vision of *sales automation done right.*

How Interactions Occur

Customer interactions are the forum for communication between all departments in the company and the customer. This book is about sales automation, so we focus more on the way salespeople, in particular, interact with the customer. But to see the entire picture of the ongoing customer transaction, salespeople need to review interactions from other groups within the company, in accordance with good CRM practices. In addition, salespeople will add another piece of information about their interactions, one that will show us the story of the sales process as well as the relationship.

Most people think of interactions as two-way—two people in conversation, face-to-face or on the phone. In sales, there is no better way of assessing the true feelings of the customer. Each party can address the issues of the other in real time. Interactions can also be one-way. One-way interactions occur when one party contacts the other not knowing if there will be a response. Examples of one-way interactions are e-mail or voice mail. There may be a response, in which case, the interaction has become two-way. Sometimes one-way interactions stay one-way. There could be no response, and as we know all too well, this is not uncommon in sales!

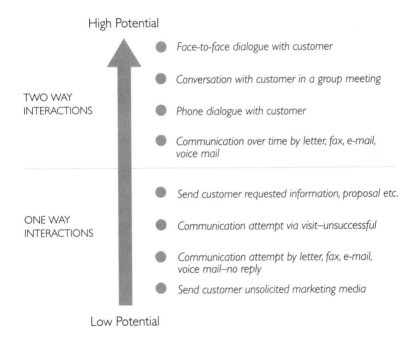

Figure 14-1: The value of interactions

Some forms of one-way interactions don't seem like interactions at all. Consider a purchase order, sent by the customer to the sales department on the successful conclusion of a sale. This is an important one-way interaction of the customer with the company. The company should immediately acknowledge the order (some don't), in which case the interaction has become two-way. In the sales department, information requests, quotations and proposals are in the same category.

As Figure 14-1 shows, customer interactions differ widely in the value that they offer to the sales process. A salesperson should always strive for high value in their customer interactions, face-to-face discussion being of the highest value. This is not always possible and there will be times when resorting to lower value contact such as phone and e-mail may be necessary. Ultimately, the job will get done in a variety of ways, but the salesperson who is able to articulate their story to the customer in the most direct communication channel will be the most effective.

Recording interactions is an essential of good sales automation, but there is one more important thing to do. The interaction must be **classified**; otherwise a vital part of the historical record is missed.

Relationship or Opportunity Focus?

Towards the end of Part Two during the discussion on the two most important competencies, we showed how salespeople fall into four different types according to their natural inclination to sell using two distinct styles. One style is focused on developing and maintaining a healthy relationship with the customer—the theory being that the better that relationship is, the greater chance of winning the sale. The other style is different; it centers on using selling skills to become more effective in the sale, and there is less emphasis on the relationship. Neither style used alone is the right way to go; you need a balance between the two. The possible combinations resulting from how the two selling styles are used lead to the four salesperson types shown in Figure 12-2 at the end of Chapter 12.

The conclusion was that the goal should be to reach Quadrant Four. The Quadrant Four salesperson is comfortable with using either selling style, and what's more, can vary the mix to one degree or another within a single customer interaction to fit the circumstances. The result is two distinctly different types of customer interaction dependent on whether a salesperson's *emphasis* is on relationship building or skilful selling. This is shown in Figure 14-2.

Consider a customer who has no *current* reason to buy. There may not be an immediate need, but there could be future business. Good salespeople will maintain their interactions with the customer with the object of retaining goodwill. These interactions will be **relationship focused**. Sometime in the future, the customer may start another buying process, and the salesperson needs to switch modes. This is a precious opportunity to win a sale and every skill in the book needs to be mustered to fend off the competition. In the sales opportunity the salesperson must be **opportunity focused**. In the period after the sale is won, leading up to the next opportunity, emphasis moves back to the relationship.

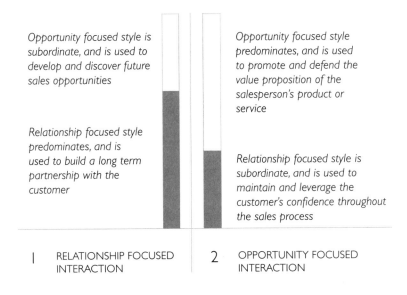

Opportunity focused style is subordinate, and is used to develop and discover future sales opportunities

Opportunity focused style predominates, and is used to promote and defend the value proposition of the salesperson's product or service

Relationship focused style predominates, and is used to build a long term partnership with the customer

Relationship focused style is subordinate, and is used to maintain and leverage the customer's confidence throughout the sales process

| 1 | RELATIONSHIP FOCUSED INTERACTION | 2 | OPPORTUNITY FOCUSED INTERACTION |

Figure 14-2: Relationship and opportunity focused interactions

This *dual personality* of the customer interaction suggests a way to take advantage of the direct benefits of sales automation while still maintaining the requirements dictated by CRM. Determine the essence of the interaction—is it more about relationship or opportunity? Answering this question is effectively *classifying* the interaction.

Relationship focused interaction: An interaction where the salesperson's *primary* objective is to measure, nourish and build the relationship with the customer. Note: True selling skills will still play a background role in laying down the groundwork for future sales opportunities, but relationship focus has dominance over opportunity focus. See Figure 14-2, (1).

Opportunity focused interaction: An interaction where the salesperson's primary objective is using true selling skills to win the sale from the competition. Note: To buttress the ongoing sales effort, attention has to be maintained on the relationship to ensure customer confidence, but the drive is towards winning the opportunity. See Figure 14-2, (2)

A couple of examples will show how this subtle association with the selling process changes the nature of the relationship focused interaction:

"I visited Mr. Parker to see how things were going. He is completely satisfied with the service we have given him, and doesn't see any need for more printers for at least another year. He was glad I called."

This is a relationship focused interaction. The call was made to ensure that the customer was getting the performance from the product that was expected. The salesperson assumed that there was not a current competitive sales situation; the intention was to ensure that both product and service were up to expectations. The salesperson probed for future possibilities, but the principle concern of call was the relationship.

"I visited Mr. Parker to see how the new demonstration printer was performing—we have to remove it next week. It appears that last week the competition brought one of their new models in to demonstrate against us. It performed well and Parker was impressed—we will have to revisit our strategy, as the decision will be made in two weeks."

This interaction obviously draws some attention to the state of the relationship, but there is a *critical* difference to the earlier example. Yes, the salesperson is checking out that the demonstration printer is working for the customer, but in addition, *this* is a sales opportunity. The salesperson is here to sell, observe, and monitor the ongoing sales strategy, in case it needs reshaping. The interaction is *opportunity focused*.

To classify an interaction as it is entered into the sales automation system, all the salesperson needs to do is make the decision of, "Is this interaction associated with an ongoing sales opportunity?" If so, it should be logged as an opportunity focused interaction. That's all there is to it. Even though all interactions have some degree of relationship focus, *in a sales opportunity*, there's no choice; significant interactions are opportunity focused.

Critical Interactions and the Sales Process

Opportunity focused interactions can occur outside of the sales cycle, but generally it's not a good idea. Salespeople who try to be opportunity focused when the customer has no thought of buying anything are asking for trouble. This is the downfall of the Quadrant 3 salesperson who is part of the discussion in Chapter 12. This salesperson is not good at developing rapport with the customer, but rather, tries to use aggressive selling skills, even when there is no desire on the part of the customer to buy. This salesperson over-actively tries to create a sales opportunity when there is no need for one to be there.

If there isn't a need to buy, the customer should not be sold to. Remember, relationship focused interactions permit selling skills to be used with caution, to discover or develop potential business when the chance comes along.

> Proposition
> Opportunity focused interactions that happen within the sales cycle are important enough to be labeled *Critical*.

This is one of the most important premises of *sales automation done right*. On the surface it's simple, but sometimes it's difficult to grasp the significance. Critical (opportunity focused) Interactions are important enough to get a special name because they are *critical* to the execution of the **sales process.**

Salespeople are all aware of sales process, but the term is somewhat overused and often misunderstood. We know from our discussions of CRM that process is important. Process, in the context of "sales process," is the best set of strategies and tactics that will achieve the sale. Tactics are the building-blocks for execution of the strategy, and tactics are played out through the Critical Interaction.

> Proposition
> Critical Interactions are the raw implementation steps of the strategy to win the sale. They form the backbone of the sales process.

This is why we put so much emphasis on the Critical Interaction—it is essential to the execution of a winning strategy. This goes down to the very roots of the direct benefits of sales automation, which we laid out in

Part I. The computer understands the sales process through the information coming from the Critical Interaction. If we don't label an interaction as critical when it goes into the Customer Knowledge Store, the computer can't distinguish it from other information that has been put there to fulfill the vision of CRM. Why do we need to distinguish it? Because then we can easily extract a chronological list of Critical Interactions, which is the same thing as reviewing the sales process as it unfolds. In *sales automation done right* we define the sales process in terms of the Critical Interactions necessary to get the selling job done.

The sales process: A proven, repeatable and well-established set of Critical Interactions through which the sales team implements their strategies and tactics to win the sale.

Most sales teams work to some kind of sales process, but often it is not documented and each salesperson may have their own variation or interpretation. As soon as the team becomes automated, it is essential that a reliable sales process gets developed and stored in the computer to be replicated in future sales. The way to do this is to evaluate past sales opportunities and develop a set of Critical Interactions that have been found to lead to the best chance of success. Sales processes vary all over the map; they depend heavily on the product and its associated complexity and value. Markets and buying processes also have an influence. However, all sales processes are a reaction to the fundamental way people buy, in other words, the selling process evolves as a reaction to the customer's *buying* process. The buying process is universal and simple—it is governed by a linear flow from the first stage of establishing true needs to the next stage of investigating possible solutions and finally to the stage of negotiating a final deal. The selling process is reactionary and follows the flow; salespeople must adjust their skill sets accordingly.

In building a successful sales process, not only does the *type* of Critical Interaction have to be specified, but also its position in the sales cycle and its timing with respect to the interactions that come before and after it. In general, the Critical Interaction set is sequential—the salesperson works through the interactions one by one, not moving on to the next until the current one has been completed. But, this is not always the case. Sales processes should allow for the fact that real life situations don't always follow ideal models and interactions may have to get "out of step." For instance, the sales process may include a product demonstration two-thirds of the way through the sales cycle. Doing the demo later in the cycle makes sense as it is better to show the customer what you have only after you have fully learned what they need—and that takes time. In the event that a customer demands a demonstration shortly into the sales cycle, the sales team may have to go ahead and do it. They would probably be sensible to keep the plans in place for a demonstration late in the cycle and persuade the customer that this would provide a more thorough evaluation opportunity.

Let's look at a very simple sales process and the way the Critical Interactions are set up. Figure 14-3 shows a process with eight steps, illustrating the relative positions of the interactions. Although the average sales cycle of this product may be 6 months, we've learned that the sales cycle can be shorter or longer, depending on when the sales opportunity is discovered. If the opportunity is found just two months from the end of the cycle, the salesperson has no other choice than to complete the sales process in those two months.

Notice that there is an initial Critical Interaction and a final Critical Interaction. It's assumed that an IBO cannot be generated unless some probing has happened with the customer *and* that a won or lost order can't be substantiated without contact with the customer. These two Critical Interactions define the beginning and the end of the sales cycle.

The sales process is described using the minimum number of *essential* Critical Interactions to fit the sales cycle, and this is the best way for the sales team to construct the formula. Salespeople may be tempted to add more Critical Interactions to this ideal process, but most will not subtract from it. It's understood that there will be many *supporting* interactions, over and above the ones defining the procedure. The process is developed using high value interactions that are principally face-to-face. These will be backed up with lesser value interactions such as phone or e-mail.

Why take the trouble to build a sales process? Because it provides a benchmark by which to gauge performance—performance of the overall sales teams but also the individuals within it. Salespeople have their own way of doing things, and could be successful because they have discovered a different way to navigate the sales cycle. If someone finds a better way to do it, then they should share it so everyone can benefit. Conversely, if an individual's sales are deteriorating because they are not following the ac-cepted best approach, they need to be brought back on course. Using a standard, universally accepted sales process is the easiest way to do this.

Interactions

1: *Initial interaction*

2: *Visit, establish needs, introduce solution*

3: *Visit, deliver initial proposal and budgetary pricing*

4: *Visit, executive level presentation to decision maker group*

5: *Factory visit, demonstrate product using customer's procedures*

6: *Phone or visit, assess customer's reaction to factory results*

7: *Visit, submit final proposal and determine customer's position*

8: *Visit, negotiate final deal*

Figure 14-3: Simple sales process built from a set of Critical Interactions

A major benefit of drafting a sales process is to develop a framework on which to hang tactics used in the sales strategy. The lowest level denominator in the sales strategy is the customer interaction. Moving forward through the sales cycle in a structured manner is the best way to make the strategy hap-pen. The structure can only be realized through a well-crafted and credible sales process.

Once the Critical Interactions that form the sales process have been agreed to and locked, the progress of the salesperson in the sales cycle should be compared and measured against it. In *sales automation done right* this is easy because we have classified the interactions.

Some Further Thoughts

Before we leave the Critical Interaction, there are a couple of things worth noting. Firstly, the Critical Interaction doesn't have to deliver positive infor-mation. Consider the following example:

"I called the customer and she told me the competition did a better demonstration than us."

This information is negative, but it's better to *know* what is going on. Review the information and modify the strategy if necessary. Maybe another demonstration attempt will turn the tide.

Secondly, just like all other interactions, Critical Interactions can be one-way or two-way as expressed in the following example. One week away from the close of an important sale, the sales team is feeling that the deal will be lost to the competition. As a desperation measure, it has decided that the customer will be called and offered a healthy discount. The customer is unavailable by phone. An e-mail is sent outlining the new deal. This e-mail must be recorded as a Critical Interaction. It can affect the outcome of the sale, although this won't be known until there's a reply from the customer.

The best way to see how customer interactions are essential to the goals and objectives of both CRM and SFA is to examine a detailed example, which is presented in the next chapter.

Points to Remember

1. The two distinct selling styles of opportunity focus and relationship focus are used together in various degrees in all customer interactions.

2. This leads to two types of customer interactions, either relationship focused or opportunity focused, according to which selling style is dominant.

3. Interactions that are dominated by opportunity focused selling and which occur in the sales cycle are called Critical Interactions.

4. The sales process is built up from a set of well-defined Critical Interactions that has historically been found to work well in previous sales opportunities.

CHAPTER 15

Putting Interactions to Work

A Case Study

The Customer Knowledge Store holds all of the company's recorded inter-actions with the client. Before the CRM initiative, the information resided in racks of manila file folders in bent-up file cabinets distributed through the offices and overflowing to stacks in the warehouse. The information was there, but the knowledge wasn't; no one knew how to get it. It would have taken an army to assemble and review the data, if they could even find it in the first place. Now the information is sitting on a couple of shiny hard drives in the computer room, just waiting for someone to extract the knowledge.

The sales department has access to this strategic, *digital* source of cus-tomer records. They have contributed the results of their interactions like all others in the company. Now they need to harvest the rewards. They can slice, dice and filter the information any way they want, but they invariably will be guided by two overriding questions: "What is the current state of my relationship with this customer?" and "How am I doing in this sale?" This idea was first introduced in Chapter 4 in the form of a proposition. Here, we discussed how the health of the relationship is driven by the principles and vision of the CRM initiative, whereas information showing the strategic progress in a sales opportunity is definitely the realm of SFA. Fortunately, the Customer Knowledge Store can deliver the knowledge needed on both these distinctly different but very important issues, by filtering based on our classification of interactions.

The best way to see how this works in practice is by looking at our ongoing example of the business relationship between Smith Print Corporation (Smith PC), a manufacturer of high quality commercial printing equipment, and their largest account, Global Digital Printer Network (GDPN), a company specializing in all types of print production from mass produced to publish-on-demand.

Smith PC has two major product lines. High Speed Printers are used for fast run, low volume work. The typical price is around one hundred thousand dollars and the average sales cycle is six months. Industrial Copiers are high throughput devices and have sales cycles ranging from one to two years and prices from one-half to a few millions. Smith PC employs specialist sales teams for each product group, as the customers tend to be quite different. But, because GDPN delivers such diverse services, they are customers for both product lines, sometimes in the same facility. Smith PC's largest competitor is Universal Registration. Universal has competitive products for everything in the Smith PC price-list.

The President of Smith PC wants to see how things are going with the GDPN account. He opens up his CRM software and it takes him to his Customer Knowledge Store. Figure 15-1 shows the information that he might see—a chronological list of interactions that happened over a three year period between Smith PC and GDPN. We are showing just 40 interactions that occurred; there could be many more in a normal business. The President could also see information from all departments, but in this case, he has chosen to focus on Front Office: marketing, sales and service.

This list looks intimidating and it is not meant to be studied intensely. It's presented here as supporting material for the case study. This is the *raw* data, and at the end of the day, it is a large part of what CRM technology is all about. If a current business question needs to be answered, the powerful analytical tools that are usually a part of CRM systems can be used to take a close look at a narrower slab of the information. But often, the material needs to be reviewed in its entirety before it's even possible to pose the correct question.

Each row of the table in Figure 15-1 shows summary information of an interaction that occurred between someone in Smith PC and its customer, GDPN. The essential information in the summary is the interaction date, the participants, the interaction type and a short description of what happened. The interactions have been numbered for convenience, but the date is more important as a classification.

Behind each interaction summary there are further details that the president can drill down to if he wishes. For instance, if the short description indicates a quotation has been sent, the actual quotation should be no more than a few mouse clicks away. For a particular interaction, the President may want to see the salesperson's detailed call report to examine details of what was discussed—this kind of detail should be easily available in any CRM system. He can view the information directly on his computer display or in a paper report. Accessing the computer directly is best, because knowledge unfolds dynamically as the President drums up new ways to query the data. The power of the CRM (SFA) system is judged by the speed and ease with which customized knowledge can be obtained from the database—the Customer Knowledge Store.

The quality of the short description is very important. The short descriptions collectively present an overview of the big picture and provide the user with a quick grasp of what happened. That's why it is good practice to create accurate and precise summary descriptions as the interaction is entered into the system. The guiding concept should be, "If anyone else were reading this, would they get a true feel as to what went on in that interaction?"

What can be seen from these 40 interactions? The first thing that pops out is the most important—the relational history with the customer. If the President's objective is to see firsthand how his Front Office team as a whole is representing his company to the customer, this chronological history of interactions from the Customer Knowledge Store has the best chance of giving him that.

A quick review shows that there is a lot of activity in the account. The President sees entries from marketing (interactions 4 and 23). In particular, marketing found an excellent lead at one of their trade shows that eventually turned into a sale. The service team is keeping up with preventative maintenance and emergency calls (interactions 11, 21 and 26). Both sales teams seem to be active as there have been three orders within this time frame. But it gets a little tough to see at a glance how well the sales process went and what was necessary to close the sale. How are the salespeople coping with

#	Date	Participants	Short Description of Interaction
1 R,C	Apr 3, 2003	Rick, HSP Group Call from John Parker	Their No. 1 customer has expanded and will be giving them twice as much business. They are historically Universal customers, but lately, reliability and service has been poor. Parker thinks that Universal needs some competition. They need two of our Type 560 printers; the order goes to us or Universal. (Note: This is the initial interaction for IBO #1212)
2 R,C	Apr 10, 2003	Rick, HSP Group Sales Support Request	Sent John Parker full information package on Type 560 printers.
3 R,NE	Apr 14, 2003	Rick, HSP Group Call to John Parker	Not in—left message.
4 R	Apr 14, 2003	Angela, Smith PC Marketing E-mail to John Parker	E-mailed flier "Printing Today" Mass e-mailing of the new Smith PC product line flier.
5 R,NE	Apr 18, 2003	Rick, HSP Group Call to John Parker	Again not there, this time I left a voicemail.
6 R,C	Apr 25, 2003	Rick, HSP Group Meeting with John Parker	They like the Universal printers that they are using, but the limited functionality of single color production is a problem. Looks as if the Type 560 is just what they need.
7 R,C	May 2, 2003	Rick, HSP Group Call from John Parker	Concerned about moving away from Universal. Reinforced to him that 560 had the single color ability that he needed; says Universal salesperson also claims their new model will do it.
8 R,NE	May 16, 2003	Rick, HSP Group Call to John Parker	Not in—left message.
9 R,C	Jun 16, 2003	Rick, HSP Group Meeting with John Parker and Susan Brown	Susan is their Chief Operator. I showed her photos of the new operating controls on the 560. Her experience is entirely with Universal machines. She definitely wants a demonstration of our product.
10 R,NE	Jun 20, 2003	Rick, HSP Group Call to Susan Brown	No reply—left message.
11 R	Jun 20, 2003	Bill, Smith PC Service Site Visit	Regular Preventative Maintenance call on their 3 old Type 300 printers. Still chugging away but now expensive to service.
12 R,NE	Jun 23, 2003	Rick, HSP Group Call from Dept Secretary Re: Susan Brown	Susan has the flu and is expected back next week.
13 R,C	Jul 10, 2003	Rick, HSP Group Call from Susan Brown	To set up a demonstration at their site on Aug 4. John and the VP Production will also be there.
14 R,C	Aug 4, 2003	Rick, HSP Group Demonstration for John Parker, Susan Brown, Joe Small (VP Production)	Five hour demonstration. Showed how well the limited single color mode worked. Did four complete book blanks. All parties pleased with speed and ease of operation. Universal will demo next week. Left 560 with them.
15 R,C	Aug 11, 2003	Rick, HSP Group Call to John Parker	Followed up on our demo and Universal's. The Universal printed slightly faster but had many software failures. John is worried that it might not be reliable enough. He wants a proposal on two of our machines with a maintenance contract.
16 R,C	Aug 15, 2003	Rick, HSP Group Sales Support Request	Proposal sent: $190,000 including a five percent discount.
17 R,C	Aug 25, 2003	Rick, HSP Group Call to John Parker	Follow up on our proposal. He likes it but Universal is 20% cheaper. Having a tough time convincing Joe Small that they should buy our product.
18 R,C	Sep 5, 2003	Rick, HSP Group Meeting with John Parker	Discussed our advantages over Universal and showed him that our superior uptime would save him money over a five year span (first trial close). John is still concerned about the price.
19 R,C	Sep 15, 2003	Rick, HSP Group Call to John Parker	Offered John our Blue Star maintenance program at no extra charge (second trial close). He felt this could be enough to persuade Joe Small that we should get the job. I suggested a meeting with himself and Joe Small, and he agreed.
20 R,C	Sep 25, 2003	Rick, HSP Group Meeting with John Parker and Joe Small	After a lengthy discussion on the merits of our proposal, I offered a further discount of 5%, if they would take our demonstration printer (third trial close). Joe agreed and called purchasing to confirm the deal was done. (Note: This is the final interaction for IBO #1212)
21 R	Sep 26, 2003	Bill, Smith PC Service Site Visit	Installation and training on Type 560. Successful install. One toner crate missing; will get Rick to deliver.

Figure 15-1: Customer interactions between Smith PC and GDPN over a three year period

#	Date	Participants	Short Description of Interaction
22 R	Dec 12, 2003	Rick, HSP Group Meeting with Susan Brown	Took in a bunch of our 2004 calendars for Susan's group. She is thrilled with the 560 and prefers it to their Universals.
23 C	Feb 6, 2004	Angela, Smith PC Marketing	Met Shirley Vine from GDPN at Print Show Las Vegas. She manages the Quality Publication Division. Needs an Industrial Copier. Urgent requirement. (Note: This is the initial interaction for IBO #2010)
24 C	Feb 27, 2004	Steve, IC Group Meeting with Shirley Vine	Took information package. GDPN wants to boost their capability for full color products. The CL-250 would probably fit their needs but I can't determine if they have the $500K that's needed.
25 C	Mar 15. 2004	Steve, IC Group Call to Shirley Vine	Suggested she join me on a visit to JF Jones who have our CL-240 in their production department. Shirley was enthused at the prospect.
26 R	April 16, 2004	Bill, Smith PC Service Site Visit	Six month warranty check up on T-560, SN 560 – RE214 98-V. No significant issues. Customer seems pleased with the performance.
27 C	May 14, 2004	Steve, IC Group Visit to JF Jones Facility—Shirley Vine and Joe Small, Ralph	Visited the Jones facility. Brought along Ralph from Technical Service to assist with the demonstration. Shirley brought Joe Small (VP Production)—says he has met and is impressed with Rick from our HSP Group.
28 R	May 24, 2004	Rick, HSP Group Meeting with John Parker	Routine check up call to see if all is OK. John is happy; our service group has done a great job in keeping the 560 working trouble-free. John knows about Steve's potential sales to the Quality Publication Division.
29 C	May 31, 2004	Ralph, Tech. Support Meeting with Shirley Vine	Worked out the software protocol for the CL-250, as it would be used in her shop. I'll send this to the factory for use in her evaluation visit in (I hope) September. Says that she is definitely going to the Universal plant.
30 C	Jul 16, 2004	Steve, IC Group Meeting with Shirley Vine	Shirley's request will be put in front of the board of directors at the end of the year. The buying process has to be complete by then. I suggested she plan to go to our factory in October. She will try to fit it into her schedule.
31 C	Sep 6, 2004	Steve, IC Group Call to Shirley Vine	Gave Shirley the final details of the trip to the Boston factory. She will fly down the day before; Joe Small will also be there. Ralph will be there earlier to get things set up.
32 C	Oct 4, 2004	Steve, IC Group Visit Boston Factory—Shirley Vine, Joe Small, Ralph	We spent full day running tests. Throughput is better than their specification. Shirley perceived complexity in the software. I explained that we had several usability settings.
33 C	Nov 5, 2004	Steve, IC Group Meeting with Shirley Vine and Joe Small	Delivered the proposal and spent all morning reviewing with Shirley and Joe. They seem OK with it and will take it to next board meeting.
34 C	Nov 12, 2004	Rick, HSP Group Call from Susan Brown	Needs another 560 printer; putting it into 2005 budget (purchase Feb 2005). Needs an updated proposal including maintenance contract. (Note: This is the initial interaction for IBO #1230)
35 C	Nov 22, 2004	Rick, HSP Group Meeting with Susan Brown	Needs to repeat the package that they purchased before, but this time, need the long term toner option. We are not alone in the bidding, Universal is in there too.
36 C	Dec 6, 2004	Rick, HSP Group Proposal sent to Susan Brown	Same configuration as before but with the long term toner option. List price on total package.
37 C	Dec 10, 2004	Steve, IC Group Meeting with Joe Small	Reviewed final proposal. Giving us the order—forwarding details to purchasing.
38 C	Jan 14, 2005	Steve, IC Group Call to GDPN Purchasing	Called purchasing and got a contract number! The order is ours. (Note: This is the final interaction for IBO #2010).
39 C	Jan 24, 2005	Rick, HSP Group Call from Susan Brown	Her budget has been approved. Wants to move quickly. Universal have offered her a deal on a demonstrator at a ridiculous price. Wonders what we can do—needs a call back soon.
40 C	Feb 4, 2005	Rick E, HSP Group Call to Susan Brown	Offered the existing 560a demonstrator with a full one-year warranty at a 3% discount. Susan said to go ahead and place the order. (Note: This is the final interaction for IBO #1230)

Figure 15-1: Continued

new customer demands and increased competitive pressure? The investment in the development of the new CL-250 instrument in the Industrial Copier group should help give an edge.

Smith PC's sales teams are on the road most of the time, and work from their homes. The two teams rarely connect with one another, and this is one of the president's concerns. He thinks there could be cross selling opportunities that are being missed because his two sales teams have been acting autonomously. This is the principle driver for his initiative in rolling out a CRM system throughout his company. The CRM tool promotes the sharing and interchange of information through access to data such as Figure 15-1. The President hopes that this facility, along with backup training, will encourage sales representatives to be on the lookout for business for their opposite team members, thereby differentiating themselves by offering combined package deals to larger customers.

Fortunately for the President, the sales automation component of his new CRM tool was done right. His sales teams are *classifying* their Critical Interactions. Within this period of three years, there have been three active sales opportunities represented by three sales opportunities. IBOs 1212 and 1230 are for the High Speed Printer Group and 2010 is for the Industrial Copier Group. Note that one IBO starts before the other has ended—a common situation for companies with different product groups and sales teams.

He sees that IBO #2010 is for the CL-250, his new baby. So he asks for just the interactions that contributed to this particular sale. The computer gives him just that—a chronological list of the critical interactions between Smith PC and GDPN from the start of the sales cycle on Feb 6, 2004 to the date of the award of the order, Jan 14, 2005.

To reinforce the connection between the Critical Interaction and the sales process, we've placed the Critical Interactions for IBO #2010 on the sales cycle diagram that we've used throughout the book (Figure 15-2). The interactions are numbered as they are in Figure 15-1. Although it is not so obvious in our simple example, interactions will start to get more frequent in the latter half of the sale. This is common in the sales cycle. As we enter the stages of proving and closing, the relationship between the salesperson and the customer is maturing. Both parties have a goal of getting to the end of the sale with the best deal having been made, and frequent meetings and discussions are the norm.

These are the actual Critical Interactions that occurred. If the President wants to, he can view them against the ideal set of Critical Interactions that forms the sales process for the Industrial Copier product. But in this case, he doesn't need to—he can see easily that Steve has made an excellent effort in the sale.

Interactions

23: *Angela (Smith PC marketing) meets Shirley Vine (GDPN) at trade show*

24: *Steve (Smith PC IC group) visits Shirley Vine for initial probing visit*

25: *Steve visits Shirley to suggest visit to a Smith customer's facility*

27: *Steve, Shirley, Joe Small (GDPN), Ralph (Smith PC Technical Support) visit Jones facility*

29: *Ralph and Shirley meet for discussion on technical issues*

30: *Steve visits Shirley to discuss budgeting and possible visit to Smith PC factory*

31: *Steve phones Shirley to confirm dates for factory visit*

32: *Steve, Shirley, Ralph and Joe visit factory for demonstration of CL-250*

33: *Steve visits Shirley and Joe to discuss final proposal*

37: *Steve visits Joe to negotiate last details*

38: *Steve calls GDPN purchasing and receives contract confirmation*

Figure 15-2: Critical Interactions from IBO #2010

Linking Interactions

The President has viewed the data in the Customer Knowledge Store in two quite different ways. The first is through a list of *all* interactions with anyone in the account sorted in chronological order. This view of the information has provided a general picture of what's happening in the account. We said in the previous chapter that all customer interactions will have some degree of relationship focused selling style, even those that are Critical, where opportunity focused selling dominates. So, in order to build a view of the information from the Customer Knowledge Store that portrays a history of Smith PC and GDPN, all interactions must be associated (or linked) to the customer contact to which they belong. Because in *sales automation done right*, the contact is linked directly through to the account via the core competency hierarchy, the Smith PC President can see the relationship history of the entire account.

Proposition
All interactions contribute in some degree to building the customer relationship, and should be *linked* to the contact (and therefore through the account) to which they belong.

The second view that the Smith PC President reviewed showed just the Critical Interactions from a specific IBO. In order to be able to construct this view there must be a link between a Critical Interaction and its sales opportunity.

Proposition
Critical Interactions, in addition to being linked to the contact, should also be linked through to the IBO to which they belong.

These two valuable views of the same data are only possible if the sales automation system classifies and then links the different types of interactions through to the contact and the sales opportunity.

Showing Critical Interactions in the context of their unique sales opportunity makes it easier to strategize the sale. It seems simple doesn't it? But remember, to do it, you need to classify the interaction as critical when you enter it into the computer. Most people have a "Contact Management" mind-set, assuming that any information remotely connected to the customer contact should be stored with the contact record and viewed along with it. This works well for monitoring the customer relationship, but something more must be added if our attention is focused on what's going on in the sale.

Viewing a sales opportunity's Critical Interactions chronologically is a way of evaluating how the *sales process* is playing out. It's the ability to see the strategic steps that have carried the sale to this point that makes the Critical

Interaction so valuable, and worth the few seconds of effort in classifying the interaction when it is first recorded.

Recording Interactions

A common criticism leveled at sales automation is that entering information into the computer can become an administrative burden. Often, salespeople will go on the defensive and ask, "How do I find time to make face-to-face contact with the customer if I am required to sit in front of a computer all day?" Whether or not this accusation is justified depends a lot on the design of the sales automation system.

SFA relies on information contributed by the sales team—information gleaned from interactions with the customer. What is the criteria for deciding which details should be recorded? Here, it is necessary to steer a fine line between too little or too much. Too little information won't supply the automation system with enough "fuel" to provide assistance in the sales process, and too much information leads to data entry overload. The system should be flexible. Some salespeople love to record endless paragraphs of information and others prefer the bare minimum. The software should accommodate both. Each sales team should define the minimum amount of strategic information that it would like "captured" in an individual interaction, and make this clear to everyone.

Remember, we are dealing now with a shared database, one that is mission-critical to the sales team and the whole company. The database should contain sufficient knowledge to satisfy the Customer Relationship Management objective. It should also contain the raw information on every sales cycle of every sales opportunity that the company works on.

Proposition
Critical Interactions build knowledge of the progress in the
sale, and the sales team needs to share them. The recording of
Critical Interactions should be *mandated*.

At a minimum, Critical Interactions must show the skeletal information of what happened as it *impacts the strategic direction* of the sale. If people want to flesh out their entries, that's up to them. Shared information is only powerful if the *entire* team contributes; one missing piece can create a distorted picture for everyone.

When it gets to relationship interactions, things can be loosened up a bit and the sales team can be allowed to police itself. Everyone should be motivated enough to want to share ground breaking customer information with the rest of the team. One of the greatest criticisms coming from salespeople who have not had the luxury of a true electronic information-sharing environment is that they don't know what is going on. Having it should provide enough incentive for them to get information into the system.

Proposition
Relationship focused interactions vary in their value. The sales team should have a common understanding as to which ones must be recorded.

The value of a relationship focused interaction depends on the insight that it provides in our overall knowledge of the customer. Some have high value and some have low value. Consider these examples: "I found out today from the general manager that the budget for copiers is doubling over the next twelve months," or "The VP Engineering said that his department is closing down next year because of the downturn in sales." Both these pieces of information could have a profound effect on future sales, and should be recorded so anyone who might be affected can hear about it—the information is extremely valuable to the future efforts of the sales team.

But this one is not so important: "I met the Controller of GDPN at the show last week, but time did not allow us to talk business."

None of these examples directly affects the strategic direction of a particular sales opportunity, and are therefore relationship focused, rather than opportunity focused. Still, in many cases, relationship focused interactions can yield good strategic information for the sales team.

Non-Essential Interactions

Interactions 3, 5, 8, 10, and 12 are interesting. Why do we record an interaction of the type, "Not in—left message with secretary?" In interaction 3, there is no dialogue between the salesperson and the customer. The interaction is one-way, and stays that way because the salesperson had to call twice more to get a response. The answer is that even though some relationship focused interactions are unimportant, we still may want to record them!

Many salespeople like to record this kind of information for their own peace of mind to prove that they are working, even though there may be no tangible results. In general, this information is not important for the company or the sales team to see, but may be needed purely for the salesperson's record keeping. The problem is that in the shared environment of *sales automation done right*, these unimportant (or Non-Essential) relationship focused interactions can quickly subject the system to information overload. Critical Interactions are hidden in the mire of too many calls that are made to Mr. Parker, only to find that he is not there!

If this kind of interaction is trivial, why do we need to record it, especially if it clutters up our precious Customer Knowledge Store? We don't—but be careful. Calling Mr. Parker between 8:30am and 9:00am for five days in a row with no reply may present us with the knowledge that he never gets to work until 9:30am, and that he is easy to reach after that. So, mixed up with all this Non-Essential and unimportant chaff may be some useful knowledge about the customer. There is a way to deal with the problem of clutter, and that is to tag or classify the interaction when it is entered into the SFA system. Then we can filter out the stuff that obstructs the view of our opportunity or current status with the contact or the account. In Figure 15-1, these interactions have been given the label "NE" for Non-Essential, to distinquish them from relationship focused ("R") or Critical Interactions ("C").

To summarize, as interactions are vital when it comes to creating a historical record of our partnership with the customer, it is well worth the extra effort to classify them before they go into the Knowledge Store. If they are related to our efforts to win a current sales opportunity, they are Critical. All others are relationship focused, some of these may not have sufficient value to justify recording (Non-Essential).

Critical Interactions will take on a new level of importance as we explore the idea of the "Sales Environment" in later chapters, but now, back to the sales cycle.

Points to Remember

1. All customer interactions provide useful information on our relationship with the customer (they use some degree of relationship focus selling style), and should be linked to the contact, and therefore through to the account.

2. Critical Interactions (opportunity focussed selling dominates within the sales cycle), should also be linked to the sales opportunity in order to retrieve information on the progress of a specific sale.

3. Not all information is created equal. Your sales automation system should be discriminating in accepting, tagging and storing information from the sales team. It should question the user about the relative value of the data being entered.

4. In determining which interactions other than Critical to record, remember that too much information often blocks the essentials and becomes a data entry nightmare.

CHAPTER 16

Fundamental Skills of Selling

Only three? Tell me more

So far, a story is evolving about what happens in the sales cycle; hopefully a story that is in tune with the requirements of sales automation to provide *direct* benefits. We've precisely defined the length of the sales cycle and set up a scheme for determining which customer interactions are exclusively in the realm of the sales process. It's now time to talk about *how* we sell, specifically which skills are most important.

The selling process depends on the customer interaction, more accurately, the Critical Interaction. In front of the customer, **selling skills** are used to progressively build the case on which to win the sale. It's interesting that we need to talk about the skills of selling in a book on sales automation—isn't this best left to the tactical sales training books? By considering how fundamental skills are used, and when they are used in the sales cycle, it is going to be possible to show that all sales cycles divide logically into three sequential stages that are quite different.

The sales cycle *must* develop through these stages, stage one must happen before stage two which must happen before stage three. They cannot take place in any other order, and if the salesperson tries to make this happen, the sale will be in jeopardy. In *sales automation done right* these stages are referred to as *phases*. Later chapters will show that any sales cycle, no matter if it is for reasons described earlier, abnormally long or short, will still have the three phases. This idea will help us develop the sales method to the point where the computer will become a valuable tool to overcome the headaches associated with managing the sales cycle, described in Chapter 11.

The Buying Process

The three phases of the sales cycle are a reflection of the natural evolution of the customer's **buying process**. Neil Rackham, in his book *Major Account Sales Strategy* describes how buying decisions follow a process that follows three distinct stages.* Customers follow the same basic set of rules when they buy, and it is from these rules that the process is determined. When a salesperson is involved with an opportunity, they adjust their selling skills to react to, or match, the customer's buying procedure. It's no surprise that the buying process flows naturally through three distinct phases, and that's why there are three phases to the sales cycle. So how does the buying process work?

The customer's decision to buy something is always fueled by a need. The recognition of the need and the decision to do something about it forms Phase One of the buying process. The need emanates over a period of time until the point that the customer decides to take action, and the salesperson is called in for assistance. The customer usually wants to review solutions from a number of vendors, making the situation competitive. The discussion with suppliers involves questions and answers, to-and-fro between customer and salesperson. When each understands the other's position, it's time to move on to Phase Two.

In Phase Two, the customer seeks assurance that proposed solutions will indeed solve their problems. This is the time when salespeople demonstrate the capabilities of their products or services. At the end of Phase Two, the customer aims to have enough information on all available options before moving on to Phase Three.

In Phase Three, it's time to negotiate a deal. The customer will be looking for value, which is the right combination of suitability and cost. The salesperson will be anxious to secure the order within the confines of good business practice.

This is a highly simplified outlook on sales transactions as seen *from the the customer's point of view*. But how does it appear from the salesperson's perspective?

* Neil Rackham, *Major Account Sales Strategy* (McGraw-Hill, Inc. 1989).

Phase One of the Sales Process

The customer is experiencing some kind of need; something is missing: an improvement must be made, a process has failed, order has to be put into a business process, a vital instrument has malfunctioned, throughput must be improved by a factor of two. Pain is felt and something must be done about it.

Enter the salesperson. Discussion occurs to see if the salesperson may have a solution. The need may be redefined, scaled up in scope, or even reduced. Sometimes the salesperson even negates the need by recommending a different way of doing things, and by doing so, builds trust with the customer.

Phase one is a *sounding out* process between the customer and the salesperson. Listening is important for both the salesperson and the customer. Asking questions is important too, because the buyer and the seller have to learn what each brings to the table. Challenging ideas is also another significant aspect of this exchange; customers can be wrong in their expectations and may have money they need not spend.

We can't sell anything to the customer unless we know what they want. That sounds obvious, but it is surprising how often salespeople fall into this trap. A salesperson must know *all* the facts, issues, emotions, politics and everything else that could affect the outcome of the sale. To do this, they need to *ask, question, listen, examine and watch*; this skill is probing.

Proposition
The first phase of the sales process is dominated by the
fundamental skill of *probing*.

When we probe, we identify and isolate the needs of the customer. Then we are in a good position to gauge which of our product offerings would be the best fit (if any). Until we know exactly what the customer needs, we cannot set ourselves up for the full impact of the next fundamental skill. Even the best salesperson does not know instantly what the customer's needs are. This process takes time. It may take many interactions and a lot of time in the sales cycle to establish this. Then there is the frequently occurring possibility that the customer doesn't even know what they want. We then don the hat of business consultant and assist with formulating the requirement. In general, the process of probing takes up a lot of time in the sales cycle—more than each of the other fundamental skills.

Phase Two of the Sales Process

The need has been identified as closely as possible and now, the mission starts toward finding a solution. There will usually be many options, each with its own pros and cons. There may not be an exact match between need and solution, as each one is multifaceted. Sometimes, the customer's demands can't be spelt out uniquely; it will be surrounded by nuance, perception and inexactness. Salespeople have to fight through this to find the best way their product can fit the bill. They must always do this with honesty and integrity—they will not survive in sales if they break this cardinal rule.

The goal is to devise the best set of matching needs and product features that will solve the customer's requirements and to prove how that match works.

Proposition
The second phase of the sales process is dominated by the
fundamental skill of *proving*.

To prove effectively, the salesperson must *tell, demonstrate, show, convince and persuade*. The predominant skill of Phase One, probing, has set the stage for Phase Two. As Phase One evolved, more and more was learned about the customer's exact requirements until the right time came for proof that there was an available solution. The customer may still have objections with some of the aspects of the proposed solution. Proving skills will be needed to unearth the objections, bring them into the open and negate them, if possible.

Phase Three of the Sales Process

The customer is longing to get on with things, and so is the salesperson. Enough proof is on the table, and a decision has to be made. But before that, the final details have to be wrapped up. If it is a fine decision between a number of suppliers, there may be many negotiations to determine the best *value proposition* for the customer. At this point, the salesperson must remove any barriers standing in the way of the customer awarding the business and ask, "If my product does everything to satisfy your needs, will you give me your business?"

The skill of checking the customer's final intentions to purchase and negotiating a final conclusion is called closing.

Proposition
The third phase of the sales process is dominated by the
fundamental skill of *closing*.

The eventual goal of closing is that the customer indicates your solution is ideal for their needs, and that you have won the order. Before this happens, the salesperson may have to go through a sequence of interactions of asking for the order, only to be confronted by barriers that the customer perceives in going ahead with the purchase. Each barrier has to be negotiated away until there are none left; then the sale is won. Each one of these tests to see if the customer is ready to make a decision is called a *trial close*.

Summary

We've identified just three fundamental skills of selling: Probe, Prove and Close. To some, this may seem radical but when put to the test in actual sales situations, the model works extremely well. The ability to probe, prove and close depends on acquiring a more broad based skill set which will be generic across the three fundamentals. For instance, diplomatic, strategic, interpersonal and attentive skills work hand-in-hand with the fundamental skills.

As we go forward, we are going to call the three phases the Probe Phase, the Prove Phase and the Close Phase to identify them with each dominant skill.

Notice that we used the term *dominant* and not *exclusive*. This is because the three skills are not used by themselves. It shouldn't be thought that each phase is self-contained and autonomous. In fact, it's not like that at all. The selling process (like the buying process) is fluid, and there are leaks across the phases. There are three naturally evolving processes that evolve, emerge, and develop over time in juxtaposition with one another. This will become much clearer in the next chapter when we take the model of the three skill phases further.

Points to Remember

1.   The salesperson reacts in unison with the customer's buying process.

2.   The buying process has three distinct stages, which imposes a corresponding three phase sales cycle.

3.   *Sales automation done right* defines three fundamental skills of selling, probe, prove, and close, which are the foundations for all other skills that may be used.

4.   Each of the three phases of the sales cycle is dominated by one of the three fundamental skills.

CHAPTER 17

The Three Phases of the Sales Cycle

At this point in the sale, which skill should I be using most?

The idea of the three fundamental selling skills is an important contribution towards an attempt to build a **model** of what happens in the sales cycle. Later in Part 4 we will see how all the pieces of the model come together. This chapter assembles the first parts of the puzzle by showing how the three phases of the sales cycle are a direct consequence of the changing behavior of the fundamental skills as the sale progresses.

Over the next few pages, it's important to realize that even though the sales cycle is shown as a simple and continuous straight line, it is really composed of the discreet Critical Interactions played out between the customer and the salesperson over time. In each interaction, the salesperson will use two, or maybe three of the fundamental selling skills, but never just one. The choice of skills used, the way the skills are used, and the focus placed on each skill follows a predetermined pattern that is governed by the conversation between buyer and seller through the natural evolution of the sale. These parameters will differ considerably depending on the current position in the sales cycle and will be quite different in the early stages, through the middle stages to the later stages.

Additionally, this pattern is applicable to all sales that have significant sales cycles, independent of industry, market, product or service. In other words, by the time we have reached Part 4, we will have developed everything to define a *generic* model of the sale.

The Degree of Focus

As a starting point, look at a Critical Interaction between customer and salesperson as the sales cycle draws to a close. This extract is obviously contracted, but is representative of what often occurs.

Salesperson: "Now that you have tried the CL-190 copier successfully for a week in your office, can I place an order for you, to get you one before the factory closes for the holiday?" (Closing)

Mr. Parker : "It performs very well, but my Support Manager thinks the footprint is too large for the new copier room."

Salesperson: "Who is your support manager? (Probing) Maybe you would introduce me so I can describe our moveable CL-190 copier cart that frees up desk space." (Proving)

In this scenario, Mr. Parker raised an objection with the footprint being too large. With some probing, the salesperson found a way to overcome the objection using their proving skill. The probe and prove skills were used to *support* the dominant closing skill.

Proposition
In any Critical Interaction, the fundamental skills are not used alone; they depend on the support of one or both of their companion skills.

We will see later that for most of the time, just two skills are used—probing and proving. In the final stages of the sales cycle, all three skills are used in the interaction. At any point in the sales cycles the usage of any one of the skills will vary, and we need to develop the pattern that shows its behavior from the start of the sales cycle through to the end. To do this, we use a *gauge* of how much any one skill is needed in a single interaction. This is called the **degree of focus**. For instance, if a salesperson assesses that for half the time spent in a meeting the commitment has been to probing, then the degree of focus on probing is 50%. Let's say that it is early enough in the sales cycle that no closing was attempted. Then our model would say that the balance of the meeting was committed to proving—therefore the degree of focus on proving would also be 50%.

The rule is that the percentages for the degrees of focus of each of the three fundamental skills in a single Critical Interaction add up to 100%. In a way, the skills compete with one another for attention. If the use of one skill in the interaction becomes excessive, a partner skill will suffer.

Remember, we are developing a *model* of what happens in the sales cycle, and models attempt to describe reality in mathematical or graphical form. After an interaction towards the end of a sale the salesperson may determine that the degree of focus on closing was 85%. If the salesperson is backing up the closing efforts with some probing, he or she may feel that the probing effort deserves a degree of focus of 10%. Then the rule that our model uses says there must be a degree of focus on proving of 5% (85+10+5=100).

The model is this precise because it needs to work for the computer. Salespeople don't need this precision, and it's interesting to speculate if they are able to judge the degree of focus in the usage of a fundamental skill. When the full model has been developed it will show that there is an optimum way to progress through the sales cycle, and strong deviations away from this path are dangerous. Salespeople should be conscious of the way they use the fundamentals skills of probing, proving and closing in each high value Critical Interaction spent with the customer, and try to keep within the guidelines described by the model. The best way to do this is to *plan* ahead for each meeting with emphasis on what needs to be accomplished and to plan using a framework determined by the three fundamental skills.

For example, if it's early in the sales cycle, the salesperson will know that probing must be a major focus, and they should develop a detailed list of issues that must be uncovered and addressed that are specifically related to probing. The model will show that some proving will be needed too, and a similar list of proving issues should be drawn up. During the meeting with the customer, the lists should be reviewed and items should be checked off as they are handled. Afterwards, the results of the meeting can be scrutinized to see what was accomplished and what was not. It's surprising how well salespeople using these planning techniques can quantify their performance in terms such as, "insufficient probing" or "proving too early" or "no attempt to close." Planning for Critical Interactions is the best way to ensure that some value is achieved in the precious time in front of the customer, and it is often the most neglected aspect of good selling.

There is no suggestion here that a salesperson should determine that they will go into a meeting and spend *precisely* 43% of their time probing and 57% of their time proving. But salespeople should make themselves aware of the trends and patterns that emerge from the model we develop over the next few pages, and test real selling experiences against them. In most cases, we guarantee that the basic ideas of the model will be validated.

Developing the Broad Strokes

Using some basic knowledge and experience about the sales cycle it is possible to start laying down some important behaviors of the fundamental skills. Fig 17-1 shows how this is done. The figure shows the familiar sales cycle with some Critical Interactions—in this case, we show just six. There will undoubtedly be more Critical Interactions than this, but we've picked these six as important marker points in time, where shifts occur (or don't occur) in the usage of the fundamental selling skills. Every sales cycle is marked by an initial interaction and a final interaction (1 and 6 respectively). Interaction 2 occurs about one-quarter of the way through the sales cycle, and interaction 3 is about half-way through. Interactions 4 and 5 straddle the three-quarter point, where things begin to liven up in the home stretch.

There is a vertical axis to show the degree of focus, going from 0% to 100%. At each interaction we've shown vertical bars, the heights of which represent the degrees of focus of probe, prove and close, as used in that particular interchange between salesperson and customer. The following discussion outlines the reasoning behind the ways that the degrees of focus change.

Interaction 1: This is a new sales opportunity. In other words, the customer doesn't already own our product and is not familiar with our company. The focus on probing must be very high—it's unreasonable to expect the customer to volunteer information about the issues that affect their potential purchase. They probably won't even know all of them, and will want to garner some of the expert advice of the salesperson. This is a good process for relationship building, but to get it to happen, the salesperson must *probe*. In these early interactions, probing is the dominant skill, and the salesperson has to forcefully reject letting the urge to *prove* get in the way. The problem is that most salespeople want to do exactly that. But the mission of the salesperson in these early stages of the sale is to *listen* and to *question*, two of the basic components of the probing skill.

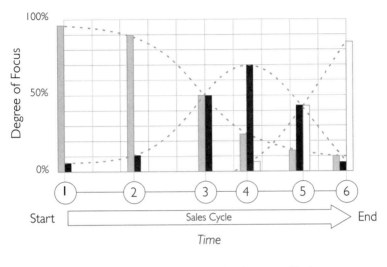

Interaction	Probe	Prove	Close	Total
1	95%	5%	0%	100%
2	90%	10%	0%	100%
3	50%	50%	0%	100%
4	25%	70%	5%	100%
5	14%	43%	43%	100%
6	10%	5%	85%	100%

Figure 17-1: How the fundamental skills are used throughout the sales cycle

Yes there will be a need to prove, but only as a response to questions asked. The need to prove will not be proactive, but more reactive. The customer might ask the salesperson questions about their company's viability. How long have they been in business? Do they have a local office? Do they have service? To establish credibility, the salesperson must prove.

Interaction 2: We're a quarter of the way into the sales cycle. We're starting to compile information from the customer, and the idea of our possible solution is beginning to gel. But as more details get spelled out, more uncertainties are raised, and must be dealt with by an increased level of proving. Not much has changed though, and we have to force ahead by probing, with the comfort that the better we can do this over our competition, the easier it will be in the later stages of the sale.

Interaction 3: Half the available time for selling has elapsed and a number of important Critical Interactions have occurred. So far, the interactions that have occurred amount to a few hours in front of the customer. Challenges and issues have been drawn out for discussion by probing. Notice that until now, probing has been the skill used most, not surprising, as in a significantly large sale, it takes a lot of time over a number of interactions to discuss and identify the customer's exact needs. During this period, proving is needed to react to issues that need identification or clarification. The more that is known about what the customer is searching for, the more effort is needed to validate the salesperson's understanding of the need and their capability of satisfying it. In Interaction 3, the point is reached where the two skills, probing and proving, are used with equal focus. From here on, the emphasis shifts to proving—the need has been identified, and the solution has to be tested and evaluated.

Interaction 4: We are approaching the three-quarter mark of the sales cycle. This is the point where we should have finally proven everything to the customer about our product and service, and how well it fits the requirement. The use of the proving skill has peaked. Theoretically, there is no reason now that the customer should not make a decision, based on the evidence that has been brought forward over the past few interactions, and the closing skill has to start coming into play. But few sales really end here; the viability of the salesperson's solution has been fully tested, and been found to do the job. Now the details of the deal have to be negotiated, especially those that determine value to the customer.

Interaction 5: We've moved on a bit in time from Interaction 4, and are starting to use the closing skill. In fact, our dependence on proving is diminishing, and focus on closing is increasing—in this interaction the two are roughly equal. We've proven enough for the customer to make a decision, and we are trying to determine if they are comfortable with that. To do this, of course, we have to keep probing. If barriers are discovered, they must be dealt with, which involves some proof. Why, after all this time, and very near to the end of the sales cycle, is there still a need to probe? The answer is because the circumstances surrounding the sale are always changing. Nothing should be taken for granted at this point in the sale, as anything can happen without warning.

Interaction 6: This is the last interaction in the sales cycle, and the emphasis has to lean heavily on closing. There is no reason that the customer should not commit. The timing is right—the customer says a decision must be made. The salesperson must directly solicit the commitment from the customer, and if it is not forthcoming, check the reasons why. Probing is used to check for objections, and proving is used to overcome them. Probing and proving support the skill of closing.

This simple exercise leads to a few key observations:

- The focus on probing is very high in early interactions, and falls off through the sales cycle to its lowest point at the end. Probing is a skill that is needed in some degree or another throughout the entire sales cycle.

- Proving has low focus in early interactions and reaches a maximum at a late stage of the sales cycle. From there, the need to prove falls off until it reaches its lowest focus at the end of the sales cycle.

- The need to close begins only when the customer has sufficient information to make a comfortable decision. This can only happen when the focus on proving starts to reach its highest point. From here on, the attention paid to closing intensifies until the final interaction in the sale, where it reaches a maximum.

These general ideas lay out the basis for the behavior of the skills throughout the sales cycle along with the dependence of one skill on another. Now it's time to fill in the dots, and that's exactly what has been done in Figure 17-1. By joining the bars that represent probe, prove and close between successive interactions, we construct three curved lines that represent the behavior of each of the fundamentals skills throughout the sales cycle. To further test that the model's behavior is precise, Figure 17-1 includes a table showing the degrees of focus of each skill, and how at each interaction, they should total to 100%.

The Three Skill Phases

Using the above guidelines, we have developed a model of how the probe, prove, and close skills are used at any point in the sales cycle. The patterns of behavior, or **skill curves**, are again shown in Figure 17-2. The idea is to pick a point on the sales cycle which corresponds to when the Critical Interaction occurs. A vertical line struck from this point will intersect the skill curves at the degree of focus that is appropriate for this point in the sales cycle.

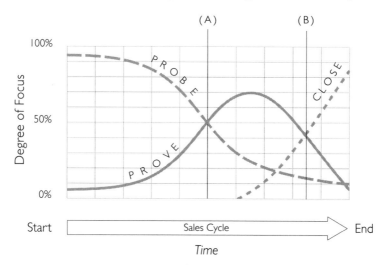

Figure 17-2: Probe, Prove and Close skill curves

For example, line (A) represents a point about half way through the cycle. In a Critical Interaction at this point, a salesperson should be using the probe and prove skills about equally (50%). Notice that the model suggests that no closing be attempted at all at this time. In an interaction represented by line (B) a salesperson would be probing with a focus of around 14%, proving at 43% focus, and closing at 43% focus. The important interaction at the end of the sales cycle has the salesperson heavily focused on closing (85%), and supporting this effort is probing at 10% and proving at 5%.

Each skill follows a well-defined curve or pattern. Again, please remember, this is a model and should not be taken too literally in its application to actual selling. However, the model has been used in thousands of sales opportunities over many years and has been found to have high *qualitative* value. Let's do a reality check against the model:

- Should the emphasis in the early stages of the sale be on learning as much about the customer's needs as possible?—Yes.

- Will some proof of capability be needed even in the first Critical Interaction with the customer?—Yes.

- Should salespeople attempt a close in the early stages of the sales cycle, before they have established the exact details of what the customer wants?—No.

- Should salespeople try to prove their solution before they have probed sufficiently to see how they can provide something that fits the customer's exact requirements?—No.

- Does the process of proving to the customer mature in a seminal event such as a demonstration of performance, or proof of concept, late in the sales cycle?—Yes.

- Is it unwise to move this event forward in the sales cycle?—Yes.

- Can the process of closing start as soon as the customer is comfortable with the level of knowledge of the proposed solution to make a decision?—Yes.

The reader should test the model in this way to see how it works for their unique sales process, but it should safely stand up to examination.

Figure 17-2 hints at another important outcome of the idea of the three fundamental skills. The lines (A) and (B) represent *transition points* in the sales cycle. From the start of the sales cycle until point (A) has been reached, only two skills come into play—probe and prove. There is an interplay between these two skills (remember that the degrees of focus of each skill add to 100%). As the probe skill goes down in focus, the prove skill goes up. At (A), the prove skill begins to overtake the probe skill in focus. Up to this point, the probe skill has been dominant. The portion of the sales cycle measured from the start to the point where proving becomes dominant is called the **Probe Phase**.

During the time that elapses between transition (A) and transition (B) the dominant focus is on proving and is called the **Prove Phase**. During this period, proving reaches its maximum point of focus, which is where the use of closing commences. The focus on closing increases until it surpasses that of proving which occurs at transition point (B).

The **Close Phase** spans the time from transition point (B) to the end of the sales cycle. It is dominated by focus on the close skill, but still has varying degrees of usage of both probe and prove skills.

Proposition
The behavior of the three fundamental skills in the sales cycle
leads logically to the idea of three sequential phases, each phase
dominated by one of the skills.

This links right back to the conclusions of Chapter 16. There we showed that there are three quite separate stages in the *buying* process and each stage is mirrored by a similar phase in the *sales* process. Our analysis of the way the skills behave reinforces this idea, and also tells us something about the relative spans of the three phases.

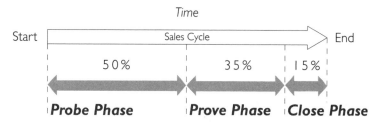

Figure 17-3: The Probe, Prove and Close Phases of the sales cycle

The way the skill curves interact in Figure 17-2 produces relative lengths of the Probe Phase, Prove Phase and Close Phase at 50%, 35% and 15% respectively. A simplification is shown in Figure 17-3. The exact values don't matter so much but experience shows that most sales cycles follow the pattern that the Probe Phase occupies at least half of the sales cycle and is longer than the Prove Phase, which is in turn, longer than the Close Phase. This idea of being able to take a sales cycle of any length and divide it into three sequential stages, each of which focuses on a fundamental skill is very important to *sales automation done right*.

The Importance of the Skill Phases to Sales Automation

The three skill phases are an elegant way of removing the issue of *time* from the sales cycle. All sales cycles, six weeks, six months or even six years will have three distinct skill phases. A specific phase is always the same percentage of the sales cycle (50% for probe, 35% for prove, and 15% for close). So with the six-week sales cycle, the Probe Phase is three weeks, for the six-month sales cycle the Probe Phase is twelve weeks and in the case of the six year cycle the Probe Phase is three years. The message is clear—no matter what the length of the Probe Phase (weeks, months or years), the priority must be on *probing*.

As the computer knows the date the sale started, along with the projected end date, it will always know which skill phase the salesperson is in at any given point of the sales cycle. This becomes very important when looking for a way to prioritize long lists of current sales opportunities, which will be covered in detail in later chapters.

If the Duration of the Sales Cycle Changes

At the start of the sale the salesperson is asked to forecast the date that the sale will end. That projection will undoubtedly change a number of times as the sale progresses. Because of the uncertainties involved in the buying process especially with complex sales and long sales cycles, the forecasted conclusion of the sale can vary enormously. Whenever the forecasted closing date changes, the computer will calculate a new trio of skill phases. How well does the model handle this, and what is the impact on the salesperson? Figure 17-4 shows the answer.

The dotted line represents the position in the *current* sales cycle which was determined to be six months long when the IBO was logged. Today, the salesperson is roughly in the middle of the Close Phase. The salesperson does a regular check with the customer to see if things are still on track, only to find out that funds are on temporary hold and are not expected to be released for another three months. The salesperson changes the expected date of close in the computer, and the sales cycle is recalculated to nine months.

Now, notice what the computer does in *sales automation done right*. The skill phases, Probe, Prove, and Close, are **scaled** in relation to the new sales cycle.

In the new sales cycle the point that represents *today* has been pushed back to one-third of the way through the Prove Phase, and to a point where the Close Phase hasn't even started. Do things really happen this way in real life? It turns out that they do.

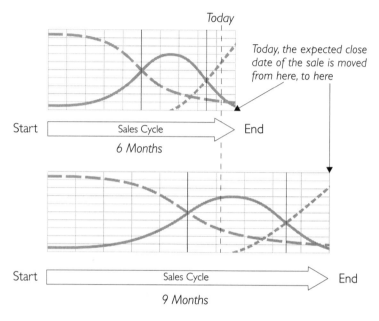

Figure 17-4: The effect of extending the sales cycle

As soon as they learn that things are delayed and the sales cycle has been extended, the salesperson must change their strategy in the sale. If they were leading in the sale at this point, it can no longer be assumed that things will remain the same. The competition has more time to turn the sale around, and our salesperson has more time to lose it! On the other hand, if the salesperson was trailing the competition, the news is good and there is more time to turn the tables. In either case, getting pushed back on the prove curve towards the need to do more proving makes sense. The customer has time to forget some of the benefits raised to this point and the competition can start to cast doubts about the product. When the sales cycle gets extended this much, the salesperson must step up the emphasis on proving to the customer.

It also makes sense that we should pull back on our efforts of closing to concentrate on our need to prove. The rescaled model shows that this is exactly what happens.

Proposition
If the predicted sales cycle length changes, the usage of the three fundamental selling skills should be adjusted accordingly.

When the sales cycle gets *extended*, the model will move us *backward* in the skill phases, and we will have to redo some of the work we have already done.

In the event the customer hastens the progress of the sale, the sales cycle gets *shortened* and the computer will scale down the skill phases according to the new sales cycle length, and the model will move us *forward* in the skill phases and we have to make up for lost time with some extra effort.

Working Consistently Through the Sales Cycle

The sales cycle must be worked with the same degree of energy in each of the skill phases. This should not be confused with using the fundamental skills equally throughout the sales cycle, as we have seen, that is not what should be done. We should be just as active in the Probe Phase as we are in the Prove Phase and Close Phase. Many sales representatives make the mistake of spending too much time in the later stages of the sales cycle at the expense of building a good foundation in the Probe Phase.

It goes without saying that mastery of all three fundamental skills is necessary to win the sale. But using them proportionally throughout the *whole* sales cycle is just as important. The sales opportunity should be discovered as early as possible and resources allocated consistently through to the end.

Points to Remember

1. It is possible to derive the three phases of the sales cycle by looking at the way each skill behaves thoughout the evolution of the sales cycle. In any one phase, one of the skills will be dominant.

2. Dividing the sales cycle into three phases, each with a dominant skill, provides a valuable device to "normalize" the effect of time, making it

easier to analyse a portfolio of widely varying sales cycles at different points in their development.

3. All three phases of the sales cycle deserve the same amount of attention and must be worked with the same degree of intensity.

CHAPTER 18

Grading the Opportunity
Probability—The Vital Percentage

The idea of three distinct phases of the sales cycle is derived naturally from the way the fundamental skills are used as the sale progresses. The three phase model turns out to be a convenient way to analyze a portfolio of sales opportunities with varying sales cycle lengths. Most salespeople are faced with handling just this situation, and there is a real possibility that some opportunities can get overlooked or neglected if their sales cycles are abnormally short or long. What's needed is a foolproof way of prioritizing this list of opportunities. The three phase sales cycle is the first element in the equation to get us there. The second element is **probability.**

Each sales opportunity has its own unique *value*. Value determines the answer to the question "How much time am I prepared to put into this one?" There are many factors that contribute to the value of an opportunity, but the most important is probability. There is a varying degree of confidence associated with the sale until it is finally won or lost, and one of the main requirements of the sales team is to classify this probability of winning the sale in numerical terms, for instance, "The sale is 80% certain."

Assigning probabilities to sales opportunities is a grading process. A low grade indicates a poor chance of winning while a high grade implies a good chance, or an easy sale. It is important to understand that the value of an opportunity (or its probability) almost always changes as the sale progresses. A good salesperson will always work their opportunities to move them higher on the value scale. A sale that is thought hopeless at the start can eventually be won through good selling and a little bit of luck.

The Probability

Probability answers the question, "Are we going to get this sale?" This means that the probability is a percentage number, such as 50%, 80% or 100% (the sales team very rarely puts down 100% as their chance of winning the sale; that would be jumping the gun a bit!). Probability is a number, so it poses one of the worst traps to the sales team—trying to accurately gauge complex sales situations consistently in numerical terms.

Why is there so much concern about assigning probabilities? What difference does it make that a sales opportunity that is discovered today and will finalize a year from now has a 30% or an 80% chance of being won? The answer is that an assessment of probability is a momentary evaluation of the salesperson's potential success in the sale. It is a simple number, but also an important one. The nuances of every issue that has bearing on the sale must be considered and integrated into a single probability number. This is not easy to do, and some salespeople are more talented at it than others. There are those that don't take it seriously enough and make a poor job of assigning probabilities. However, it's difficult to be delinquent throughout a sales career, because the sales team not only lives by current performance but also by future predictions. If those predictions are consistently inaccurate, there are usually dire consequences.

Salespeople should realize that the exercise of evaluating a sale to pin down probability is extremely useful in managing their portfolio of sales opportunities. Each opportunity will have a probability associated with it, and the probability will change as the sale unfolds. Maintaining the list of opportunities with accurate up-to-date assessments of probabilities is the first step in allocating personal resources effectively. This ensures that no time is wasted on one situation at the expense of another. Salespeople understand that some sales are easier than others. That does not mean that the opportunity list should be sorted in descending order of probability and worked from top to bottom. There are sales automation systems that do just that, and it's dangerous. As we discuss in later chapters, factors other than probability also need to be taken into account.

Probabilities form the core data for sales forecasts. Companies don't like to work in the dark and will always want to know the business to be expected in the future. The dynamic of the sales cycle invites frequent changes, so it's not unusual to forecast every month. This means that in the span of a six-month sales cycle, the probability could be reassessed at least six times. Monthly and quarterly forecasts are the norm, but yearly forecasts will always be required, and if year-end is looming, weekly and even daily forecasts come into play.

Accurate is a word that gets a bad rap when it comes to forecasts, because sales forecasting can be an inexact science. Open sales opportunities predict future revenue and good financial planning requires an estimate of future business, so forecasting won't go away. It wouldn't be so bad if salespeople were consistent with their forecasts (either consistently high or consistently low). Once the sales manager has a handle on the trend, it's easy to build in a factor to bring the forecast into line.

But, often, salespeople are not consistent and their forecasts can vary according to the day of the week on which they were constructed. So far, the discussion is on individual salespeople, but things get worse if the consideration is consistency across the team. It's very tough to even out inconsistencies when dealing with a mix of different salespeople. This is where a good manager should review each forecast and put their own spin on it. The ceaseless chore of assembling and presenting meaningful forecasts is the bane of every sales manager.

But there is an answer. Sales automation provides the foundation for sharing, which should encourage everyone to work off the same page. If everyone uses a standard, sound method that they respect and understand, forecasting has a much greater chance of being consistent. In the following sections, we will attempt to devise a method of deriving probabilities which removes some of the vagaries from the forecasting process and which can lean on the computer for help.

Problems with Forecasting

Sales automation should make it easier to assign a probability to the opportunity, but it can't when bad methods are used. Let's take a quick look at the most common ways of handling probabilities.

Ask for a number. Just take the easy way out and ask the salesperson for a number between one and one hundred. The answers will come back all over the board. What is the difference between 43% and 37%, especially if the numbers are from two different salespeople? Many systems operate this way, and the sooner you move away from it, the better. The easiest way to smarten up this system is to limit the options. Given the difficulty of looking into the future, how accurately is it possible to forecast to within plus or minus 10%? Limit the possibilities to 10%, 30%, 50%, 70% and 90%. Given serious thought, most sales managers would agree that it is a tough job to be more accurate than this. If not, more comfort can be had by giving salespeople concrete criteria with which to predict the numbers. For instance, 30% may mean "Wants the product, but has a low chance of getting budgeted."

Base it on milestones. Award a percentage probability on reaching defined milestones in the sales process. For instance, if you've done a demonstration, which is the fourth major milestone in the sales cycle, you have an 80% chance of winning the sale. It's difficult to understand the validity of this method. It's tempting to say that it's based on averaging out the previous history of sales opportunities, but this can't really be the case. Nothing takes account of how well the sales team sells. Simply because a milestone has been reached, there's no guarantee that the sale will be won. Consider the example where a customer has a favorite supplier but has to go through a competitive purchasing process with three other vendors. All the vendors are put through exactly the same process with exactly the same sales cycle. After getting 80% of the way through the process, can they all claim an 80% chance of winning the sale? No, the customer's favorite will have the best chance of winning, and the others probably don't have much chance at all. The situation is not much different even if the customer has no clear favorite. The fact is that the chance of winning depends mostly on how well the selling has been done, and the milestones don't have much to do with it.

Do a quiz. A variation on the previous method is to ask the salesperson to check off answers to a series of questions as the sale progresses, such as "Have you done a preliminary proposal?" or "Have you presented to the key decision maker?" or "Has a demonstration been done, and what happened?" A formula adds up the answers and awards a percentage chance of success. This can be a useful technique, but it can be taxing to the salesperson if it is imposed for every opportunity. It is best reserved for a "back-up" confirmation that the initial intuitive evaluation of the probability is right.

So, what's needed? Well, some method based on the sales representative's personal evaluation of events surrounding the opportunity is best. After all, there is no better judge of results than a participant in the customer interaction. But the method has to smooth out all the possible results governed by the personality of the salesperson, their emotional state when they submitted their forecast and dozens of other issues that affect a personal assessment of "Will we win this sale?"

A Better Way to Do It

We're going to rely on the salesperson's ability to judge the sale and to try to measure their instinct about whether the sale will be won or not. Remember, the goal is to look for a numerical value of the probability, but we don't want to ask the salesperson directly for that number. Part of the answer lies in asking the salesperson easy but penetrating questions about crucial elements of the sale and to limit the number of possible replies. The other part of the puzzle is to compose the probability value from two quite different questions concerning the sale. The computer will take the answers and compose the numerical probability.

Two very effective questions are "Will it happen?" and "Will we get it?"

Will It Happen?—Will We Get It?

"Will it happen?" simply means "Will this sales opportunity go through to completion?" Many sales don't—they start off just fine, with the customer making an honest attempt at the buying process, only to get stymied by issues such as funding cuts, changes in needs or even company politics. When salespeople are asked to provide a probability, they have to take these factors into account in their answer. We suggest that these particular issues be the subject of a completely separate question—"Will it happen?"

Let's ask the salesperson to answer the question "Will it happen?" and limit the answer to a choice of a High, Medium or Low chance. What's more, the criteria for determining the answer can come from the help system of the sales automation solution.

"Will it happen?" has nothing to do with the competitive side of the sale. It is an estimate of the customer's ability to do what they say they will do, that is, to buy something. Let's look at some examples. This customer interaction is the initial one, in which the sales representative is first told of the intention to buy.

Customer: "This new technology looks interesting. I don't really need it, but I'll add it as an addendum to my budget for next year." In this case, "Will it happen?" is Low.

Customer: "I really need this new product badly, but my boss is tight with the budget these days. I'll have to be very persuasive." In this case "Will it happen?" is Medium.

Customer: "The old CL-50 died today, we'll fix it once more, and then junk it. We'll need a new one soon, otherwise there is always the threat that the line will go down." In this case "Will it happen?" is High.

A common question concerns the situation where "Will it happen?" is Low—if this is the case, why worry about working on this sales opportunity at all? Quite simply, it's a gamble not to. If you stay away and the competition doesn't, you are effectively shortening your sales cycle. When you next get involved, you have a lot of catch-up to do. It's possible that "Will it happen?" will change from Low to Medium or High. You should stay on top of the sale and be ready should this happen. Logging the opportunity will ensure that it doesn't get forgotten.

There are a few very important aspects of the opportunity that sales-people need to be consciously aware of throughout the progress of the sale. We are going to call these the *IBO Essentials*.

Proposition
The first of the IBO Essentials asks the question, "What
are the chances that this sale will go through to conclusion
(Will it happen)?"

The other question that supplements "Will it happen?" has to be "If it does happen, will we get it?" Again the choice is a High, Medium or Low chance.

The answer to this question takes into account the degree of competition surrounding the sale and how well you can sell against the competition. There are three possible answers to this simple question, which assists our drive for consistency. Again, let's look at some examples using the initial interaction with the customer.

Customer: "I have two of your machines, both of which have given me a load of trouble. This time, I'm going to give the competition a chance." In this case "Will we get it?" is Low. We have our work cut out for us to turn this decision around.

Customer: "I'm new to this game. It seems from your product information that your solution is the same as your competitor's." In this case "Will we get it?" is Medium. We have to prove that we are better than the competition. If we are successful, the "Will we get it?" moves up to High.

Customer: "I've been told to add another machine to the line. I've got six of your Type 560s; I'm immediately starting the process of buying another one, but it will have to go out for tender." In this case "Will we get it?" is High, but we should not get complacent!

Proposition
The second of the IBO Essentials asks the question, "Will we win this sale over the competition (Will we get it)?"

Using this method, we have separated the issue of winning the sale into two separate and independent parts, each of which can only be answered in one of three ways. This is going to deliver a method of deriving probabilities that will be more consistent and more accurate across the entire sales team.

Completing the IBO Essentials

There is just one more IBO Essential, and that was covered in the discussion of the sales cycle in Chapter 11. A few reasons were outlined on why it is so important to be attentive to when the sale will *end*. *"When will it happen?"* determines the actual length of the sales cycle and enables the computer to calculate which of the three phases of the cycle we are in: Probe, Prove or Close.

Proposition
The third IBO Essential asks the question, "What is my best
guess of when this sale will close (When will it happen)?"

"When will it happen?" completes the trio of descriptors that will give us the ability to characterize the opportunity in some dramatically new ways. The three IBO Essentials are vital to *sales automation done right*. If the computer is rigorously updated throughout the sale on just these three pieces of information, it will be able to perform magic behind the scenes.

It is important to recognize that the IBO Essentials are estimated by the salesperson. All the factors that surround the sale will govern the way that the IBO Essentials are assessed. When the salesperson is determining these three critical pieces of information, they are integrating all the many pieces of knowledge gathered about the sale during interactions with their contacts.

The Probability Matrix

We've just said that the answers to "Will it happen?" and "Will we get it?" give the raw data to the computer to calculate the percentage probability. The easiest way to see how this is done is to plot the answers on a three-by-three grid called the Probability Matrix. One axis of the grid represents the three possible answers to "Will it happen?" and the other axis represents the three possible choices for "Will we get it?"

In Figure 18-1, you can see that there are nine possible answers to the two questions, each answer is a unique point on the grid and is called the Probability Index. When first using this system, it's best to adopt a standard way of referring to a particular square, for instance, to refer to the answer to "Will it happen?" first. This makes square (index) number 3 a High-Low, or High "Will it happen?" and Low "Will we get it?" Following this idea, squares 9 and 7 are High-High and Low-High respectively. Hopefully, we won't get too many of Probability Index 1, which represents Low-Low.

This sounds fine, but where are the numbers? Every sales team needs a number to define the percentage probability. It's no use filling in High-High, or Med-Low on the forecast sheets at the end of every month. With *sales automation done right* there will be no more forecast sheets. The forecast is assembled daily in the computer with the ebb and flow in the portfolio of sales cycles. But we still need a number like 50%, or 80%. For instance, a $50,000 order with a probability of 50% has a potential value of $25,000.

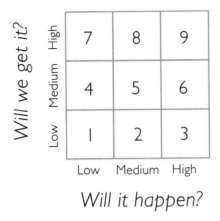

Figure 18-1: The Probability Matrix showing the nine Probability Indices

In assigning percentages to the Probability Matrix, it's possible to take either the scientific approach or to just assign numbers driven by gut feel as to what each combination means for a particular industry and market. Most sales teams will probably use a combination of both.

Let's say we make Low to be 20%, Medium to be 50% and High to be 80%. For each square, we can then multiply the two probabilities together, for instance High-Low is 80% multiplied by 20%, or 16%. Medium-Medium would be 50% multiplied by 50%, or 25%. If we use the same values for High, Medium and Low on each axis, Probability Indices 4 and 2, 8 and 6, and 7 and 3 will be the same value, so this method distils the nine possibilities down to six. This is OK because six possibilities are about as much as we need or can handle; it just isn't practical to forecast with more accuracy than this. What's good is that the computer does all of the background work. Just decide whether your sales opportunity is a High "Will it happen?" and a Medium "Will we get it?" and the computer will calculate that it is a 60% probability.

Even though science dictates that two independent probabilities of 50% will lead to a 25% (one in four) chance of something happening, many sales managers won't want the Medium-Medium case to be as low as 25%. This is not a problem because forecasting is not an exact science—make it 40%. Figure 18-2 shows a completed grid where the sales team has tinkered with science, but has come up with numbers that it is comfortable with, and that work well in practice.

Will it happen?

Figure 18-2: Numerical probabilities assigned to the Probability Indices

The method behind the Probability Matrix has a much better chance of getting sales opportunities tagged with consistent percentage probability numbers. Once consistency has been established, it is much easier to refine the actual numerical percentages using accumulated sales data.

A Few Words on Forecasting

Many companies use a "weighted" value for their forecast. This simply means taking the actual value of the IBO and multiplying by the percentage probability. For example, a salesperson submits one IBO on their forecast for an Industrial Copier, with a value of $500,000, a High "Will it happen?", a Low "Will we get it?" and an expected date of July 2005. The computer calculates the percentage probability to be 25% and weights the actual value by this number. In other words 25% of $500,000 (or $125,000) is entered for July 2005.

This thinking is okay if your business has a product line where each sale is more or less the same value and a lot of sales are processed per month. If you have a variety of product values with some IBO values going very high, you will get errors with this method. A small percentage probability of a very large order can skew your overall weighted forecast. A meager 10% chance of getting a million dollar sale still puts $100,000 into the forecast.

If you are faced with this problem, it is worth supplementing the weighted forecast with a "binary" forecast from the salesperson. A binary forecast is just what the name implies; there are only two options. The salesperson is required to make a decision whether the sale will be won or not. Theoretically, these forecasts should be made only with a "Will it happen?" of High. With this type of forecasting, the example of the million dollar IBO with the low chance of happening would not make the forecast. The binary and weighted methods should be tested against each other over time to gauge how well they match. SFA systems should provide alternative methods of forecasting; the sales team can then choose the one that best fits the needs of the company and its products. The only real way to test forecast accuracy is to store forecasts over time and compare them against what really happened.

Points to Remember

1. Asking salespeople for numerical assessments of winning is asking for trouble. The results will be inconsistent and inaccurate.

2. Basing forecasts on historical data is dangerous—history does not always repeat itself in business!

3. You are more likely to get a straightforward, objective response when you ask the salespeople a few simple questions about the sale, and let the computer calculate the probability numbers.

4. The essential information on the IBO is contained in the answers to three simple questions: "Will it happen?", "Will we get it?" and "When will it happen?"

5. Be careful which method of forecasting you choose. Test weighted forecasts against binary estimates.

CHAPTER 19

Priorities

Working the list

The previous chapter presented a way to deal with probabilities that will inject more consistency into projecting future business. The idea of *probability* is needed to create another valuable parameter of the sales opportunity, which is *priority*. Some sales methods confuse probability with priority—both words begin with "pr" and end in "y," but that's about where the similarity ends.

Salespeople are constantly faced with the question of how to best allocate their time. The most pressing demands on their time and skills come from the list of sales opportunities that they are currently working on. They must *work* the list. To do that effectively, the list must be prioritized, because some opportunities are more appropriate to work on than others. Consider two of the terms used to define priorities, for instance, "This one is *hot*. You'd better set up an appointment now!" or "This one is *cold*. Come back to it in a few months." How much science is used to determine hot, cold or warm? Probably not much.

Some sales teams use probability alone to prioritize their opportunities. Salespeople are asked to sort their list by probability with the highest at the top and the lowest at the bottom. Then they are told to start at the top and work their way to the bottom. As we see later, this method is dangerous and using it can actually lead to lost sales. Something other than probability is needed to correctly define priority and it turns out this parameter is closely (but not completely) related to *time*.

The Opportunity Portfolio

We are going to call the list of opportunities the **Opportunity Portfolio**. The word portfolio better expresses the potential business value that lies within the opportunities that have the ability to be won or lost.

Managing the portfolio can have some real challenges, and we will go into the major reasons why. Many salespeople manage their portfolio in their heads, with varying results depending on capability and experience. The average portfolio contains between ten and one hundred opportunities so it's not too difficult to see why, at the upper end of this scale, some business could get overlooked.

Logging the opportunities into the computer is a good way to start getting the portfolio under control. The next step is using the computer to automatically *prioritize* each opportunity using a few fundamental parameters, so it can then proactively guide the salesperson as to which to work on first. This chapter shows how to do that, but first let's look at the scale of the problem we are dealing with.

Problem—Sales Cycle Spread

There is a *natural* length for the sales cycle, resulting from the fact that any product in a given market takes a certain time to sell. This time depends on the product and the market. Low cost, high turnover products take a short time to sell. Complex and expensive products take longer to sell. Institutions such as government or universities may take longer to purchase than a similar sale to private industry. But at the end of the day, the sales team will have a pretty good idea of what their *average* sales cycle should be under similar conditions.

But "average" infers that there may be exceptions, either abnormally long or abnormally short cycles. Short sales cycles are driven by urgent customer need. Long sales cycles happen when customers experience problems in the buying cycle, such as funding, or maybe their needs are not that strong. So, there are reasons why deviations exist in the time it takes to buy and sell a product.

But in Chapter 11 we explored how salespeople can self-inflict variations into the length of the sales cycle. The *actual* sales cycle is dependent on when the salesperson finds or recognizes the opportunity. In fact, the majority of salespeople arrive at the opportunity after the customer's buying process has begun.

Figure 19-1 is an example of what happens. Salesperson A has the longest sales cycle (sales cycle A) but still has missed fifteen percent of the available time to sell (the customer's sales cycle). Salesperson C is "in too late" and has less than half the time to sell than Salesperson A. Here are three different sales representatives in the same sales opportunity and they each have quite different sales cycle lengths to contend with. Exactly the same thing applies to the average salesperson who, in spite of best intentions, finds their opportunities at various points in the customer's buying process (the customer's sales cycle). Because this happens, there will be a spread in the sales cycles within the salesperson's Opportunity Portfolio. The better the salesperson, the more likely the spread will be narrow because they will generally discover the opportunity early. Bad salespeople will also have a narrow spread in their portfolio, but as they are always "in too late," the sales cycle will always be too short. In between sits the average salesperson with a portfolio of sales cycles that vary over a wide range. This kind of portfolio is tricky to handle. How can even the best salesperson handle the situation without a sheet of paper and a calculator—or a computer?

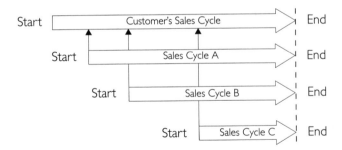

Figure 19-1: How three salespeople discover the same sales opportunity

Figure 19-2 shows actual information on the opportunity portfolio of a scientific instrument salesperson. There are one hundred open IBOs in this portfolio, where *open* means that the customer is in the buying process and has not yet made a decision. The sales cycles range from five weeks to two years—a tremendous spread—let's take a look at why.

Along the bottom axis there are twenty "bins," each representing an increment of five weeks. The first bin represents sales cycles that are up to five weeks in duration, the second bin represents sales cycles between five and ten weeks long, and so on. Each IBO is allocated to the bin appropriate for its sales cycle. For instance, if the sales cycle is 17 weeks, it goes in the bin that represents 15-20 weeks. If the sales cycle is 78 weeks, it goes in the bin representing 75-80 weeks. There are 12 IBOs in the bin representing 15-20 weeks, and 1 IBO in the bin representing 75-80 weeks.

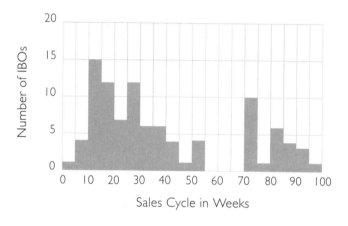

Figure 19-2: The opportunity load of a high tech salesperson

There are two distinct "clusters" centered around 25 weeks and 85 weeks. This is because the salesperson is responsible for selling two quite different types of products—"instruments" and "systems." Instruments have an average price of around $50,000 and are easily installed and put into operation. Systems cost typically $150,000 and take much more discussion and negotiation with the customer before the sale is finalized. They are also more complex, need collaboration with third party suppliers, and require ongoing support and service contracts after the sale. Consequently, the sales cycle for systems is much more involved and therefore longer than that of instruments. The difference in sales challenges is reflected in the sales cycles of the two product lines. The average sales cycle for instruments is 25 weeks, and for systems it is 85 weeks.

Let's home in on the cluster representing the average sales cycle for instruments. Even though the average sales cycle of instruments is 25 weeks, the spread for this salesperson is from as low as 5 weeks to as high as 60 weeks. This is the effect of "late arrival" to the customer's buying process, discussed earlier.

Proposition
There is usually a wide spread in sales cycles lengths in the salesperson's Opportunity Portfolio because of two principal effects: product mix, and entering the sales cycle late.

The point of this discussion is that the average salesperson will have an Opportunity Portfolio with sales cycles that vary all over the place. The sales cycle represents the only time in which the selling process can occur. If sales cycles are vastly different, then this process of selling has to be condensed or stretched by the salesperson to make it fit. This can be very difficult *unless* opportunities are logged and regularly monitored. Then, they must be *prioritized*. Fortunately, *sales automation done right* can help, but first, the methods to characterize sales cycles must be developed.

Problem—Where to Use the Skills Next?

Another challenge to the salesperson is having to manage multiple opportunities which are at different phases in their sales cycle—some in Probe, some in Prove and some in Close. Figure 19-3 looks at a typical opportunity portfolio and maps out the sales cycles of fifteen sales opportunities over the course of a year, along with their Probe/Prove/Close skill phases.

Some sales cycles start and finish in the year (1, 2, 6, 8, 9, 10, 11, 13, 14, 15), but some are incomplete, having started in the previous year (3, 4, 5, 7, 12). One of the opportunities is ongoing from the previous year, and does not finish in this year (3). Remember, the Probe, Prove and Close Phases occupy 50%, 35% and 15% of the sales cycles, as described earlier. Three lines map out points in time: one at the end of March, another at the end of June, and the other at the end of September. Look at the first "time slice" at the end of March. The salesperson has to concentrate on probing—eight opportunities are in the Probe Phase, one is in Prove, and none are in Close. At the end of June the focus moves towards proving—now, four opportunities are in the Probe Phase, six are in Prove and one is in Close. September is the month of the Close—here there there are four opportunities being closed, four are in Prove, and only one is in Probe.

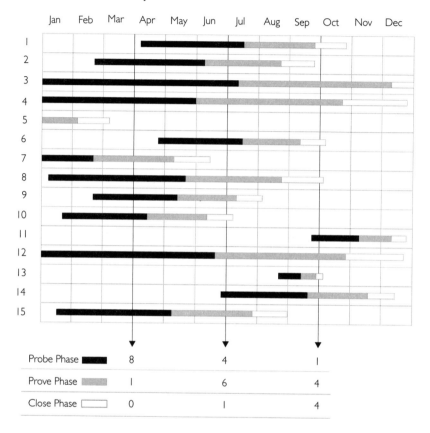

Figure 19-3: Use of the fundamental skills across the Portfolio at different times

Here, there are just fifteen opportunities. The typical number for a hard working salesperson is fifty to one-hundred! Which opportunities do they tackle first—the ones in the Probe, Prove or Close Phases? The answer is to work them *consistently* using a sensible method of prioritization. The easy solution adopted by many systems is go to the ones that are closing first, but if this happens at the expense of spending time with opportunities in the earlier stages of Probe and Prove, the penalty will come later. If you don't probe, you can't prove effectively, and if you haven't proven there will be no way to close.

Revisiting the Importance of Phases

In the previous chapters, we showed that dividing the sales cycle into three skill phases brought an easier way to handle the problematical spread. Let's pick up on this again to see how it becomes significant in establishing priorities.

What we proposed earlier was that any sales cycle, be it six weeks or six months, has three phases. In each phase, one fundamental skill of selling is used dominantly. This concept has the effect of "normalizing" time. What do we mean by that? Take the six-week sales cycle for example—its Probe Phase will be 50% of the six weeks, or three weeks. With the six-month sales cycle, the Probe Phase is three months or twelve weeks.

This line of thinking makes it easier to answer the question of "What point are we at now in the sales cycle?" Why not say "I'm two weeks into the sales cycle?" Because, this doesn't tell us much unless we know the other factor—the length of the sales cycle. Are we two weeks into a six-month sales cycle, or two weeks into a three-week sales cycle? Each has a very distinct meaning and implication. Two weeks into a six-month sales cycle means that we are in the early stage of Probe. Two weeks into a three-week sales cycle means that we are in the late stages of Prove.

Building Priority

We can now put together the factors that determine priority. One of these, *probability*, has been discussed already. Obviously the probability that a sale will happen has an influence on the resource we devote to the opportunity. But another consideration is **time**.

Probability has to be assessed regularly through the sales cycle, because it invariably changes. If an opportunity has just been found and rated as a low probability, it would go to the bottom of the list that categorized high probabilities at the top. Does it make sense to give it no attention? Of course not. It should be worked because it's just the start of the sales cycle and there is an opportunity to move the probability higher. On the other hand, the same opportunity found at the end of the cycle, and assessed to be a low probability, should be given low priority because there is little time left to turn things around.

Consider an opportunity with eighty percent probability. Does it deserve the same amount of effort one week into its six-month sales cycle as it would one week before the deal closes? No—in the first case there are over five more months left, meaning work just needs to be done to protect the sale and cover bases. In the second case, there's only one week left, and the customer has made up their mind. Maximum effort should be given to booking the sale.

These examples show that priority should be considered in the context of time, which translates into *point in the sales cycle*. The idea of skill phases gives us the way to put *time* into context with point in sales cycle.

Proposition
The priority that is attached to a sales opportunity is determined both from its probability and the current phase of the sales cycle.

This proposition says that we can calculate priority from the IBO Essentials. "Will it happen?" and "Will we get it?" give us probability, and "When will it happen?" determines which phase we are in. The value of the Essentials can't be overstated. Just three simple pieces of information are all that's needed to characterize the sale and prioritize it in the Opportunity Portfolio.

Points to Remember

1. Sales automation solutions can assist in prioritizing the salesperson's workload, specifically the allocation of time. To do this, there has to be a sensible prioritization of the Opportunity Portfolio.

2. If your current sales automation methodology handles priority purely by sorting your opportunity list from high probability to low probability, it's time to consider other options!

3. Low probability sales that are in early sales cycle need attention. There is a chance that, with work, they can be moved to a higher probability value.

4. Rather than talking about being six weeks into the sales cycle, get used to saying "Which skill phase am I in—Probe, Prove or Close?" This gets rid of the problem of dealing with diverse sales cycle lengths.

5. *Probability* combined with *skill phase* equals *priority*.

CHAPTER 20

The Priority Cube

What is this . . . the Theory of Relativity?

Marrying probability with skill phase into a meaningful priority gets as close to physics as we dare in a book about sales. Yes, we are going to explore three-dimensional space! But don't feel alarmed; with some examples of some typical sales situations, everything will make sense.

At the heart of all of the discussion in this chapter is the notion that the importance attached to a sales opportunity should be influenced by time, specifically the current point in the sales cycle. It's surprising how many salespeople are not conscious of this, but once understood, this basic idea provides an excellent way to prioritize the Opportunity Portfolio.

Now we are going to follow the path of all good scientists by testing a few *extreme* conditions before we come up with a general answer.

Some Examples of Setting Priorities

When setting up a prioritization scheme, it's best to keep the number of priority categories on the low side rather than going for too many. In the case of probability we finished up with six possible numerical percentage values. In the case of priorities we start off with four categories but go on to define a special case that will put the number up to *five*. The objective will be to take a list, for instance, of fifty opportunities and sort them into five groups by assigning one of five priority categories to each group. The opportunities in Priority I are the most important, they should be worked on first; those in Priority 2 should be worked on second, and so on. Let's look at some examples.

Example One

The salesperson discovers a sales opportunity and estimates the sales cycle to be six months. These are the early days and we are in the Probe Phase—the concentration is on probing, backed up by a little proving. The salesperson thinks that this sale has a *Low* chance of happening as this customer has a history of applying for budgets which do not get approved. But in the event that the customer does get funding for the project, the salesperson rates the chances of getting the sale also as *Low*, because the customer has traditionally purchased a competitor's product. Figure 20-1 shows the Probability Matrix for this sale.

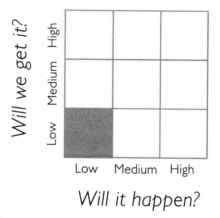

Will it happen?

Figure 20-1: Salesperson evaluates opportunity as a Low-Low

A Low-Low opportunity corresponds to a scant 10% on the Probability Index. What priority should the salesperson assign this opportunity in relation to the other forty-nine in the Opportunity Portfolio? With some sales automation systems, this one would go to the bottom of the pile, but *sales automation done right* actually awards a *Priority 2*, not quite a Priority 1, but still pretty high up there! Why?

Even though the sale seems to have a Low chance of happening, there could still be a small chance that it will go through. Can the opportunity be totally ignored? If the answer is no, then the salesperson had better do something about it. Backing away from the sale is a surefire way of killing any chance they may have of winning it. Even though the competitor might have an edge at this point, anything is possible in the next six months—one of their products may give the customer trouble, or their best salesperson may quit! In other words, this sales opportunity has *potential* value, and by using best selling skills now, it may be possible to increase that value. In other words, the salesperson should strive to move "Will we get it?" from a Low to a Medium or a High. That's why this opportunity is given a Priority 2; some work put in now may pay off later.

At this point, we introduce an idea that will be picked up and expanded on in Part 4, and that is the computer can be made *smart* enough to remind the salesperson of specific circumstances that crop up in all sales cycles. These simple, concise messages are referred to as *intelligent advice*. In the case of Example One, where the salesperson is in the Probe Phase and allocates a Probability Index of Low-Low, the message is "Even though your chances look slim—invest the time now to improve your position should this sale go to completion." Although these are simple messages, they can be life-savers for the harassed salesperson who is lucky (or unlucky) enough to own one of those portfolios that has a large spread in sales cycles. Remember, no matter the length of the sales cycle, the selling process has to go on as planned, and has to fit the available time to sell. Under these circumstances, it is easy for salespeople to forget the basics, but a flash of intelligent advice when conducting the monthly review of the Opportunity Portfolio is often enough to ensure nothing gets overlooked.

Let's continue with Example One. Now consider what happens in the next phase, which is Prove. The salesperson still feels very negative about the sale, and is unwilling to retract the initial assessment of Low-Low. But this is after fifty percent of the sales cycle has passed. We have to assume that all the work that the salesperson has put in to try to ratchet-up the probability has been unsuccessful. This opportunity is becoming greatly diminished in value, and because of this, we are going to take it down a notch to a *Priority 3*. The intelligent advice message also takes on a more negative tone: "Low probability sale. Don't waste too much time on it."

Moving on to the Close Phase, nothing will change our salesperson's assessment of the sale—it will probably be stalled before completion because funds won't be forthcoming and the competitor still has a strong foothold. This is after most of the sales cycle has passed! There's no option other than to move this sale further down on the list—it goes from a Priority 3 to Priority 4. But to reinforce the futility of working on an opportunity that is of such Low value *late in the sales cycle* we rename Priority 4 to *"Leave it alone!"* The advice message could not be more direct: "You are confident you will *not* get this sale. Check your evaluation, is it correct? If so, walk away." There are almost certainly better opportunities in the portfolio that need attention. There is one caveat—the salesperson must be one hundred percent sure about their assessment of "Will it happen?" and "Will we get it?" before taking this step.

Example Two

In the second example, the salesperson has just found another sales opportunity, again with a six-month sales cycle. The Probability Matrix is shown in Figure 20-2.

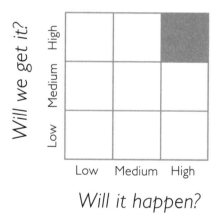

Will it happen?

Figure 20-2: Salesperson evaluates opportunity as a High-High

In this case the customer already happens to be a loyal user of the salesperson's product but needs additional capability and must buy more. Funds are available, but the purchasing department is enforcing a competitive bidding process. Our salesperson thinks that this opportunity warrants a "Will it happen?" of High and "Will we get it?" of High. This translates to a probability percentage of 80%.

This is the Probe Phase and things are looking good. The salesperson is confident that as the customer has already made a commitment to the product they will, in fact, buy again. As funds are available and the need is High, this sale is likely to happen. This opportunity is assigned a Priority 2 and not a Priority 1 as might be expected. Since things are heavily stacked in the salesperson's favor, there is no intensive selling to do. Why spend additional time finessing this opportunity when there are so many others that need attention? The best thing is to go into "maintenance mode." The salesperson must stay close enough to the situation to know if the competition is making inroads; ultimately, the sale will be won if the salesperson just puts in enough effort to keep the customer moving in their direction. The advice message is positive but cautionary: "This customer wants your product and will probably go ahead. But don't get complacent—you are still in the early stages of the sales cycle."

In the Prove Phase, nothing much has changed, other than time is running out. The salesperson is holding on to the original evaluation and still thinks it is a High-High. We still leave the opportunity as a Priority 2. The advice message becomes a bit more upbeat: "Keep the momentum going. Eliminate any possible obstacles or objections. You are in a commanding position. Get ready for an early close."

In the Close Phase, the salesperson is still prepared to rate this opportunity as a High-High. So, why wait around? The sale is going to happen soon, and the customer wants the product. The mission is to close the sale quickly and move on to another opportunity. The opportunity now becomes a Priority 1. The advice message reinforces the plan: "The customer wants your product and is ready to buy. Waste no time—close this sale and move onto the next."

Example Three

The salesperson sees this opportunity differently from the previous two examples. There is an excellent chance that the sale will happen. That is, at the end of the sales cycle, the customer will make a purchase; therefore "Will it happen?" is rated as High. But the salesperson thinks that the competitor has the edge, and rates the chance of success as Low. Figure 20-3 shows the Probabiliy Matrix. The Probability Index is a High-Low and this is the Probe Phase with a lot of time left. For the same reasoning used in Example One, this opportunity should be given a high priority—it's possible that the salesperson can use the Probe Phase to improve their position. But this sale has a higher value than that in Example One, because the rating on "Will it happen?" is High rather than Low. Therefore the opportunity is assessed as a Priority I. The advice message is: "Sale will happen but you are not highly favored. Work hard to discover issues that will make your proposal better accepted."

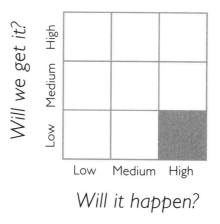

Will it happen?

Figure 20-3: Salesperson evaluates opportunity as a High-Low

In the Prove Phase, the salesperson still sees the circumstances around the sale as unchanged. The sale will definitely happen, but chances of winning remain very low. Something dramatic needs to be done to take advantage of a sales opportunity that will go through to completion, only to have the competition win. This is where we introduce the fifth category of priority, which is called "Breakthrough needed."

In sales, breakthroughs often do occur with appropriate effort. The salesperson may have a brand new product that has leapfrogged the competition in performance or they can bring in a factory expert for help, or even offer to send the customer to the factory to prove capability. The salesperson can virtually give the product away by massive discounting—not the most favored strategy, but one that is used in closely protected and dominated markets.

The advice message changes appropriately: "The sales cycle is developing, but you are still not well positioned. Now is the time to pull out all stops and try to distinguish yourself."

If things don't change by the time we reach the Close Phase, the need for a breakthrough is even more urgent. We keep the "Breakthrough needed" priority and emphasize the need for action in the advice message: "At this point, the competition look like they will get this sale. Only something dramatic can rescue the situation!"

Let's revisit the snippets of intelligent advice to see how they are constructed.

"Time is running out (you are in the Close Phase) and this customer will almost certainly buy something ("Will it happen?" is High) from the competition ("Will we get it?" is Low). You need to do something to turn things around (Breakthrough strategy needed)."

"The customer is ready to buy ("Will it happen?" is High) and wants your product ("Will we get it?" is High). Waste no time; close this sale and move onto then next (you are in the Close Phase)."

"This customer will probably go ahead with the purchase ("Will it happen?" is High) and wants your product ("Will we get it?" is High). Don't get complacent—this is just the early stages of the sales cycle (you are in the Probe Phase)."

"You are confident that this sale won't happen ("Will it happen?" is Low) and if it did, your chances are poor ("Will we get it?" is Low). Check your assessment once more, and if there's no change, just walk away (you are in the Close Phase)."

Notice the different nuances in the messages that are possible by looking at the two probability components, "Will it happen?" and "Will we get it?" in the context of which skill phase we are in, Probe, Prove or Close. We've pulled out just a few instances of the unique combinations of "Will it happen?", "Will we get it?" and skill phase—just how many of them are there? The answer lies in the Priority Cube.

The Priority Cube

There are three options for "Will it happen?" (High, Medium, Low), three options for "Will we get it?" (High, Medium, Low) and three options for skill phase (Probe, Prove, Close). The number of unique combinations of these three important factors is *three* times *three* times *three*, or twenty-seven. Figure 20-4 shows this in the form of a diagram which we call the Priority Cube.

The Priority Cube is merely a device to illustrate what we have been talking about thus far. The importance we attach to an opportunity is dependent on the probability of getting the sale and the position in the sales cycle.

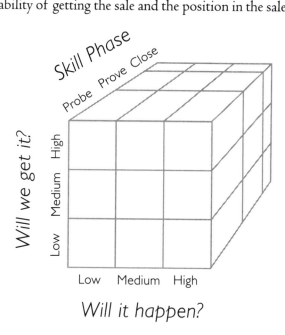

Will it happen?

Figure 20-4: The twenty-seven point Priority Cube

The front face of the cube is divided into nine squares which are determined by the three possible answers to the questions "Will it happen?" and "Will we get it?" that constitute the now familiar Probability Matrix. Then we add a third dimension, which is skill phase with the three possible options of Probe, Prove or Close. It's easy to see that the Priority Cube is composed of twenty-seven sub-cubes, each one representing a unique combination of

"Will it happen?", "Will we get it?" and a skill phase. At any point in the sales cycle you can be only in one of these sub-cubes.

In Figure 20-5 the cube is shown "opened up." In the left hand column is the Probability Index first described in Chapter 18 (Figure 18-1). These are the values on the "face" of the Priority Cube. Each index represents a unique combination of "Will it happen?" and "Will we get it?" For instance, a Probability Index of 3 represents a value of High for "Will it happen?", and a value of Low for "Will we get it?", and is referred to as a High-Low.

Each intersection of the Probability Index *row* with the skill phase *column* represents a sub-cube and in each one, we've analyzed the set of circumstances concerning probability and phase of the sales cycle to come up with priority values and advice messages, just as we did in the above examples. The subtle differences between a sub-cube and its neighbors are reflected in the priority value, nature and tone of the message, and reflect the overall gut feel about the sale as expressed by the salesperson in the context of how much time has passed in the sales cycle.

Let's test the Priority Cube again by extending our examples a little differently. In the first cases, we looked at situations where the salesperson's assessment remained unchanged as we passed through the Probe, Prove and Close Phases. We were effectively picking a particular Probability Index from the left column and following across a single row through the three phases. What happens if the salesperson changes the probability from one phase to the next?

In Example One, the salesperson initially believed that the customer would not be successful in funding his project and set "Will it happen?" as Low. Remember, this customer is a friend of the competitor and therefore the salesperson rates the "Will we get it?" as Low. We assessed a Priority 2 in this Probe Phase with the idea that the salesperson should put enough effort into the opportunity to move his competitive position from Low to Medium or High. Let's see what happens as we move to the Prove Phase. At the start of the Prove Phase, the salesperson still sticks to their assessment of Low-Low. Because we've moved on in time and things still appear bleak, the priority is set from 2 to 3; after all, this looks to be a time-waster. But then the scenario changes a little. The salesperson bumps into an associate of the customer who divulges that this time, management is looking favorably at

Prob Index	Probe	Prove	Close
1. "Will it happen?" - **Low** Will we get it"? - **Low**	"Sale won't likely happen, but worth investing time to position yourself if it does." **Priority 2**	"Low probability sale. Don't waste too much time on it." **Priority 3**	"You're confident you will not get this sale. Is your evaluation correct? If so walk away." **"Leave it alone"**
2. "Will it happen?" - **Med** Will we get it"? - **Low**	"There is a reasonable chance the sale will happen. Probe to uncover issues that will advance your chances, or obstacles that might be hindering you." **Priority 2**	"This sale may happen. The customer has to know why your proposal is better than the competition's." **Priority 2**	"A potential time-waster. Check your evaluation. It's time to move on to more productive opportunities" **"Leave it alone"**
3. "Will it happen?" - **High** Will we get it"? - **Low**	"Sale will happen but you are not highly favored. Work hard to discover issues that will make your proposal better accepted." **Priority 1**	"Sales cycle is developing, but you are still not well-positioned. Now is the time to pull out all stops and try to distinguish yourself." **"Breakthrough needed"**	"At this point the competition looks like they will get this sale. Only something dramatic can rescue the situation!" **"Breakthrough needed"**
4. "Will it happen?" - **Low** Will we get it"? - **Med**	"Low chance that the sale will happen, but we are early in the sales cycle. Extra effort to differentiate yourself will pay off if the situation improves." **Priority 3**	"Low chance sale and we are positioned in the center. Try getting higher customer favor. Don't waste a lot of time." **Priority 3**	"Cover your bases. You're in reasonable shape to make the sale if it happens." **Priority 3**
5. "Will it happen?" - **Med** Will we get it"? - **Med**	"You are well-positioned in a sale that has a reasonable chance of happening. Probe now to improve your competitive position." **Priority 2**	"This sale may happen. Need to strongly differentiate yourself from the competitors to improve your chances at winning this sale." **Priority 2**	"There's still hope for this sale. Overcome any objections and be prepared for a strong close." **Priority 1**
6. "Will it happen?" - **High** Will we get it"? - **Med**	"High probability sale. Use your best probing skills to put yourself ahead of the crowd early in the sales cycle." **Priority 1**	"The customer still doesn't see you as a highly differentiated solution. Convincing now will vastly improve your chances later." **Priority 1**	"You are still not differentiated from the competition. Probe for objections, prove capability and try to close this order." **Priority 1**
7. "Will it happen?" - **Low** Will we get it"? - **High**	"You are highly favored, but the chances that the sales will happen are low. Probe enough to protect your position." **Priority 3**	"Do enough to ensure that you stay in front of the pack, in the event that the sale does happen." **Priority 3**	"Cover your bases. Customer wants your product. Be ready to close if the sale goes through." **Priority 3**
8. "Will it happen?" - **Med** Will we get it"? - **High**	"Maintain your strong position with the customer. Ensure the situation is as you think it is." **Priority 2**	"You are well-positioned to win. Do enough to maintain your position." **Priority 2**	"Stay close to the customer. You're in an excellent position to make a sale if it goes through." **Priority 2**
9. "Will it happen?" - **High** Will we get it"? - **High**	"Sale is very likely to happen and it looks as if you will get it, but don't get complacent and spoil your leading position." **Priority 2**	"Keep the momentum going. Eliminate any possible obstacles, objections, etc. You are in a commanding position. Get ready for an early close." **Priority 2**	"The sale is yours—make the close and move onto the next." **Priority 1**

the submission and the associate's personal opinion is that the project will fly. The salesperson realizes that although this is second-hand information, it should not be discounted and they decide that "Will it happen?" should move from a Low to a Medium. The Probability Index is now Med-Low (number 2). Checking Figure 20-5 shows that this means a move from row one to row two in the Prove Phase and the priority is escalated from a 3 to a 2 to reflect the higher probability.

A few months have passed and we move to the Close Phase. The customer calls our salesperson to say that one of the competitor's products, recently purchased, is giving trouble in its warranty period. The customer, understandably upset, can no longer be dependent on one supplier and vows to give our salesperson this sale—things have to change starting with this purchase. Our salesperson is excited, but not too excited because sometimes, customers react emotionally and calm down as time passes. But after some sober second thought, the salesperson thinks the time has come to crack this account, and moves "Will we get it?" from a Low to a Medium. This moves the Probability Index to a Medium-Medium and moves us to the fifth row down in Figure 20-5 to Index 5 and the Close column. We move the priority up from 2 to a 1. Some extraordinary effort put into this opportunity, even though the probability has been assessed as not that high (40%), could win the sale and it deserves extra effort from the salesperson. Here there is an inference which may sometimes be taken for granted—combined focus on specifics of the sale with increased effort on selling skills can turn run-of-the-mill sales opportunities into winners.

So that's how the Priority Cube works. It was developed using direct experience in sales opportunities over a fifteen year period. Readers should check the reasoning, and if they need added proof, they should test the logic out on their own real-world sales experiences. When doing this, it's enlightening to look at a few opportunities that "strayed from the norm."

The Computer Takes Charge

Everything we have planted into the Priority Cube can easily be plugged into the computer, ready for it to recognize and to react. The ammunition that the computer uses is the information stored in the IBO Essentials. If the IBO Essentials are recorded and updated as the sales cycle evolves, the computer can allocate one of five possible priority values to each opportunity, along with a reminder of where to be vigilant in the sale. Let's see how that works. The IBO Essentials are "Will it happen?", "Will we get it?" and "When will it happen?"

"When will it happen?" is the date that the salesperson is forecasting for the sale to end. The start date is the date when the sales opportunity first gets logged. Using this date and the projected end date, the computer can calculate the *actual* sales cycle, and the skill phases of Probe (50%), Prove (35%) and Close (15%), and so it knows which column of Figure 20-5 to go to.

"Will it happen?" and "Will we get it?" are the other two Essentials that define probability. Each can have a value of High, Medium or Low and lets the computer locate the Probability Index value in column one of the matrix shown in Figure 20-5.

Armed with the row number and the column number of the matrix, the computer locates the priority and determines what to look out for. It sounds simple, but this is a 1 in 27 chance of hitting a very special combination of salesperson enthusiasm and position in sale, along with the ability to contribute sensible suggestions on how to prioritize and go forward. Computers always know what day it is, which means that as soon as the salesperson turns on the computer, it will know the current phase of every opportunity in the portfolio. Using the current probability assessment ("Will it happen?", "Will we get it?"), the computer will assign a meaningful priority. Remember that the Priority Cube shows that the priority can change from phase to phase in the sales cycle, *even though the probability remains the same.*

If the Opportunity Portfolio is large, there could be a lot of opportunities under Priority 1. If this is the case, other factors affecting priority come into play. What is the cash value of the opportunity? What are the actual days, weeks, months left to the end date? What is the strategic value of the sale? How long has it been since the last customer interaction? Some secondary sorting has to be put in place within each priority category. If this is done thoughtfully and in line with the specific objectives of the sales team, the salespeople can work their sales opportunity list safely from top to bottom, confident in the knowledge that they are maximizing their chances of winning more sales over the competition.

Points to Remember

1. There are 27 unique situations that can pop up in our model of what happens in the sales cycle (which means that there are many more in the real world!)

2. Each of these situations should be considered in their own light and assessed with one of five priority values.

3. The computer can remove the burden of time management within the Opportunity Portfolio, and *proactively* update priorities as conditions change.

CHAPTER 21

The Sales Environment

Everything we have to know to win!

We're at the end of Part 3, in which we've gone a long way in characterizing the sales opportunity. Although developed with sales automation in mind, this material is applicable to the everyday understanding of the sales opportunity, even outside of the framework of the computer. Much of it depends on the science of selling; we've taken some of the cornerstones of the science and reformatted them in a way that makes sense to the computer.

Now the discussion continues in a direction that is the most important in determining success or failure for the salesperson. What happens in the sales cycle itself?

The Importance of Information

In Chapter 14, we saw that Critical Interactions are the essential components of a reliable sales process because they provide the environment for the dialogue between the salesperson and the customer. In this dialog, **information** is exchanged which shapes the strategies that salespeople use in their efforts to win the sale.

Strategy is central to good selling. A strategy is a well-defined plan to get from where we are now to where we want to go. The plan is a series of action steps, forming a strategic *path* and leading in a strategic *direction*. For salespeople, the end is always the objective of winning the sale. If they don't have information about everything concerning the sale, they are flying blind and can't develop a winning strategy. Strategic selling is founded on **knowledge** of what's going on in the sale formulated from the information picked up in the Critical Interaction. With good information coming in, strategies can be developed or modified on the fly. The process is ongoing—strategies are initiated, refined, discarded, and reinvented, depending on the ebb and flow of the sale.

The Sales Environment

Information and knowledge are intimately connected. Knowledge is **understanding** built up from accumulation and analysis of information. Salespeople need knowledge of *everything* that can affect the sale. Who is making the decision? Is more than one person involved? How much funding is available? Is there any competition? Who are they? How well am I doing in this sale? How do politics work in the customer's organization? How important a player is the customer in these politics? And so on, and so on. There is an awful lot of stuff to know. For the sake of convenience, we throw all of the answers to these questions into a grab-bag of information that's called the **Sales Environment**.

Sales Environment: A term to describe all aspects and circumstances surrounding the sale that will ultimately determine its outcome.

The Sales Environment is the **factual** description of all the issues that affect the sale. Of course, no one person, the sales representative, the customer or anyone, *knows all the facts*. The customer may believe that funding can be secured, but the CEO of the company may have absolutely no intention of providing it. The salesperson may think that they will win the sale even though they are actually disliked by the customer, who has no intention of buying the product.

Proposition
All things being equal, the salesperson with the most knowledge
of the Sales Environment will win the sale.

The proviso here is "all things being equal" because even the sales team with the most knowledge about the sale won't win if they don't know how to formulate and execute the right strategy, or if their selling skills are not up to par.

There are a few important things about the Sales Environment that are vital to understand:

- The Sales Environment *changes* as the sales cycle progresses. As salespeople weave their way through the sales cycle, the issues that determine the sale constantly change, which will alter the Sales Environment.

- Salespeople's perception of the Sales Environment may be quite *different* to what it really is. In customer interactions, salespeople must seek all the facts that determine the Sales Environment. It's easy to get it wrong, but the closer it can be understood, the better.

- Salespeople have the power to *influence* the Sales Environment. That's a given since they are *half* of the sales equation (the customer fills the other role).

- The Sales Environment contains the answers to the questions "Will it happen?", "Will we get it?" and "When will it happen?"—The *IBO Essentials*.

Discovering the Sales Environment

Salespeople function within the Sales Environment. They are an intimate part of it, as are all other players: customers, competitors, advisors, users, and more. When the sales cycle starts, the interactions between these parties begin, and the complex dynamic of the Sales Environment unfolds. It's like a play by Shakespeare—but this isn't acting.

The challenge confronting salespeople is figuring out what the Sales Environment really is. At this point, our story links back to earlier discussions on fundamental skills—the skill of *probing* is used to discover facts surrounding the sale. Figure 21-1 shows this in a simple way; the circle on the right represents what the Sales Environment really is while the circle on the left represents what salespeople think it is. The *gap* between the two represents the knowledge that separates perception from reality. Salespeople have to work hard to narrow this gap. A certain way to do this is to probe as much as possible.

Influencing the Sales Environment

How can salespeople influence the Sales Environment? By using the fundamental skills of *prove* and *close*.

If the customer doesn't understand an important feature of the product, the outcome of the sale may tip towards the competition. The performance and the value must be *proven*, which can move the balance back to the salesperson and change the Sales Environment. The skill of proving is an important agent of change within the Sales Environment and it has to be mastered.

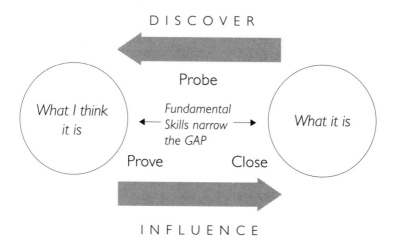

Figure 21-1: How the salesperson interacts with the Sales Environment

The skill of *closing* can have a more dramatic effect on the sale because it has the power to bring a win, eliminating the Sales Environment.

Successful proving and closing puts the mark of the salesperson on the Sales Environment. Influencing moves the Sales Environment to where the salesperson *wants it to be*.

Proposition
Fundamental selling skills are used to narrow the gap between the salesperson's perception of the Sales Environment and what it really is.

Developing a strategy that works depends on getting as much information on the Sales Environment as possible, and probing is the way to do it. The strategy is then executed by proving and closing. Strategic selling depends heavily on interacting with the Sales Environment.

Lessons Learned in Part 3

This discussion on the Sales Environment concludes Part 3. We've covered a lot of material, all of it being interconnected. The result is a characterization of the sales opportunity that is conveniently suited to being understood by the computer. These ideas are important to understand as we move forward into Part 4, which will deal with a method of figuring out, as accurately as possible, what the Sales Environment really is. They are important enough to warrant a recap, and Figure 21-2 helps us with that.

Starting with the **sales opportunity**, it is vital to recognize its existence as early as possible. It's not acceptable to log a sales opportunity into a sales automation system at the point where the customer's request for quotation ends up at the door. Getting into the sale as early as possible is one of the most important factors in winning the sale. Accordingly, our advice is don't be *reactive* in addressing customer's needs, but be *proactive*. Sales automation helps here; once the sales opportunity is logged into the computer, there is a constant reminder that selling effort is needed.

Every sales opportunity has a unique set of issues and circumstances that determine its outcome, which for simplicity is dubbed the **Sales Environment**. We've condensed all of the information associated with the Sales Environment into three crucial concerns for the salesperson, which we call the **IBO Essentials**. The answers to these three questions determine the value of the IBO. If the best "gut-feel" response is assigned to each Essential as the sale develops, opportunities get labeled with a priority that places them in a natural hierarchy of importance in which the salesperson has confidence.

The IBO Essentials each have a contribution to developing the story further. "**When will it happen?**" determines the length of the **sales cycle**, and is obtained by subtracting the "date entered" from the expected close date. The sales cycle is then divided into the three **Skill Phases** using the rule of 50%/35%/15%. Now, at any point in the sales cycle, the computer knows which of the fundamental skills should be dominant—in other words, which skill phase we are in.

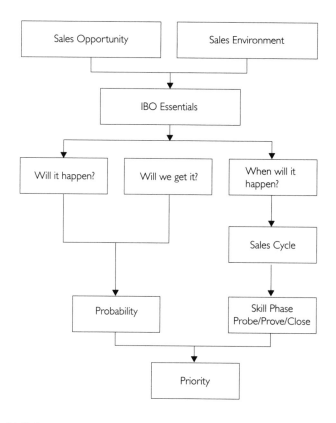

Figure 21-2: Summary diagram showing the methodology introduced in Part 3

The other two IBO Essentials contribute to the important issue of **Probability**. Probability is derived from **"Will it happen?"** and **"Will we get it?"**. Assigning a *one out of three* value to each of these Essentials in the Probability Matrix leads to the computer tagging each opportunity with one of six unique probabilty percentages.

The only work left to do is to meld together the two parameters of probability and skill phase to come up with **Priority**.

Figure 21-2 helps to focus on connectivity between the various pieces of the story, and points out the tremendous importance of the IBO Essentials. The information embodied in the three Essentials provides so much value in managing a heavily populated portfolio of sales opportunities. Two of the Essentials provide a consistent evaluation of chances for success, which is fundamental to accurate forecasting. The other Essential provides the answer to how much time is left to sell, and to the skills needed at a certain time in the sales cycle. The three Essentials combined provide a value of importance to each opportunity, such that salespeople can intelligently work one opportunity in relation to another, knowing that their precious time is being used to the best effect. The IBO Essentials are so interdependent that if you take away one of them, most of their value disappears. Probability alone is not much help in sorting the Opportunity Portfolio, because you also need consideration of the sales cycle. The wonderful thing about the computer is that it can do all the behind-the-scenes calculations in the process outlined in Figure 21-2 while keeping a constant eye on time, and it can do it for all the sales opportunities in the portfolio. All the salesperson has to do is to update the IBO Essentials throughout the sales cycle whenever the Sales Environment for a particular opportunity changes.

The computer can help out in another important way. It can perform a reality check on the salesperson's views of what the IBO Essentials are.

Proposition
The IBO Essentials are derived from knowledge of the Sales Environment. The more detailed the knowledge, the more accurate the answer.

Determining the IBO Essentials is not easy. Many issues within the Sales Environment can collectively contribute to what the Essentials should be. Issues may not be factual and could be open to interpretation. The salesperson's gut feel on whether "Will it happen?" is Low, Medium or High depends on their ability to seek out and identify the many factors that can contribute to the answer. Only detailed knowledge of the Sales Environment can ensure a correct handle on the IBO Essentials. Seasoned salespeople may get it right, whereas a rookie may not.

Regular updating of the IBO Essentials is a good exercise because it forces a rethink of the Sales Environment. Salespeople typically check out their feelings about a sale in discussion with their peers or managers. The Sales Environment for the opportunity in question is dissected under close scrutiny by both parties, with each trying to poke holes in the other's interpretation. The objective is to get down to the facts, and to challenge the assumptions that have been made, to see if they hold water. Here are some of the issues that might get addressed:

- "Are you sure that you've talked to all of the decision makers?" (Affects "Will we get it?")

- "Are you sure that we will get an order in May and not June?" (Affects "When will it happen?")

- "Will he get Board approval for a purchase this time around?" (Affects "Will it happen?")

- "Are you sure that the customer has an urgent need for our product?" (Affects "Will it happen?")

- "Do we know all the competition involved in this sale?" (Affects "Will we get it?")

- "The customer says we will get the order. Will Purchasing allow the award to come to us without going to tender?" (Affects "Will we get it?")

- "Is the customer telling us the truth when she says she is the sole decision maker?" (Affects "Will we get it?")

- "Have you had enough face-to-face meetings with this customer to do some serious selling?" (Affects "Will we get it?")

- "The customer has already started work on a new research wing to house all of this equipment." (Affects "Will it happen?")

Notice that the information in the above exchanges consists of fact, observation, interpretation or perception. But this is the raw material that the sales team has to deal with. The number of meetings with the customer is fact, and it is either enough or not as judged by the sales team. The new research wing is fact, and the sales team can form their own impression of whether it will be completed, or get delayed through factors such as funding cuts. How well the competition is doing is perception, based on the salesperson's exchanges with the customer, as is the urgency of the customer's need. These notions about the sale come from integrating a myriad of issues within the salesperson's mind—and the human mind is particularly adept at this. The best salespeople observe the Sales Environment, are sensitive to it, and build the insight necessary to assess it correctly. Then they develop their strategies to manage it.

It also helps if the salespeople can easily bounce their ideas off a willing listener because they cannot conduct strategies in a vacuum. Now here's a proposition that will cause a stir in the crowd.

Proposition
The computer can be used as a useful tool to question assumptions that are being made by the sales team about the Sales Environment.

This infers that the computer can take the place of the "willing listener." Before this could happen, the computer would have to have a level of understanding about the performance of the salesperson in the sale. Is this possible? It is, if we narrow the scope to the "science" of selling. In fact, we are not narrowing the scope too much—the science provides most of the building blocks needed for successful strategic selling. But first, we need to develop the technology that provides the intelligence that the computer requires, which leads us conveniently into Part 4.

Points to Remember

1. The Sales Environment contains all the information needed to build sales strategies, and a better understanding of the Sales Environment than the competition will lead to more sales

2. The salesperson *discovers* the Sales Environment using the skill of *probing*.

3. The salesperson *influences* the Sales Environment using the skills of *proving* and *closing*.

4. The IBO Essentials are contained in the Sales Environment. To provide the answer to an IBO Essential, the salesperson evaluates and considers all contributing issues from the Sales Environment and then forms a final conclusion.

5. Determining the IBO Essentials *forces* salespeople to re-evaluate and assess changes in the Sales Environment.

The Technology of Sales Automation

CHAPTER 22

Intelligent Response

The computer understands what we are up against?!

Part 4 looks at some different technologies that impact sales automation—not just those that we are familiar with, such as the Internet, notebook computers, or wireless communications. They are important, but so is the technology of the *application* itself. The application is the software, or the programming which gives the computer an understanding of the *sale*. An idea was introduced earlier where the computer could act as a sounding board to test out the tactics used in a given sales opportunity. In the next two chapters we'll explore a way that this can be done. Fortunately, most of the groundwork has been laid down in Part 3.

Information, Knowledge and Intelligence

Two of these words, information and knowledge, have occurred before. Information Technology and Knowledge Management are the cornerstones of the technology infrastructure that supports the customer related activities essential to SFA and CRM.

Proposition
Knowledge is information which has been filtered, analyzed,
dissected, beaten into shape, and stored for future use.

Information doesn't have to be composed from facts; it can also include observations or insights. Knowledge, on the other hand, implies understanding, and facts are needed to provide that, so information must be sifted for facts before knowledge can be extracted. Once we have knowledge, what do we do with it? This is where intelligence comes in. Intelligence is the capacity to acquire and apply knowledge. Salespeople bombard their computers with information on a daily basis. To make this worthwhile, the SFA application has to retrieve knowledge and present it in a useful way to help the salesperson make progress in the sale.

How SFA Systems Function

The information that the salesperson puts into the computer varies in nature and potential value. Much of it is administrative, and includes the routine documents of day-to-day business like letters, e-mails, faxes, proposals, leads, price lists, etc. Then there is information about accounts, contacts, and of course, the essential details of every interaction with the customer. Finally there is the information on the sale itself, the IBO—details of products, timing in the sales cycle, probabilities, priorities, and at a bare minimum, the IBO Essentials. Hopefully, the SFA system can put some order into all of this material using the hierarchical data structure that was shown in the discussion of the four competencies.

Computers are good at sifting, sorting, and analyzing information. This is the way most sales teams get value from their SFA system. A salesperson enters a query and the computer passes back some filtered information as knowledge. This is shown in Figure 22-1. Let's say that the salesperson wants to know where their business is coming from. One response from such a query might be "Over eighty percent of your territory's forecasted revenue comes from the Southeast." If the computer is queried on accounts, it may deliver a response of "You have visited the top performing account in your territory only once in the past six months." A query regarding product might yield "Your sales of the Type 560 Printer are one-half of what they were at this point last year."

A salesperson usually has to delve deeply into the sales automation system to find this stuff; it doesn't hit them in the face. This is knowledge obtained by filtering facts, the computer is just sifting information with careful input and guidance from the user. There is no reliance on intelligence. This is OK, but the technology can be pushed further. For example, consider this response from the computer: "You are two months into a six-month sales cycle and your main focus should be probing the customer's needs." This message implies some form of *understanding*. Part of the computer's response is mechanical—it takes today's date and figures out the current position in the sales cycle from the information on the start and end dates provided by the salesperson. But it then has to lean on *methodology* to go further—specifically, the sales method that was developed in Part 3. The method defined an *actual sales cycle* and divided it logically into three phases, the first of which occupies 50% of the cycle and is dominated by the fundamental skill of probe. So, the computer knows we are in the Probe Phase. There is nothing magical here; the method *gave* the computer this understanding by telling it something about the nature of the sales cycle, which it is then able to memorize.

Figure 22-1: Conventional sales automation

Actually, we were moving toward this point earlier in Chapter 20, when we looked at the *intelligent advice* that resulted from the Priority Cube. One of the advice messages was "Time is running out, and this customer will almost certainly buy something from the competition—you need to do something to turn things around." The computer knew that time was running out because it knew the actual sales cycle and the time that was left until close. Because of the salesperson's recent assessment of the IBO Essentials, it also knew that the competition were heavily favored. The salesperson also believed that this customer would definitely purchase some kind of solution. The computer then becomes *proactive* with its knowledge and recommends that the salesperson do something to turn things around. This simple reminder has the power to produce some last minute action from the salesperson. The computer has been programmed with data from past sales experience and when the same set of circumstances arises again in the future, it provides a similar advisory message.

The past sales experience can be augmented with a rulebook based on the science of selling. Remember, these rules have been developed by sales professionals over many years and apply to virtually all facets of sales. If the computer understands the rules, and applies them to what's happening in the actual sales cycle, it can flag deviations and point out potential traps. If the salesperson's information matches the knowledge stored by the computer, everything is OK. *Sales automation done right* calls the process we have just described **Intelligent Response Technology**.

Intelligent Response Technology: A computer system that compares *actual* sales progress against what is considered to be ideal, and makes recommendations on strategies for improvement.

At the heart of the Intelligent Response is a simple notion. First, provide the computer with a bank of knowledge based on established principles that define the overall picture of a perfect sale. Then, essential information collected from Critical Interactions with the customer is used to record the *actual* progress in the sale. This is compared against the understanding of what should happen—the difference between reality and ideal is referred to as the **gap**. The computer goes on to provide constructive information back to the salesperson on how to strategize to *minimize* the gap. Figure 22-2 shows how this works. The picture is similar to the last figure showing conventional sales automation, but with an important difference—there are now two sources of information going into the computer, the salesperson, and a new concept called the **Sales Model**.

The computer compares this with its understanding of what should happen—the difference between reality and ideal is referred to as the **gap**. The computer then feeds constructive information back to the salesperson on how to minimize the gap. Figure 22-2 shows how this works. The figure here is similar to the last figure, which showed conventional sales automation, with the exception that there are now *two* sources of information going into the computer, the salesperson, and something we call the **Sales Model.**

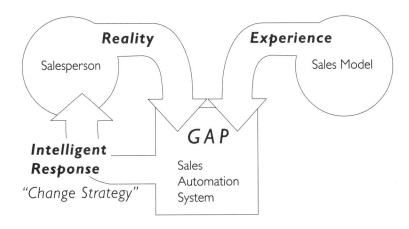

Figure 22-2: Adding the Sales Model—with gap

The Sales Model: A description of the essential events and characteristics of the sales opportunity which the computer can refer to for an understanding of the sale.

The diagram shows the situation just described—there is a gap between what *has* happened in the sale and what *should have* happened. The gap gives the computer the necessary information to make recommendations on potential ways to improve the salesperson's strategy to win the sale. This information is called the **Intelligent Response.** What if there is no gap—the situation shown in 22-3? Information about the current status of the sale matches with previous experience in similar circumstances. The computer's Intelligent Response is a *careful* reaffirmation that the salesperson is OK.

Some will say, "Why do we need an Intelligent Response? We know what we are doing. Everything is under control." But is it? The average salesperson in just about any industry is confronted with from ten to over one hundred open sales opportunities at one time. Isn't it possible that something could slip through the net? The fact is, good salespeople are very busy, and a great danger is that because of everyday pressures, a sales opportunity may get overlooked. Through Intelligent Response, *sales automation done right* tries to ensure that this does not happen.

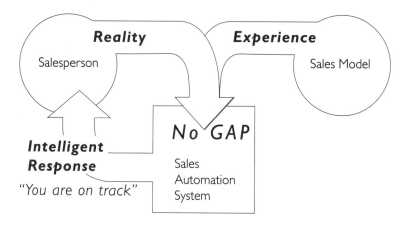

Figure 22-3: Adding the Sales Model—with no gap

The Sales Model

In the scientific world, a *model* is a set of descriptions that define a real life experience, and which can be tested and proven on the computer. The corollary is that the computer, having understood the model, will be able to pass back some useful knowledge to the outside world. For Intelligent Response Technology to work, we have to model what happens in the sale. In past chapters, we have described all of the components that are needed to do that. There are four raw ingredients which are used to create the Sales Model: Time, Skills, Interactions, and Information.

1. Time: Discussions of the sales cycle in Parts 2 and 3 highlighted the importance of time in describing the sale. When does it begin, and when does it end? What is the timing of everything that happens within the duration of the sale? Any model of the sale must take time into account. Fortunately, the computer has a built-in clock, and tagging every event with a time label is seamless and flawless.

2. Skills: The model looks at the buyer-seller transaction and shows how it flows logically through three distinct phases, and each of these must be matched with a fundamental selling skill. The model takes into account

the *timing* of these skills and shows that the three phases of the sales cycle are divided roughly into a Probe Phase of fifty percent, a Prove Phase of thirty-five percent and a Close Phase of fifteen percent. The model also shows how the sales skills are used *together*. Probing and proving are used to differing degrees throughout the sales cycle. Closing only begins when most of the proving has been done, and all three skills are used in the critical Close Phase.

3. Interactions: Opportunity focused customer interactions that take place within the sales cycle are labeled as Critical. The information flow from Critical Interactions leads to the understanding of the sale, which means that sensible sales strategies can be put in place. The ideal set of Critical Interactions, developed from previous sales history, forms the sales process which is an important part of the model. The type of interaction (visit, phone, demo, proposal, etc.) and the approximate time of occurrence in the sales cycle are plugged into the model. We don't have to be concerned with being too accurate to get the value from Intelligent Response Technology.

4. Information: The Critical Interaction is the means through which the sale unfolds and gets understood, using as much information as we can get. The computer needs this information, but it will only take it in a structured way that is governed by the science of selling. The information in the model is an amalgamation of the best practices of selling and the learned experiences from past sales opportunities.

Figure 22-4 shows the four components of the Sales Model laid out on the familiar sales cycle diagram.

The Sales Model and the Sales Environment

How can the Sales Model store a picture of *all* of the information associated with a complex sale? The answer is that it can't. But based on the eighty/twenty rule, it is safe to say that eighty percent of the knowledge that determines a sales strategy comes from twenty percent of the information gathered by the salesperson. *Sales automation done right* prods the salesperson to get this information, and compares it to the Sales Model.

Proposition
The Sales Model offers a framework for the computer to
understand the Sales Environment.

When salespeople are *discovering* the Sales Environment, they will use the fundamental skill of probing. The Sales Model says that probing is used throughout the sales cycle, but with different degrees of focus. One of the key components of probing is the asking of *questions?* The computer can test the success of the salesperson in establishing the Sales Enviroment by doing its own probing, that is, by asking the salesperson the right questions. The next chapter will describe one set of questions that attempts to get this done.

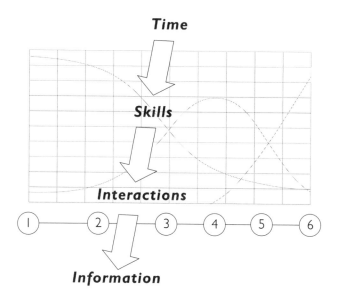

Figure 22-4: The Sales Model

Points to Remember

1. For the computer to understand what's going on in the sale, it must reference a sales model that as accurately as possible describes what an ideal sale should look like.

2. The Sales Model provides the computer with the *understanding* that it needs to become *intelligent*.

3. A model of the sale can only be developed from a foundation of strong sales methodology.

4. The sales model can be constructed using four important elements: Time, Skills, Interactions and Information.

CHAPTER 23

Establishing the Sales Environment

Question and Answer time!

This chapter illustrates an example of how Intelligent Response Technology can be put into practice. It deals, for the most part, in the information gathering process. Information leads to knowledge of the Sales Environment and is the first raw ingredient of the Sales Model. The story will build as the sales cycle progresses and more Critical Interactions are completed. The Sales Environment must be broken down into issues on which the salesperson can develop knowledge or opinion, that, in turn, can be reported to the computer. Take a simple example: "Today, I met with the purchasing agent and learned that he had recommended that the decision be delayed by six months." When this information is fed into the computer, the Sales Model is evaluated, and the length of the sales cycle is recalculated, along with the skill phases. The computer then informs the salesperson that the phase has shifted backward from Prove to Probe, and strategies should be adjusted as necessary. For instance, the salesperson may elect to reduce "Will it happen?" from a High to a Medium, which in turn will change the probability, and maybe the priority.

It is possible to devise a set of generic questions that have a good chance of sketching out the Sales Environment as the sale progresses. The questions can be stored conveniently in the IBO section of the sales automation software, and reviewed regularly, usually before or after Critical Interactions with the customer. Answers to the questions are quantified by the computer and a meaningful response is sent back to the salesperson.

Devising the Questions

The trick in this exercise is to have *enough* questions, but not too many—the salesperson should not be burdened with excessive data entry. Questions have to be carefully chosen and phrased; there can be no ambiguity in understanding them. The sales automation application's help system can be referred to for clarification.

The Sales Environment defines everything that contributes towards *truthful* knowledge of the sale. This means an unbiased truth—not skewed by the views of the salesperson or the customer. The salesperson often has to work hard to get the most accurate assessment of the Sales Environment. If information on the decision making process has not been unearthed, this fact must be acknowledged and the reasons evaluated. The competition could be winning, and that too, has to be admitted. If the salesperson feels that "The customer doesn't like me," they must come to grips with the idea and strategize the sale around it. Much of the information surrounding the sale will involve emotions, likes, dislikes, personalities and relationships. Salespeople must be as objective as possible when they try to define these factors accurately. Intelligent Response Technology works well when salespeople are totally *honest* about issues that affect the sale, especially those that question their performance.

Salespeople often resolve uncertainties with the sale by brainstorming with peers and managers to get fresh ideas. Sometimes, salespeople are too close to the sale to be able to see discontinuities staring them in the face, whereas a third party might instantly spot the issues. Our objective is to employ Intelligent Response Technology to be that third party, using a set of questions that are based on the fundamentals of selling. These are ideas and methods that have been around for a long time, and are by no means the be-all and end-all. They are also generic, and applicable to a wide range of sales situations, and relevant to a good cross section of businesses. Take them as *one* set of questions to get to grips with the Sales Environment; likely, there are many other possibilities.

The questioning process will also be framed around the three fundamental *skills*—the second raw ingredient of the Sales Model.

Getting Computer Feedback

One of the most important considerations in implementing Intelligent Response Technology is how to effectively get the computer's message back to the salesperson. An important way that *sales automation done right* does this is by using the IBO Essentials. Remember, it has already been suggested that the answers to IBO Essentials are *contained* within the Sales Environment.

We will use just two of the Essentials, "Will it happen?" and "Will we get it?" The third Essential, "When will it happen?" is mostly the domain of the salesperson, and they should try hard to get that one right. When salespeople are asked to provide their assessment of "Will it happen?" or "Will we get it?" they must rely on their knowledge of the Sales Environment to give them the answer. This often involves distilling countless pieces of information. While good salespeople will be able to do this, it is not easy, and requires experience. After we've gone through the exercise of forming the questions that will discover the Sales Environment, it should be possible for the computer to construct its version of "Will it happen?" and "Will we get it?"—where it can *test* the salesperson's gut feel on the Essentials. The kind of response we are looking forward to from the computer is, "You think this one is a High-High, but I think you are wrong. It's a High-Medium and this is why."

Probing for Information

The Sales Model says that probing is done in different degrees throughout the sales cycle. In the beginning stages, probing is intense, as nothing is yet known about the sale. Nearing the completion of the sale, virtually all probing has been done and most information is known, but perhaps not all, and that's why a little probing is reserved right until the end. The most dominant factor to good probing is the ability to question, followed closely by an associated ability to listen. Remember that the Probe Phase is the longest of all, at roughly half the sales cycle. Within this time period, the attention to probing is dominant, and it is normally expected that answers to most of the direct probing questions listed later will be known by the end of the Probe Phase. This is not always the case because some information may be difficult to get, and some influencing factors change during the sales cycle. The salesperson should revisit the questions regularly throughout the whole sales cycle, and the best time to do so is after making any Critical Interaction with the customer.

Need?	Choices	Affects
How well have you established the customer's need for this product/service?	Unknown A little Average A lot	"Will we get it?"
What is the customer's level of need for your product or service?	Unknown Low Normal Urgent	"Will it happen?"
How well does your product fit the customer's requirement?	Unknown Low Medium High	"Will we get it?"
How well does the price of your solution match the customer's budget?	Unknown Matches Higher Much Higher	"Will we get it?"
What are the chances that the customer will receive funding?	Unknown Low chance High chance Very high chance	"Will it happen?"
What is your familiarity with the customer and their organization?	Low Medium High	"Will we get it?"
How strong is the competitive pressure in this sale?	Unknown Low Medium High	"Will we get it?"
Who are the competitors?	List known competitors	"Will we get it?"

Figure 23-1: List of general probe questions

Figure 23-1 shows eight general questions that try to fill in the details behind the basic sales issues. Does the salesperson have a solution to match the customer's needs? Is it affordable? How well does the salesperson know the customer? Is there any competition? Who are they? And so on. In some cases the salesperson just ticks off the appropriate answer from a simple list, for instance, Unknown, Low, Medium or High. In other cases, actual information needs to be entered, such as naming the competitors. If the salesperson does not list any competitors, the computer assumes that he or she does has not been successful in probing to find out (remember, there is always at least one competitor—the option for the customer to buy nothing).

The answers to these kinds of questions are indispensable toward the ongoing effort to win the sale, but some of them are invariably neglected, even by the most experienced salespeople.

Who?	Influence?	Choices	Relationship?	Choices	Affects
Who is the economic decision maker in this sale? Name...	What is the degree of influence of the economic decision maker in this sale?	Unknown Low Medium High	How is your relationship with the economic decision maker?	Unknown Bad OK Good	"Will we get it?"
Who is the technical decision maker in this sale? Name...	What is the degree of influence of the technical decision maker in this sale?	Unknown Low Medium High	How is your relationship with the technical decision maker?	Unknown Bad OK Good	"Will we get it?"
Who is the user decision maker in this sale? Name...	What is the degree of influence of the user decision maker in this sale?	Unknown Low Medium High	How is your relationship with the user decision maker?	Unknown Bad OK Good	"Will we get it?"

Figure 23-2: Probing for information on decision makers

The questions in Figure 23-2 begin to set the stage to probe for information on the decision makers in the sale, so that later, the salesperson knows they are proving to the *right* people. In some sales there may be just one decision maker, but it's not uncommon to have more, and if they are not technically making the decision, they may well be influencing it. The salesperson has to pay special attention, not only to finding out who the decision makers and influencers are, but also to selling all of them on the merits of the product. If there are multiple decision makers, each will have their own agenda. Usually one is interested in value; whether the solution is going to work and if it is at the right price—this is the *economic* decision maker. One may be interested in the usability of the solution—this is the *user* decision maker. If the solution is a machine or a device, there will be someone who is concerned not only with performance, but also serviceability and reliability—this is the *technical* decision maker. In some industries there will be other decision makers to consider, but in this example, we are using just three.

Our probing questions are designed to identify the decision makers. If none are listed, it is assumed that the salesperson doesn't know who they are (which adversely affects "Will we get it?"). If there is just one decision maker, they will effectively be adopting all three roles. Not only have we asked specifically who the decision makers are, we've asked what issues are important to them in their purchase (Figure 23-3). It might be price, or best value, or even performance at any price. It might be ease of use of an instrument, machine, or device. It could even be the smallest package that will meet the specification. Whatever it is, the salesperson has to identify the decision maker's issues, and later, make an effort to *prove* that the product will alleviate those issues.

Next we ask for the influence that the decision maker has in the purchasing process. Some will have much more influence than others. Obviously these issues rely on the subjective opinion of the salesperson, and the correctness of the answer depends a lot on their own experience. The next issue to be resolved is how well the salesperson relates to the particular decision maker—the better the relationship, the greater the chance of winning the sale. The answer to this question is one of those where the salesperson has to search inwardly to come up with their best evaluation of how well they get along with a contact. This is not easy to do, as no one likes to admit that the relationship may be bad.

Evaluating Degree of Proof

It's no good gathering information on the sales background if nothing is done with it. As the Sales Model shows, there must also be an ongoing effort to *prove* throughout the sale. The computer must test to see how successful the proving is, and to do this, it asks the salesperson directly, as shown in Figure 23-3. Previously, we've asked what is important to each of the decision makers. Now the salesperson is asked to give their best estimate of how well they have proved that their solution fulfils the decision makers' concerns. This is another one of those soul-searching questions with which the salesperson has to fight to be objective. The more confident they are that they have successfully proven, the greater the chance of winning the sale (and the higher is "Will we get it?")

Concern?	Degree of Proof?	Choices	Affects
What factors are critical to the economic decision maker in this sale? List ...	How well have you proved these critical factors to this decision maker?	I don't know Not well Reasonably well Well Very well	"Will we get it?"
What factors are critical to the technical decision user in this sale? List ...	How well have you proved these critical factors to this decision maker?	I don't know Not well Reasonably well Well Very well	"Will we get it?"
What factors are critical to the user decision maker in this sale? List ...	How well have you proved these critical factors to this decision maker?	I don't know Not well Reasonably well Well Very well	"Will we get it?"

Figure 23-3: Looking for degree of proof to decision makers

The Close Phase

The closing skill involves a lot of process. The way the computer judges progress in the close phase is to check for trial closes and their results. Chapter 16 described the trial close as a *testing* process which checks to see if the customer is ready to make a purchase. Usually, there will be a number of trial closes. Figure 23-4 shows how the process works.

In a trial close (1), the salesperson probes the customer to see if they are ready to make a decision (2). This can be done in scores of different ways, but this topic is of greater relevance in a sales tactics book than one on sales automation. If the customer says that they are ready to go ahead (3), the sale is won (4). If the customer is not ready to purchase (5), the salesperson should identify the reasons why (6). A planned strategy to overcome these objections must be devised (7), and tested in the second trial close (8)—here, the process starts all over again. It continues until the customer has no more objections to going ahead, or buys something from the competition.

The Sales Model has already been told how many trial closes are usually necessary to make a sale (based on previous sales experience). As soon as the closing skill starts, the computer regularly checks that the salesperson has entered information on trial closes, and if none have been entered, it assumes that none have been done. Once the salesperson decides to enter information on a trial close, the computer will guide them through the process shown in Figure 23-4. It can then track whether sufficient effort is being made to close and comment accordingly. By logging objections and strategies to overcome them, a history is developed that can assist the salesperson in future opportunities.

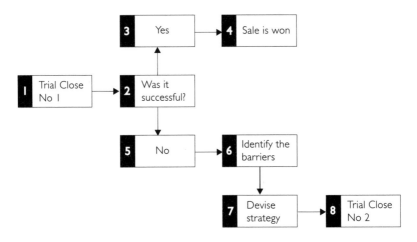

Figure 23-4: The closing process

Quantifying the Results

Now, the difficult part! Just by reviewing the three tables of questions, plus the closing process diagram, the reader knows instantly that there is a lot of information here to deal with. It may not have taken the salesperson much time to pass it to the computer, after all, there was the entire sales cycle to do it in, and most of the answers are simply a matter of checking from a list. But now, the computer has to assemble all of this information and make some sense of it. Because we are going to get the computer to develop its idea of "Will it happen?" and "Will we get it?" our task is somewhat easier than it might have been. There is now a framework on which to build the important

Intelligent Response that has to resonate with the salesperson, and hopefully be of significant value in moving the sale our way.

All pieces of data collected can impact the value of one of these two important IBO Essentials, and this has been shown in the question tables. Because the computer just appreciates numbers, we have to be able to quantify the quality of the answer to each question. Take the example of "How well does your product or service fit the customer's requirements?" The possible answers are Unknown, Low, Medium, or High. If we assign the numerical values to these answers (assuming Medium is neutral), we get -2, -1, 0, +1, and we create a measurement system whereby the computer should be able to add up all the answers and come up with the final evaluation as to whether "Will we get it?" will be a High, Medium or Low. An example on the other side, affecting "Will it happen?" is the question "What are the chances that the customer will receive funding?" The possibilities are: Unknown, Low Chance, High Chance or Very High Chance. Just like the previous example, these answers can be given a set of numerical values.

All issues have to be considered: If five trial closes are usually needed to get a sale and only one has been made "Will we get it?" is negatively affected. If competitive pressure is high, but no competitors have been identified, "Will we get it?" is again compromised. The answer to "What is the customer's level of need for your product or service?" for the most part determines "Will it happen?" But if the salesperson answers this question with "Unknown," this response affects "Will we get it?"

This kind of numerical evaluation of significance can be applied to all the information gathered through the questioning process. It's impossible to go into detail of how it can be done in the confines of this book. The important thing to realize is that a rapidly changing sales scenario can be modeled fairly accurately on the computer to establish if the salesperson is on the right, or maybe the wrong track.

Behind the scenes, the computer is assembling all the information that has been fed to it by the salesperson as they work their way through the selling process, and numerically qualifying its importance in terms of the value of the two IBO Essentials, "Will it happen?" and "Will we get it?"—High, Medium, or Low. It then goes ahead and calculates probability and priority, because both of these important parameters depend on the IBO Essentials.

This is a very effective way for the computer to communicate with the salesperson. When the salesperson is asked to rate the opportunity in terms of "Will it happen?" and "Will we get it?" they must consider everything about the sale and condense it down to one of three options for each question. It's not trivial to do this, but the human brain is typically very good at it. To try to make the computer do the same thing, we need information from sixteen questions with choices from almost a hundred possible answers.

If the computer's response on the IBO Essentials differs from that of the salesperson, the Intelligent Response kicks in with an explanation on the causes of the disparity. The salesperson can agree with the computer, or possibly disagree, but in this case, there is only one explanation—some of the answers to the questions are incorrect. This situation initiates a reevaluation of the salesperson's thinking on the sale. It is this process that effectively puts the computer in the position of a "coach," always challenging the salesperson on whether their spin on the Sales Environment is right. Remember that if the salesperson's assessment of "Will it happen?" and "Will we get it?" are wrong, the probability is likely wrong too, as is the priority, so it makes sense to *test* the gut feel on the IBO Essentials using this questioning process, just in case.

How often should the salesperson revisit the list of questions? As the sale will always follow twists and turns determined by changes in the Sales Environment, it's best to look at updates after each Critical Interaction is completed. This should not be tough for the salesperson, as there will always be follow-up needed after the interaction, and in *sales automation done right*, essential IBO information, including factors that affect Intelligent Response, are never far away from the administrative area of the software. Obviously, in the early stages of the sale, information may be sketchy. The computer can be programmed to recognize this and can allow for the gradual build-up of knowledge on the sales cycle through to the end, when mostly everything will be known.

The method described here of establishing the Sales Environment does not take into account how much work is being done in the sale, which is related to how many customer interactions are occurring and if they are following the sales process. This can, and probably should, be done. In Chapter 14, the sales process was defined as a set of Critical Interactions which have been proven by experience to be necessary to provide the best chance of winning the sale. These interactions can be entered into the Sales Model—both the type of interaction and the approximate point that it happens in the sales cycle. For instance, one Critical Interaction of this set could be a demonstration of the product roughly halfway through the Prove Phase. Another could be the presentation of the final proposal to the decision makers and the beginning of negotiations, happening one-third of the way into the Close Phase. The computer keeps track of whether these elements of the preferred sales process are happening, and flags the salesperson if things are getting behind. It's up to each sales team to decide if the Critical Interaction set represents the minimum number of interactions needed, or whether more activity should be happening over and above the critical process steps.

The Final Result

The best way to understand Intelligent Response Technology is to see it working in practice. To do that, we are going to revisit the case study from Part 3, Chapter 15.

Rick is a salesperson working for the High Speed Printer group of Smith PC. A table of customer interactions from Smith's CRM system is shown in Figure 15-1. We can see that IBO #1212 involves Rick attempting to sell a Type 560 printer to a group within GDPN who are Smith's largest global customer. This particular GDPN division, however, prefers the machines from Smith's major competitor, Universal. But during the initial call (Interaction 1 of Figure 15-1) of this opportunity, a conversation with John Parker, a GDPN manager, Rick learns that all is not well with the Universal printers in this GDPN facility. Reliability has been poor and service slow. John Parker is fed up—he needs to look at other vendors. Rick has a chance to crack the account.

Rick enters into his standard selling process. He sends an extensive product information package to John Parker and follows up with a visit (Interaction 6 in Figure 15-1). He learns that, overall, they like the Universal products, except for one very important need—single color processing on the Universal equipment is not good, and this is an important revenue source for this GDPN facility. Rick talks briefly about his new Type 560, which has strong single color capability, and John Parker is intrigued.

Rick is using the Intelligent Response Technology within his Smith PC CRM system, regularly filling in details about needs, budgets and key people in the account. After the April 25, 2003 interaction, Rick's completed Sales Environment information looks like Figure 23-5.

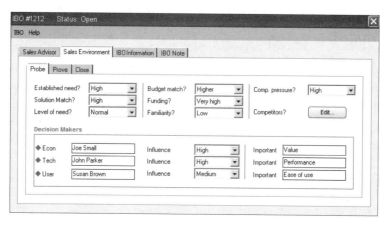

Figure 23-5: Questions during Probe Phase for IBO #1212

Rick recognizes that although Universal has lately been complacent at handling this GDPN account, they still have an advantage based on their historical track record, and the sheer volume of product in this facility. But Rick has a superior product that addresses the problems that John Parker is having with single color production. However, the other players in this deal are still unknown. Rick must meet the operators who will take charge of his Type 560, if he should win the contract. Then there is the person who controls the finances, Joe Small, Parker's boss. Rick's lack of exposure in this account is beginning to hamper his efforts.

This sale will definitely go though to completion, so Rick decides that "Will it happen?" is High. Because of his unfamiliarity with the people in this GDPN division, Rick feels uncomfortable about his chances, so he logs a "Will we get it?" of Low. All Rick has to do is to click on a few buttons to update the IBO Essentials. His assessment corresponds to a probability of 25% and a priority of 1.

The computer looks at the Sales Environment described by Rick's responses to the questions it posed and comes up with its response shown in Figure 23-6.

It is more optimistic than Rick. After all, this sales cycle is still young, and hasn't yet reached the halfway point of the Probe Phase. Rick's product really fits the customer's expectations well and there is a good chance that he will be able to use the time available to make himself more known in GDPN and probe for more valuable information. The Intelligent Response suggests probing more, and to be ever vigilant of Universal. It rates Rick's "Will we get it?" as Medium. This changes things a bit—the probability now becomes 60%. The computer still thinks that this is an excellent chance for Rick and should still warrant a number 1 priority.

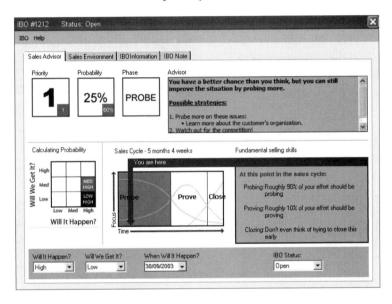

Figure 23-6: Computer's response to the information in Figure 23-5

Let's see what happens as the sale develops. Customer interaction number 17 in Figure 15-1 is actually the tenth Critical Interaction that Rick has had with the decision makers in this account. This one is a telephone call to John Parker in August of 2003, in which Rick is still probing for information that will help him with the sale. A successful on-site demonstration has happened a few weeks earlier, and Rick now has identified the three decision makers and has had the chance to develop good relationships with John Parker and Susan Brown.

Parker confirms that he personally prefers Rick's product to Universal's and says that he knows Susan is very enthusiastic about it. But he also tells Rick that the VP of Production, Joe Small, is a possible problem. Joe attended the recent demonstration and liked the Type 560, but thinks that its high price over the Universal product won't be justifiable. Parker also confirms that any deal that goes through will have to be signed off by Joe.

Rick is beginning to accumulate all the information to fill in the questions that assess the Sales Environment. Figure 23-7 shows the data entry for the Prove Phase.

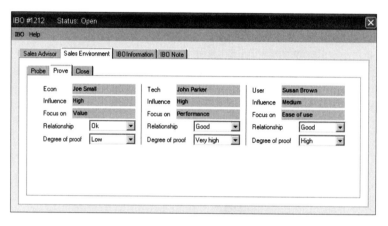

Figure 23-7: Questions during Prove Phase for IBO #1212

Rick feels confident with his efforts to persuade John Parker on the performance and value of the Type 560. He also feels that Susan Brown is convinced that the Type 560 would be advanced technology for the shop floor. But Rick sees that work must be done to build a proposal that Joe Small can believe in.

Rick's optimism takes over and he upgrades his "Will we get it?" from a Low to a Medium. Of course, the "Will it happen?" is still a High. This represents a probability of 60%, and because we are now in the Prove Phase, the priority remains at 1 (see Figure 20-5, Page 180). But, the computer's assessment differs from Rick's (Figure 23-8). In this user interface, the computer is the "Advisor."

The "Possible Strategies" in Figure 23-8 suggests areas of concern that Rick should address. Central is the economic decision maker, Joe Small, whom Rick has met only once, and Joe's concern with the price. Another issue is Rick's comparative newness to this account, and the fact that the competitor knows it much better. The "Advisor" also knows that Rick has not logged any trial closes, so it assumes he has made none. Given the fact that this is late in the Prove Phase, and the skill of closing could have been started, a suggestion is made to execute a trial close.

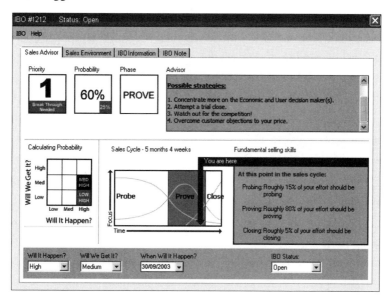

Figure 23-8: The computer's summary of the sale with advice to the salesperson, in the Prove Phase

Instead of rating "Will we get it?" as Medium, the computer sees it as Low. This downgrades the probability to 25%. More importantly the priority now becomes "Breakthrough Needed." The onus is on Rick to strategize something special for the little time that he has left in this sale. After doing some soul searching, Rick realizes that the computer is right. Unless something is done to overcome Joe Small's reluctance to pay the significantly higher price for the Type 560, this will remain an exclusive Universal Account.

Rick does know that his product has proven reliability, and Universal's new printer proved to be quite unreliable in the demonstration to GDPN. Rick does an analysis of running costs over a five year span, and finds that because of its superior reliability, the Type 560 would effectively prove less costly over its operating life than the Universal. In September, Rick takes his report to John Parker and attempts a trial close (Interaction 18, Figure 15-1). Parker is impressed with Rick's data, but knows that his boss won't accept any deal which still carries a price differential of fifteen percent over Universal.

At the end of the meeting Rick goes back to the office and enters his trial close into his computer. The computer still sticks to its case that a breakthrough is going to be needed. Now there is even less time left. Rick discusses the situation with his manager. Rick's manager wants desperately to crack this account, but doesn't want to give away too much—the Type 560 is a good product and deserves a higher sticker price than Universal's product.

The manager offers Rick a deal, in which he can present John Parker with a five-year Blue Star maintenance program at no extra charge. This is effectively worth 5% of the selling price of the Type 560. Rick will meet with Parker and attempt a trial close. But the manager mandates that Rick must pressure Parker to set up a meeting with himself and Joe Small, so that Rick can directly prove to Small the value of this deal over the one from Universal.

Interaction 19 (Figure 15-1) is where Rick executes this strategy. He lays out the value of his manager's offer. Parker likes it but still can't give Rick an affirmative answer—obviously he must still get the okay for the deal from Joe Small. Rick senses this and suggests a meeting between himself, Parker and Small. Parker promises to set this up. Later, Rick enters this interaction into his automation system and updates his closing strategies as shown in Figure 23-9. His manager is excited about the meeting with Small, and offers Rick the opportunity to use a further discount of 5% if needed to get this order. But Rick must try to sell the demonstration Type 560, which is still residing at the GDPN facility. The manager has already depreciated this unit in his demonstration inventory.

Parker comes through with his commitment to get Rick in front of Joe Small. Rick has a good chance to explain the value of his proposal, and Joe is impressed. But Joe explains to Rick that he has severe guidelines from his Corporate Team to keep costs down. He asks Rick for a further concession on price. Rick agrees, and suggests that GDPN keeps the Type 560 demonstration unit in return for an additional 5% discount. Joe breaks for a few minutes to discuss this offer with Parker, and comes back to Rick with an agreement to accept the offer. He calls his purchasing department to confirm the deal.

Rick's successful attempt with his third trial close is the subject of his customer Interaction 20 in Figure 15-1. The GDPN account now has state of the art Smith PC equipment in addition to Universal, and will be a good opportunity for Rick to sell more product going forward.

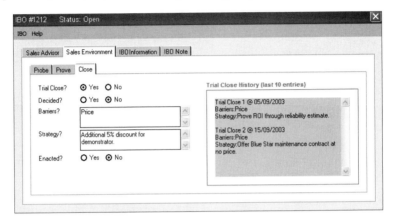

Figure 23-9: Entry of trial close strategies in the Close Phase

Throughout the six months of this sales cycle Rick has found his sales automation system of great value. Interactions were recorded and easily retrieved for Rick's regular progress reviews. Also, the computer has proved a valuable tool to cross check and validate Rick's personal assessment of his performance in the sale.

Points to Remember

1. The essence of the Sales Environment can be deduced using a series of carefully crafted questions that the salesperson should answer as accurately and honestly as possible.

2. It is helpful to phrase the questions around the fundamental skills of selling.

3. The IBO Essentials are a useful tool to compare the salesperson's gut feel about the Sales Environment and the computer's more rigorous evaluation.

CHAPTER 24

The Interface

What the salesperson sees

The user interface is the boundary between the salesperson and the sales automation system. What we see on the computer screen, and the ways in which we interact with the application are lumped under this general term. The user interface represents the "personality" of the software, and to the salesperson, the user interface is the software. What happens behind the scenes doesn't concern them, it's only the stuff that appears on the screen or goes in through the keyboard that counts.

Good interface design can make all the difference to the salesperson's perception of how well the sales automation works. The user interface can also directly impact the *quality* of the information that the user puts into the computer—for better or for worse. A bad interface can make a program a drudge to use. Given that all of the salesperson's daily administration and activities flow through the computer, this could be a recipe for disaster.

Proposition
The user interface has a major bearing on how well the SFA
application is accepted by the sales force.

A busy salesperson won't have much tolerance for sales automation software that is not intuitive and simple to use. The consequence is that they will do everything in their power not to use it. This can seriously affect the successful roll out of the software company-wide. Remember, the collaborative benefits of automation depend on *everyone* using the software, and there can be no exceptions.

In this chapter, we will look at some of the key areas where the user interface needs to be *done right.*

Reinforcing Method, Process and Data Integrity

Just as with any software, the user interface has to have some basic characteristics to be successful. The visual appearance such as font, color and layout must be appealing to the user. The functionality should be available intuitively, without constant referral to the Help system. With these attributes, users will learn to love it; without them, they will grow to hate it. Sales automation also has some special requirements of its own that should be considered. Here are some of those issues followed by specific examples.

Simplify and minimize data entry: In the course of a typical day, a salesperson can amass a sizable amount of material that they will have to enter into their computer. There will be the essential results of Critical Interactions—meetings, discussions or phone calls, along with updates on IBOs as well as entry of new ones. Then there is all the supporting information on potential deals: product descriptions, special requirements and pricing. Some of this will be standard stuff that repeats over and over, but some won't and it will need the salesperson to get into a text field and start typing. As much of the repeat material as possible should be available from pick lists or drop-down menus. Not only does this make data entry easier, but it also helps consistency. The challenge that the software designer faces is achieving the core objectives of automation (CRM and SFA) with the minimum amount of data entry from the user. It's all too easy to make the salesperson fill in loads and loads of electronic forms. If life with sales automation amounts to filling in forms every day, who would use it? The data entry burden has to be reduced as much as possible.

Maintain Quality Data: One of the founding principles of CRM technology is that a warehouse of information (Customer Knowledge Store) is maintained throughout the history of the company's transaction with the customer. If this information is incorrect, inadequate or only partial, the negative effect on the CRM vision is profound. Not only will business strategies be based on bad data, but salespeople, or for that matter, anyone in the company, will learn to distrust the system and try to circumvent it. Data integrity is very important and the interface to the software is an excellent way to assist the user to input information properly.

One of the best ways of ensuring consistency is by permitting only one way to enter information that repeats a lot. Address information, for instance, should be available only through easily accessible pick lists. The user need not type, they just have to use their mouse and keyboard to pick the data they need. The choices available from pick lists can be extended to more complex information, for instance, in setting the type of Critical Interaction, there may be options such as "Telephone call to assess needs" or "Visit to ascertain funding." All of these options available to the user must be customizable by the administrator of the CRM/SFA system, in a way that makes sense to the team.

Another way to make sure data is collected correctly is by the enforcement of rules, and using the interface to make sure the rules are followed. If a salesperson wants to enter information on a new sales opportunity, the customer's account and personal data should already be in the system and easily available through a simple look-up. If it's not there, then it's best that the salesperson should call the system administrator to enter the particulars of the new account. This way, critical data is entered only by a limited number of people who have a passion for correctness. Imagine what might happen in a large sales team of fifty people, if each one was allowed to enter account data—duplications, errors and frustration. Once correct information is in the system, the user interface can make it easily obtainable for regular data entry tasks.

Reinforce the sales method: The sales team has decided on a sales method that they will all follow. The method must be evangelized, and one of the ways to do this is through the user interface. Bring the method out front and center—that way it gets reinforced, learned, and understood every second the salesperson is using the system. Identified Business Opportunities (IBOs) are logged in their infancy if the method is followed. This means that the sales automation system can kick in early to assist in managing the Opportunity Portfolio. Every time a Critical Interaction is entered, the sales opportunity must be revisited, and the interface can force this to happen. This is the time to review the sales method to see if it is being followed and what changes need to be made. At least the IBO Essentials need to be updated, and then perhaps the Sales Environment should be checked, to see if the computer is on-side with the current strategy.

Promote and enable process: Process is a very important part of both CRM and SFA, and ensures that things get done consistently and efficiently. To make a process work properly, the computer should guide the salesperson logically through all the steps. These steps should be clearly defined and understandable (intuitive). Method and process go hand in hand—you have to have a method before you can carry out a process. Not only will process be used for the administrative side of the sales day, such as with proposal generation, pricing, or processing sales orders, it will also be used extensively whenever we bump into the sales method, as we will see in some of the examples. Fortunately, computer-based technology forces an evaluation of existing processes as the computer only understands clear multi-stepped approaches to getting tasks completed.

The next few sections show the more important examples of how the user interface can be used to reinforce some of the more frequently used methods and processes in sales automation.

Navigating the Core Competencies

Part 2 showed how a salesperson could put some order into their sales activities by looking at their workload in terms of the four competencies of Territory, Account, Sales Cycle and Contact Management. Sales automation software works best if it is designed to make the navigation through the four competencies both evident and accessible to the salesperson. Figure 24-1 shows the most obvious way to do this in a two level menu system.

In this example, the entry to the sales automation system is by a so called "portal" on which the salesperson has the freedom to include any pieces of information that they need to have access to easily and regularly. Here, the salesperson has included their latest performance data, their calendar of activities, and some information on which IBOs need attention this month. This portal screen contains the first level menu of the system, and it is organized around the familiar CRM cycle of Marketing, Sales, and Service.

Once the user clicks on "Sales," the second level menu appears organized around the four core competencies. In the figure, the user has gone a level deeper and has chosen to look at the information displayed for "Sales Cycle."

This particular screen of information is interesting. It is centered around a display of information called "Sales Cycle Planner" which has the ability to show the salesperson's IBOs sorted in order of the priority (discussed in Part 3). Here, the salesperson has selected the IBOs that fall under the "Review Second" category. The most obvious element of this display is a graphical representation of the sales cycle of each opportunity, in bar format. The Probe, Prove, and Close Phases of each cycle is picked out in a different color (in the case of this figure, grey level). This idea follows directly from the discussion in Part 3, as illustrated by Figure 19-3, of the widely varying sales cycle lengths that normally occur in the salesperson's Portfolio. The salesperson can see easily from this graphic if there is a preponderance to one skill phase or another at this point in time, and can prepare themselves for it.

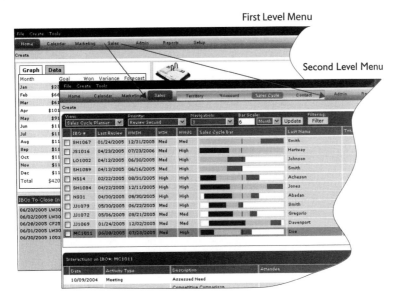

Figure 24-1: Navigating the core competencies through the main menu bar

If the salesperson wants to work their contacts, they should be able to effortlessly go to the area that has all of the contact information, sorted and sifted to make contact management easier. Once the salesperson has selected a particular contact, they should be able to go to the Account section to see that contact along with their colleagues in the *context* of the account. Then it should be possible to go to the Territory section to see the account and any others that may be in the same geography—city, state or even country. Of course, at some point, the salesperson will want to see the sales opportunities relating to the contact they have selected by going to the Sales Cycle section of the software.

The contextual or "smart" navigation through the four competencies makes the software easier to use and, of course, reinforces the part of the sales method that relates to the management competencies in their hierarchical structure.

Qualifying Leads

The process of lead qualification provides an excellent example of delivering consistency when many people are required to perform the same task. Chapter 13 went into the way leads should be classified and Chapter 4 showed that lead qualification was at the boundary of marketing and sales in the CRM process loop.

A lead is an indication that a contact may be starting the process of buying a product or service. This is the issue that has to be ascertained in the process of lead qualification. All leads should be entered into the CRM/SFA system. Even if they do not eventually get turned into sales opportunities, they must be stored as valuable sources of future business. After all, someone has contacted you to find out more about what you do—*they* have been proactive in initiating the interaction, and even if there may be no business now, things may change tomorrow. Yes, there will be some weak leads, where perhaps someone is collecting research information for whatever purpose, but these can be weeded out.

Figure 24-2 shows how the user interface can help to make the qualification process work. The salesperson goes to the lead entry area of the software. The interface presents just one question, with three possible answers—does the customer plan to buy? The answers are Yes, No and I don't know. The software is context sensitive and the interface responds differently according to the three options. This is a better way than exposing all of the possible alternatives to the user right from the beginning.

In Option 1, the salesperson has ticked off "Does not plan to buy." In other words, the lead was an excursion by the customer into the unknown, and now reality has crept in. The user interface pops back a message to the user that the "lead has been classified as poor—it will now be closed."

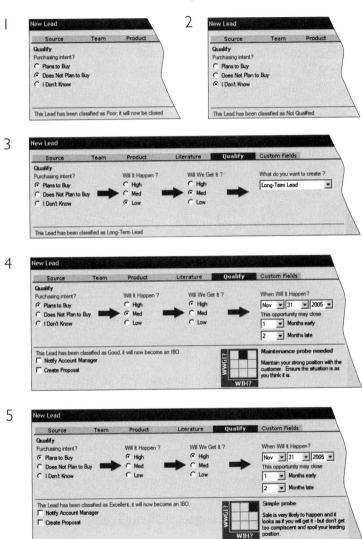

Figure 24-2: The process of lead qualification

This result will be passed back to the marketing department for analysis on the results of their campaigns. In this case, someone expressed interest, but upon close qualification, admitted to no buying intent.

In Option 2, the salesperson has found that after trying to qualify the customer, there is still uncertainty as to whether there is a serious buying intention. The salesperson clicks on "I don't know." Here, the interface sends back the message "The lead has been classified as Not Qualified." The lead is placed on the back burner awaiting the salesperson's attention to figure out what is going on.

In Option 3, the salesperson has picked the choice of "Plans to buy." The software recognizes that this means there is a sales opportunity, and it immediately goes on to display first the IBO Essential of "Will it happen?" for the salesperson to pick High, Medium or Low, and then pops up "Will we get it?" to repeat the process. In this case the computer sees that the salesperson thinks the opportunity has a low chance of happening, and it provides the choice for the salesperson to reconsider creating an IBO (with a very low probability), and maybe to store this situation as a long term lead instead.

In Option 4 the salesperson has chosen a Medium value for "Will it happen?" and a High value for "Will we get it?". " When will it happen?" is also entered through a calendar look up—notice that in this application, the salesperson has the opportunity to put a "time window" around the expected date if they are uncertain of the exact close.

Behind the scenes the computer determines that these IBO values constitute a Good lead quality and stores this information for marketing. The Probability Matrix is also shown graphically with the Probability Index shaded in. The Intelligent Response is also shown as a reminder of the implications of the salesperson's chosen IBO Essentials.

Option 5 again shows the creation of an IBO, but the IBO Essentials of "Will it happen?" and "Will we get it?" are both High. The computer posts the message "This lead has been classified as Excellent, it will now become an IBO"

Logging IBO Essentials

The previous example on lead qualification shows the user interface reacting to data entry by the salesperson. The interface is not static, but changes according to the context of the information being entered. This is a good way to make processes work, and to make them work consistently.

The three IBO Essentials embody information that creates tremendous value throughout the sales cycle (see Chapter 18). Options 3, 4 and 5 in the lead qualification example show how the Essentials are entered into the computer. The Essentials govern the sales cycle length, the position in sales cycle, the probability, the priority, the skill phase and other peripheral information of use to the salesperson. Presenting all of this within the user interface is a challenge. Figure 24-3 shows one way to do it, in the form of a so-called *dashboard*, something we have seen already in the screenshot examples in Chapter 23.

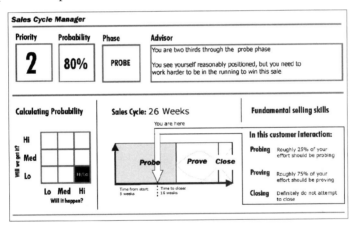

Figure 24-3: Graphical prototype of a sales method dashboard

Information is shown in the dashboard dynamically—if any of the IBO Essentials change, the dashboard will update automatically. The interface *reacts* to data entry, which is one way to relieve the potential stress and boredom that a frequent user of the software may experience. This dashboard is dominated by graphics, with only the right amount of text to provide understanding. For instance, the arrow which shows the current position in the sales cycle *moves* if the sales cycle length changes ("When will it happen?"

is updated). If this happens, the information on the fundamental selling skills appropriate for an interaction at this point also change. The priority may also be affected if the new expected date pushes the sales cycle into a different skill phase.

Entering Interactions

Figure 24-4 shows the customer interaction data entry process. Chapter 14 showed that there are some important distinctions that must be made on the nature of customer interactions. Classifying interactions in terms of whether they are relationship focused or opportunity focused is important.

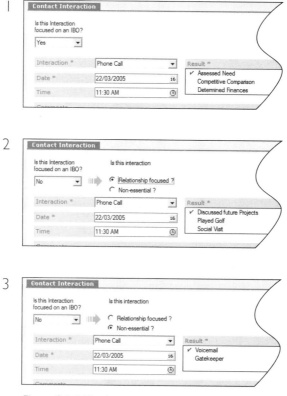

Figure 24-4: The interaction data entry process

Opportunity focused interactions that occur within the sales cycle are Critical Interactions, and form the basic elements of the sales process.

Enforcing the importance of Critical Interactions in sales automation allows salespeople to see an unfolding picture of their tactics and strategies as the sale progresses. It is important, therefore, that the user interface be designed to help the classification process.

At the start (1), the program asks the salesperson if the interaction is associated with a current open IBO. If the answer is Yes, the interaction is tagged as Critical. If the user opened the interaction from the form holding the customer information, the IBO linked with the customer is known by the computer, and the interaction is then automatically associated with that IBO number. If the customer has a number of open IBOs, they are presented, along with a description of the opportunity, for the salesperson to pick just one.

If the interaction is not related to a sales opportunity, then it is relationship focused (2) or maybe Non-Essential (3). The salesperson has the chance here to decide whether non-essential information should be stored or not. If it is stored, the software will have the capability to filter it from important business views of the data.

Note that in each form, there is a list of the most common interaction types, and these are again context sensitive. For instance the list for non-essential interactions contains "voicemail" or "gatekeeper," meaning that the call was not successful at reaching the desired individual. The list of options for relationship focused interactions contains options such as "discussed future projects" or "played golf." The intent, again, is to reduce data entry time while maintaining consistency across the organization. As always, the salesperson can type in as much information as they want in addition to the standard short description.

Showing the Hierarchy

Chapter 7 discussed how the four competencies could be described in terms of a hierarchical structure within the sales automation system. The user interface can take advantage of the hierarchical relationship in practical ways. Take for instance Figure 24-5, which shows some of the data from the case study on interactions from Chapter 15. The account, Global Digital Printer Networks is shown at the top level of the structure. The next level down shows the contacts that belong to that account: Susan Brown, John Parker, and Shirley Vine. Listed underneath the contacts are the sales opportunities that have occurred with each of them, with the Critical Interactions listed in chronological order. It's easy to see from this kind of presentation of the data the level of sales activity necessary to win the order.

Figure 24-5 is from a sales automation application that runs on Lotus Notes. Notes lends itself well to showing information in this logical hierarchical display format. Notice that in this user interface, navigation occurs using the acronym TASC to represent the four competencies. The user can switch easily between the competencies by clicking on the appropriate letter.

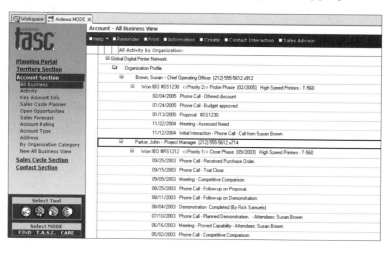

Figure 24-5: View of case study information showing the core competency hierarchy

Setting up the Sales Model

The Sales Model that was developed in Chapter 22 is important in deriving the true benefits of Intelligent Response Technology. It's a good idea to set up the ideal Sales Model for each distinct product line if the sales cycles and sales processes vary from one product to another. The Sales Model is usually set up just once and only changes if the sales team decides for whatever reason that the sales process needs to be modified. *Sales automation done right* has defined the sales process in terms of a set of Critical Interactions that have been found to provide the best path toward winning the sale. The user interface can be employed effectively to set up these interactions graphically. Figure 24-6 shows one way to do this.

The sales administrator first enters in the average sales cycle length for this product. The computer then knows the lengths of the three skill phases. Next, the set of Critical Interactions that best describe the sales process is chosen, and in the case of the user interface shown in Figure 24-5, can be dragged and dropped into place on the sales cycle graphic. For example, an initial probing visit in which a product information package is given to the customer may be called for within two weeks of the IBO being identified. A product demonstration could be called for at roughly sixty percent through the sales cycle, and so on. In this way the entire sales process is constructed interaction by interaction.

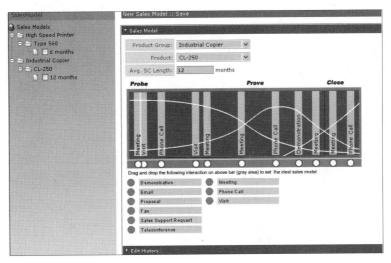

Figure 24-6: Setting up the Sales Model

The Help System

The way that help is made available in software applications sometimes comes under intense criticism. There can be concerns regarding too much or too little help available. If there is too much, the challenge is finding what you want—too little, and there is a real problem. With sales automation, there needs to be two coexistent help systems. The salesperson has to know how to use the software, but also they must know how to use the sales method. This means that the book which describes the sales method has to be available online to the salesperson—if they decide to reference it. It goes without saying that the online help system describing the sales methodology isn't much good unless there has been some formal classroom training to begin with. Unless the method has been explained, understood and validated, the salesperson won't go to the help screen for a refresher on the methodology.

If we are seeking assistance on how to use our word processor software, help is just a few mouse clicks away. Search systems are so refined that everyone can get context sensitive answers to their troubling problems. Sales automation must provide the same security. With tongue in cheek, "the methods behind the madness" must be made available easily and in the context of the current situation.

As Figure 24-7 shows, there is no problem in displaying these "methods" on any device that can run a sales automation application. Even the tiny display of the PDA can provide some valuable advice to the salesperson, although it may take some scrolling.

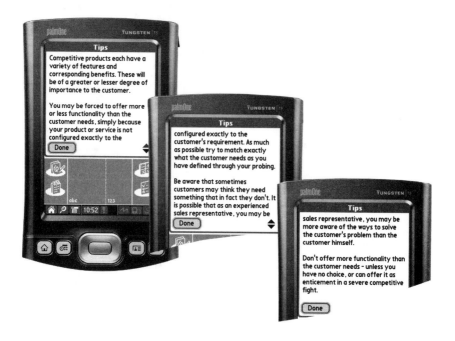

Figure 24-7: Sales method help shown on a PDA

Points to Remember

1. When deciding on a sales automation solution, pay careful attention to the user interface. The interface has a lot of impact on the potential success of the project.

2. If the sales automation system is based on a strong sales method, make sure it is reinforced through the user interface.

3. Use the interface to achieve consistency and accuracy of data entry through process.

CHAPTER 25

The Nuts and Bolts

What do I need to make it run?

Part I talked generally about the technology that makes sales automation work. The computers, operating systems, and networking infrastructures that companies use to make information sharing easy, are now well developed. They are getting cheaper to implement and easier to use. The software applications that bring CRM and SFA to life are also readily available, although *sales automation done right* would argue that more work can be done to *directly* benefit the salesperson. This chapter discusses some of the newer, more interesting innovations in technology that are impacting the way salespeople sell.

There have been recent developments in established technology, and also some new ideas that promise to provide some interesting improvements in sales automation. Technology is racing ahead so fast that no book can hope to be current with what's new. Bear in mind that the discussion that follows is a snapshot of the situation at the beginning of 2005.

Mobility

Salespeople are constantly on the move, often away from home base, but they still have to get their job done; business doesn't shut down simply because the salesperson is out of the office. E-mail has to be answered; quotations and presentations have to be put together. Daily interactions with customers have to be recorded for future reference, and past activity has to be reviewed before important meetings. Some of this is accomplished at home or in a hotel room in the evenings, but there is also a lot of spare time during the day: catching a coffee before the next appointment, waiting at an airport before catching a flight, sitting at a trade show waiting for the next crowd of attendees to come through the exhibition hall. The technology that the salesperson uses has to be *mobile*. First and foremost, this technology is the computer.

Ever since personal computers became a reality, manufacturers have tried to make them smaller in size and weight. The reason is clear—if technology transforms the way people work, they have to take it wherever they go, and in the case of salespeople, that could be *anywhere*. The notebook computer is now ubiquitous. With a weight of six pounds or less, it has the same processor, memory, disk capacity and connectivity as the machine that needs a desk to support it. Virtually all salespeople have one, you can see them being used in airports, in flight, in coffee shops and in the park. The notebook has become the essential prerequisite in the salesperson's arsenal of tools, followed closely by the software that it hosts: spreadsheets, databases, word processors and custom sales applications.

What are the issues of size when we talk about portable computers? Obviously the physical size of the notebook and its weight are very important, but when we discuss these issues, there is an assumption that the computing power is up to par with desktop PCs. Fortunately, today's notebook computer typically has the ability to handle all of the sophisticated computing tasks that the most demanding CRM or SFA applications can throw at it. But other issues are important considerations: is the screen large enough to adequately display all the information that needs to be seen? Is the keyboard large enough to type at reasonable speeds? We'll see that as the size of the computing device comes down, features such as these can get severely compromised, to the extent that the technology may not stand up to the demands of the job at hand. As computing devices get smaller and smaller, displaying and typing large amounts of information get to be a challenge. Notebook computers are shrinking and seem to have bottomed out at the three-pound level for true desktop capability and a screen and keyboard that impose no restrictions on what can be done.

For the computer to be truly mobile, access to home base is a must, both for downloading work created on the road and retrieving communications and information. The Internet is, by far, the preferred way to move information electronically, and fortunately, it's now straightforward to go online when traveling. There will be times, however, when this is not possible. As of today, it's not yet feasible to hook up to the Internet in an airplane—something that will eventually be possible, but probably not for everyone. With a six hour continental flight looming, the salesperson will probably want to get some work done. This is possible even without an Internet connection if the sales automation system has bulletproof synchronization capability. The salesperson works on a copy of the relevant part of the CRM database, and at the end of the journey, the work that has been done can be synchronized with the office. Refer to Part I for a detailed discussion on synchronization.

The Internet

The Internet and the World Wide Web have impacted every facet of personal and business life in ways that are impossible to calculate. All sizes of business now use the Internet for purposes ranging from communication, marketing, online commerce, business process, to research. In the sales department, the Internet is the communication channel of choice for the traveling salesperson to continue their administrative activities while away from the office.

After a busy day on the road, the salesperson settles down at home or in their hotel room and turns on the computer to do all of the back-up work resulting from their day's visits. Product information has to get sent out to customers, quotations or proposals have to be assembled, pricing has to be finalized and approved by managers, and perhaps, flights have to be booked for the next few days. To do all of that, the salesperson must log on to their company network through the Internet. From there, they have access to all the company files, processes, and people needed to keep the sales effort on track. Hotels and airport lounges offer high speed Internet access, and through the advent of wireless technology, discussed later, connections are becoming available in a whole variety of new locations.

The Internet has also introduced new ways to deliver efficiencies and cost reductions in rolling out CRM and SFA projects. Take for instance, web browsers such as Microsoft's Internet Explorer. Everyone has a browser because all computers come with one. Software designers are scrambling to make their applications run directly from the browser to obviate the need for proprietary client software. This lowers software costs and delivers the usability improvements that the very efficient browser brings to the table.

The ultimate end-point of immersing the CRM software in Internet and web technology is subscription computing. Many companies put off introducing CRM/SFA solutions because of the perceived expense. There definitely is an IT overhead associated with any significantly sized CRM project. The computer and networking infrastructure is usually in place, but application software has to be purchased and installation and training costs must be given consideration. Up front costs can no longer be an excuse—there are many good subscription services available that will provide immediate CRM functionality just by signing up for a monthly plan, with delivery through the Internet. There is no need to buy new hardware, or strain the capability of an already stretched IT department. All that's needed are computers with web browsers and a suitable Internet connection. Whether subscribing makes sense financially depends on your company's own situation. CRM solutions are definitely getting cheaper and easier to maintain, and hardware costs are also coming down. But subscription costs do go on forever, and once your company has revised its processes to fit the subscription-based product, it will be very difficult to leave it.

Another issue is offline usage. Synchronization is more difficult to do with web-based technology, so it's worth checking to see if the subscription service has this feature and whether it is capable enough for your needs.

Fortunately, the better CRM subscription services allow a certain amount of customization to accommodate the user's specific processes. Figure 25-1 shows the popular Salesforce.com CRM application running the sales method described in *sales automation done right*.

Wireless

Wireless phones have become a standard part of the salesperson's day, and now, wireless computing is heading the same way. The phone is probably the salesperson's number one tool on the road, followed closely by the computer.

For the traveling salesperson, wireless technology provides the capability of connecting to home base from almost anywhere. Wi-Fi, which stands for Wireless Fidelity, uses radio technology to connect computers with each other, to the Internet, or to conventional networks, without the use of wires. As long as you are within range of a base station, a Wi-Fi enabled computer can send and receive information, indoors or out, quickly and reliably. The total freedom from requiring a physical connection to the Internet is very liberating to the user, and extends computer usage to times and places never before possible. These days, notebook computers are often delivered wireless enabled, but if not, a wireless card can easily be added.

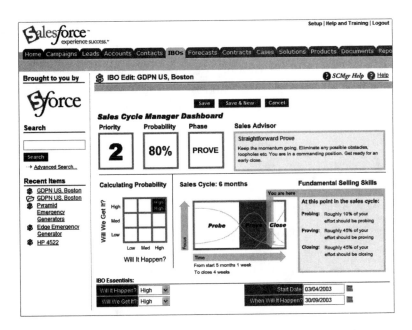

Figure 25-1: *Sales automation done right* as executed in Salesforce.com

Wireless access points or "hotspots" are now becoming common in many public places, including restaurants, coffee shops, conference centers, airports and even car rental agencies. In the future, we can expect that wireless connection will be possible throughout large urban areas and along major highways, making it possible to pull a car over in a convenient spot, grab the computer, and get to work.

An unexpected consequence of this newfound freedom for the traveling salesperson is that it has a very positive impact on the CRM and SFA initiative. Good CRM practices depend on capturing customer information and providing fast, efficient and customized service in return. If a salesperson comes out of a client meeting and heads into Starbucks for coffee, they can use this chance to log details while it is fresh in their mind. They can also research issues raised at the meeting in their company's archives, and perhaps get back to the customer with answers via an immediate e-mail. Customers are always impressed by this level of immediate attention.

Widely available remote connectivity also improves the chances of winning the sale. After important Critical Interactions with the customer, valuable newfound information that affects the strategies of the sale can be circulated to the sales team immediately. The details that impact and change the IBO Essentials are logged soon after the event, and have a better chance of being correct. Tactics can be modified on the fly—the sales teams that get online, even when they are on the road, will be further ahead than their competitors who don't. Yes, the cell phone can be used to do some of this, but when it comes to working business processes, and spreading the word amongst many different parts of the team, the computer is best.

The Personal Digital Assistant

The beautiful thing about the Personal Digital Assistant or PDA is that it wraps an awful lot of computing power into a very small footprint. A salesperson may be reluctant to walk all day on a University campus, visiting customers with a six-pound computer in their briefcase, but with the PDA, there is no excuse, as it easily slips into a pocket. It can also, just like a desk diary, be used in front of the customer, which is more than can be said for the notebook computer. Customers are usually intimidated if a salesperson gets out their computer, powers it on, and starts typing details of the meeting. But the PDA is unobtrusive, and the data is usually entered with a stylus just like putting a pen to paper. Salespeople have adopted the PDA for calendaring and contact lists, but are now searching for ways to use it to help their sales efforts.

How good is the PDA as a serious sales automation tool? It certainly pushes the bounds of displaying lots of information on a miniature screen to the limits. But a lot can be done with this tiny device. Figure 25-2 shows much of the sales method described in this book as it is successfully implemented on a PDA—three of the popular standards of PDA are shown. Just about everything we've talked about is there: lists of accounts, contacts and sales opportunities, IBOs sorted by priority, and the Probability Matrix in graphical form with dynamic display. The sales cycle is viewed along with duration, where we are now and how much time there is left. Intelligent Response technology is there too, and there is just enough room on the screen to provide a clear message for the salesperson, albeit with some additional scrolling. For storing, displaying and manipulating the *core* information that the salesperson needs at their fingertips, at any place and at any time, the PDA works just fine.

Figure 25-2: The sales cycle as shown on three different PDA platforms

There are certainly things that the PDA has problems with. Preparing proposals, writing letters or entering large pieces of information are a challenge. It's difficult to see the PDA as the primary technology tool for CRM, because there is just too much information that has to be moved around and processed electronically—but for working with a critical subset of data without constraint, the PDA is a wonderful tool for the salesperson.

The cell phone and the PDA are now converging with the possibility that one device will replace two. But because of the absolute requirement that a phone be very small, the PDA display screen will move to a smaller format than it is today, which is the single largest barrier to this device becoming the one and only computer tool for mobile workers.

A Word about the Solo Salesperson

Throughout this book, the discussion of sales automation or SFA has been in the context of the fit with Customer Relationship Management. That has inevitably led to the discussion being more focused on *sales teams* because CRM is about a common path followed by individuals within the company to serve the customer. But many salespeople don't work within this kind of environment—they work alone, because they work for themselves or very small companies. These are *solo salespeople*. The solo salesperson has no one to direct them on which technology to use, and there are also no company sponsored solutions because they choose their own. Sales automation works as well for one person as it does for a hundred. However, the solo salesperson is less involved with the sharing or collaborative side of the CRM technology tool; rather, they need only the functionality that suits just their own individual needs. There still must be lists of accounts, contacts and opportunities. There still is a need to record customer interactions and also to strategize the sale, but the need to share information with a team is no longer there.

The solo salesperson may not have the same tools as their counterparts in the big sales teams, when it comes to networks, information resources, mobile computers and limitless connectivity while on the road, but he or she can still enjoy all of the direct benefits of sales automation as they have been developed and described in *sales automation done right*. Figure 25-3 shows an application that runs in Microsoft Excel that has all of the essential features of the sales method derived in Part Three of this book. If necessary, a good deal of the method can also be used without any technology at all, other than a pen and paper. For instance, using Figure 20-5, it's possible to evaluate the current sales situation by doing some quick sums on the length of the sales cycle, current position and phase, along with an assessment of the Probability Index. We don't even need a slide rule to do this, just some basic arithmetic. But it gets difficult if we are doing it for fifty sales opportunities. It's even more difficult if our predictions for the end of the sales cycle are under constant change. In these circumstances, a computer is needed, even one with only the basic spreadsheet application. But, we know that the solo salesperson is indeed smart enough to be equipped to this level—these people are invariably trailblazers of technology.

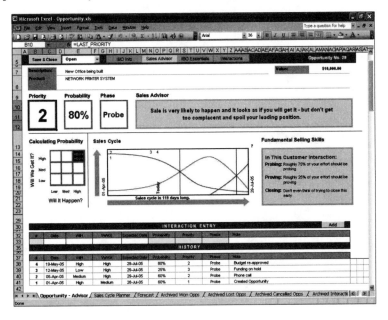

Figure 25-3: *Sales automation done right* as executed in Excel

The lesson here is that sales *effectiveness* does not depend on networks, collaborative software, communications or what have you—it boils down to salespeople using smart sales methodology with just enough technology to make it come alive.

Points to Remember

1. Good sales automation works well on all technology platforms. Determine which one is best for you, according to individual or team needs.

2. The Internet is invaluable for salesperson, and is becoming easily available even when travelling.

3. Personal Digital Assistants are powerful, small and unobtrusive. They can help a lot in managing a large portfolio of sales opportunities.

4. Sales automation isn't the exclusive domain of large sales organizations. The solo salesperson often is a trail blazer when it comes to technology, and the sales methods in this book work just fine if you fit this category.

PART 5

Conclusions

CHAPTER 26

Getting It Right First Time:

Watch out for well-known pitfalls.

Fortunately, there are a lot of companies actively using SFA and CRM, so anyone thinking of doing it at this time can sift through a wealth of experience of what went right and what went wrong. In this chapter, we look at some of the issues that, if handled badly, can scuttle a CRM project. As we are focusing on the common aspects of CRM and SFA, we will refer only to the term CRM.

In the past, CRM systems have been labeled as *transformative* technology because they literally transform business culture and the way companies operate. Not only is information free-flowing and available to everyone, but processes become well defined and smooth—they have to be, because they are electronically enabled.

The initial experience won't be pleasant if the CRM project is unplanned or out of control. The existing state of the business has to be reviewed in detail to see how the new technology will fit. Bad procedures have to be cast aside and effort given to developing new ones that will work with technology.

This chapter looks at the critical hurdles to automation. It's possible to buy a complete book on what the next few pages will cover, so don't consider it as an exclusive guide to getting things right.

Lock in the Vision

Because CRM technology influences every nook and cranny of an organization, it's important that everyone touched by it is made aware of the changes that might affect them. There should be a carefully documented and well-broadcasted vision of the new company after the transformation has occurred. A large enterprise will do this through a committee, whereas a smaller company may rely on the vision of just one or a few top executives or managers.

The main focus of the vision should be on why change is necessary, and the answer will likely be because things are not working well at present. The decision to change is usually not immediate; rather, the impact of imperfect processes, data or communication develops over a period of time, until consensus is reached that something must be done. The starting state of the business is one with which people are dissatisfied, and CRM is being introduced to change that. This is why the vision must be written down at the beginning of the project, and must include a clear description of the problems and issues that provoked the change, along with the expected improvements at completion. The vision becomes an important part of the implementation plan.

Develop the Plan

Even before the CRM system is purchased, there should be discussion amongst all the functional groups within the company that might be impacted (and that will be pretty much the entire company). The vision will begin to permeate through the organization. Just like any project, if there is no implementation plan, things are bound to go awry.

The plan will include the vision, the overview of what has to be fixed, and a detailed operational summary of how and when to do it. Key people will be assigned as stakeholders and will take charge of the piece of the project that they control or influence. Expectations have to be aligned with real tasks. Measurement criteria have to be assigned. These can vary in scope depending on the expected impact of CRM or SFA. A sales manager may set down the goal of having a day-to-day bookings forecast available from the system, one that he or she can rely on with 70 to 90 percent accuracy. Someone in sales administration may want to see all customer information in one place and virtually error proof. A CEO may demand real time information about any interaction between the company and the customer. A more general expectation may be the ability for everyone in the sales department to have nation-wide access to each other through electronic communication. CRM is so all-encompassing that each company that adopts it will have its own unique set of aspirations—the important thing is to get them written down in a plan. That way, the *success* of the project can be monitored. A good idea is to call the plan the *Success Document* to keep a focus on the ultimate objective.

Success can only be judged against initial expectations. CRM projects are lengthy, and reflection upon past progress becomes clouded if influencing factors change: the original proponents of the project may leave the company; original sources of discomfort may get fixed and forgotten about; other needs may evolve and take over the field of view. For instance, a CRM project may have an initial focus on consolidating customer information and improving response time in customer service. The expectation is that if this happens, sales will automatically go up. If over time, sales don't go up then the CRM initiative may get blamed, even though the customer service is much better. The poor sales could be caused by other independent factors—the Sales Manager could be incompetent, or the products may be uncompetitive. That's why the Success Document is so important. In order to get a value on investment, the company must record *all* the initial expectations and the frame of reference for them to be judged in the future. If expectations get modified because new barriers are exposed, they must also be recorded along with proposed methods of resolution.

Proposition
The Success Document is a *living* record of the company's efforts to embrace CRM.

Explicitly, it is an ongoing review and measurement of progress in implementing carefully planned initiatives that are calculated to resolve defined business pain points.

Much has been written about failure, rather than success of CRM projects, and much of the problem can be traced to bad or incomplete documentation of expectations and action plans, coupled with a regular review of progress against those documents.

If changes in business culture are necessary for CRM to work, these changes must be identified and become part of the "expectations" section of the Success Document. That way, some time in the future, if the CRM project is faltering because the culture was not made to change, the true reasons for potential failure are apparent, and can hopefully be remedied.

A simple example from the sales department illustrates this. One of the goals of a particular sales department was to maintain good quality of customer information, no duplicates, no misspelling, and all appropriate contact data, like phone numbers or e-mail addresses present and correct. To ensure this, the team decides that they will only let this information be entered by one person, a database administrator. They purchase their CRM system, but renege on hiring a database administrator to save some funds. In order to keep things moving, all salespeople are allowed to enter customer data any which way they want. Some do this well, but others don't. The data becomes quickly contaminated and incomplete, and everyone gets tired of using it. The Success Document would show what the true problem was. Without it, the CRM system would take the heat.

Top management must sign off on the plan and the vision. There should be provisos for what happens if there is a change in management. Often, CRM projects suffer because the vision disappears when the people who carry it leave the company. There have been examples of companies adopting CRM only to see political changes that brought in a new CEO, who then claimed that the old way of doing things on paper was the best. CRM projects were promptly shelved, which moved the company back from Wave Four to Wave One (see Chapter 6). That's why CRM is most successful in small, fast moving companies whose business is inspired by a single owner, shareholder, entrepreneur, and *visionary*.

The last piece of advice concerned with planning the CRM project is to not tackle too much at once. Yes, these projects are large, but they can always be planned to occur in a logical, staged order. If good customer data is a forefront requirement, do that first, and do processes next. The sales team may even need to move onto a common sales method ahead of the company-wide roll out to CRM. Decide the objectives, rate them in terms of importance, and then decide if the plan can accommodate a graduated installation of the project.

Hone up the Processes

Chapter 4 talks about CRM technology in terms of process and knowledge. Process is endemic to CRM systems; they live and breathe through process. But this is not process based on moving paper around from desk to desk; this is electronic process that moves around instantaneously on a computer network. Existing processes will inevitably be tweaked or changed before the CRM project gets underway. The better and more freely-flowing the old process, the easier it is to duplicate it on the computer.

Bring the groups together that are responsible for processing the customer's transaction and look how information flows between them. Is it efficient, and does it work? In a meeting such as this, current problems will surface very quickly. Moving to CRM provides an excellent excuse to get on a new page and to fix the disruptions, road blocks and delays caused by established bad practice.

Develop the Database

Inadequate, non-existent or unobtainable customer information is one of the prime incentives for companies to move to CRM. Chapter 5 discusses the Customer Knowledge Store and what should be in it. The challenge to the company embarking on a CRM project is creating a new Customer Knowledge Store from their legacy information, whatever and wherever that may be. It is probably going to come from multiple sources including paper files and computer disks from various departments, in the Front and Back Offices. In the case of the sales team, the data may be dispersed in the files of whatever Contact Management application each salesperson thinks is the latest and best.

A great danger lies in imposing a new set of data on everyone, one that is different to their own personal much-loved system, only for them to find that it has lower quality information and a load of stuff belonging to other folks that they don't want to see. Don't invent new information, take the old, then sift through and cleanse it. The more carefully and accurately this is done, the better. It's better to err on the light side rather than try to include too much of the old, bad stuff. Go into listing some sensible rules for cleaning information. Use the computer to correct batches of data or remove duplication. Establish a Database Manager who believes in the vision, and who knows that clean data is integral, and give them the power to control the situation.

Monitor Progress

The Success Document is the best way to ensure that this is done. There should be regular reviews of vision, objectives, tasks and achievements driven by what is laid down in the Success Document. In these meetings, issues are identified and a plan is set up to take care of them. The project will have tentacles reaching out to everywhere in the organization, and the best tactic is to elicit help from all the people they touch.

Lay Down the Rules

In a sharing culture, everyone has to participate, even though they may not want to initially. If there is a common vision, there can't be any deviations. By definition, most salespeople have large egos, and will want to do things their own way. If they have learned the advantages of working in a team, they will suppress the ego and join in. If they don't, they will have to be managed by rules. Anarchy cannot be the order of the day. The Sales Manager has responsibilities, and has to report performance up to the boss. This job gets tough if forecasts come through in a host of different ways, simply because each salesperson sees their own way as the best.

At the outset of the CRM project, the vision has to be carefully articulated with an acknowledgement that change is always difficult, but that the end result is worth the pain. The benefits to the individual, by working as a *team*, have to be laid down. If the team does not naturally evolve under the new environment, rules may have to be enforced to encourage the process.

One way to ease in the rules is to blend them into administrative processes. Examples of the "You can't do that, until you have done this" philosophy have been scattered throughout *sales automation done right*, and it has been found to work well in practice. One of the best uses of this is in achieving the logging of sales opportunities *early* in the sales cycle. Usually, in the early stages of their buying process, customers request product information. Doesn't it make sense to open an IBO at this point? If so, make a rule that says that any time a customer requests product information, an IBO should exist in the CRM system, and if it doesn't, then a new IBO should be created. If the salesperson finds out that the information has been requested for information only, the IBO can be removed.

Experience shows that when rules are applied through process, there will be initial groaning from salespeople, but that quickly dissipates as time goes on and the benefits materialize.

Share the Results

Everyone that the new system touches has a stake in it, and can influence its success. They have the right to know how the project is progressing. There should be regular meetings in which the original expectations are reviewed along with the current measurement criteria that determine success. If people are experiencing a bit more process to guarantee that customer data is getting better, then they should be shown directly in what way the improvement is taking place. Is there more data? Is there cleaner data? Is the transaction flowing faster? Is the information easier to retrieve? These issues will become apparent much quicker than the macro effects such as forecasting becoming more accurate or sales revenues going up.

If it Starts to Fail, Put it Right

CRM and SFA are here to stay. There is nothing mystical about it. It is just a way to do good business and if you haven't got it, your business is working under a huge compromise.

If past projects have failed, you can be sure something in this chapter was neglected or not done correctly. If your project hesitates, take a deep breath, don't panic, regroup and start again.

Points to Remember

1. Understand and recognize the initial reasons that drove the CRM/SFA project.

2. After committing to a solution, make sure to record the progress, good or bad, at fulfilling the initial goals.

3. If the project goes off course, immediately put in the measures to get it back on track.

CHAPTER 27

Final Thoughts

There's still a long way to go

This book was not written quickly. In fact, it's been over ten years since the idea first came about. The thing about creating a sales method is that it just doesn't happen overnight—it's evolutionary and the picture gradually emerges. Ideas are triggered by real problems experienced in the sales process. Attempts are made to fix them, leading to changes which, in turn, are tested in the field. In response to results from real sales experience, the ideas may be tuned, changed or added to. At some point, it's possible to take a pause, look at the results and say, "We have a method." This is what happened in devising the story that weaves its way through most of *sales automation done right*. If the ideas of the method are sound when things get started, the progress of development is a logical evolution of what's gone before. For instance, the idea of two selling styles based on relationship or opportunity focus evolved a number of years after the concept of the Critical Interaction, and yet supports the original thinking extremely well.

The fact that the story still continues is very encouraging. The book just skims the surface of what is possible from the marriage of computer and sales. There is still much to be done, and a long way to go. This chapter reflects on the changes over the past ten years and reviews what has moved forward, and what has stayed still.

Progress Made to Date

Chapter I talks about the two "faces" of sales automation, defined by *efficiency* and *effectiveness*. I hesitate to bring in the overused "e" words again, but there is no better way to discuss the cause and effect of CRM and SFA.

The efficiency side of the equation is well proven and acknowledged, and this is where most of the benefits have shown up in the past ten years. Companies have realized that the computer is an essential tool for their sales teams to react quickly and be competitive. Communication has never been better, information flows freely and work can be done anywhere, even when traveling. All of this leads to much more efficient selling, and revenues are stronger because of it. Sales efficiencies fueled by computerization are so recognized today that they are virtually taken for granted.

The same cannot be said for sales effectiveness. In fact, whether CRM is delivering the goods when it comes to sales effectiveness is an issue under constant discussion. In my opinion, true sales effectiveness has not been influenced much over the past ten years, and one of the reasons is that, somehow, SFA morphed into CRM sometime in the mid-nineties. CRM has efficiencies, not sales methodology, at its heart. Let's take another look at the true meaning of sales effectiveness.

Sales Effectiveness

The definition of sales effectiveness has to be put in terms of how well we *sell*. How strong are our true selling skills against a competitive alternative? Some salespeople are better at it than others, and some sales *teams* are better at it than others. One of the most important success factors in effective selling is sales team culture. Even a poor salesperson can get swept along by a winning team. This culture is founded on focused and visionary leadership combined with a sharing organization and sales professionals who have respect for their team and their own selling abilities. You don't need technology to make this chemistry work. All that's needed is a telephone, a pen and a pad of paper—countless companies have been doing it for decades.

CRM has unfortunately been promoted as a technology that will increase sales effectiveness, and therefore increase revenues. CRM tools are often looked upon as magic seeds sown to make sales blossom overnight. Companies blame the software if sales don't go up; I wish it were that simple. CRM *can* yield more effective sales through its SFA component. Unfortunately, a long time ago, someone managed to confuse building customer relationships with using selling skills. It's a shame, because if the original SFA definition would have been left in place, it might be easier to resolve the difference between CRM and SFA technology. SFA has to lead the way to sales effectiveness, and CRM left to take care of the efficiencies.

Customer Relationship Management philosophy has been wonderfully supported over the last ten years with technology that provides invaluable assistance with its core ideals—easily accessible and accurate customer information, the ability to tailor service to customer needs, and a universal invitation for everyone in the company to share the "customer experience." With properly implemented CRM tools, the processes that deal with the customer transaction become seamless, smooth and quick. Yes, CRM technology works, *if* there is corporate sponsorship and belief, and *if* internal business culture and process can be adjusted to fit the vision. Which of the two "e" words best fits the competencies of CRM? It has to be "efficiency." Everything is known about the dealings with the customer. All the information is freely available to the teams that need it. The customer's demands are identified and the transaction is fulfilled. Ongoing recognition of the customer and product satisfaction is established, measured and acted upon. This is everyone's idea of CRM, and it is because of the successful implementation of "efficiency."

It's time to resurrect the term "Sales Force Automation" and give it the importance that it richly deserves. Only then will we see the true potential that comes from sales effectiveness. When the difference between the terms SFA and CRM are thoroughly understood by both industry and customers, there can finally be a chance to push ahead with building sales models for computerization, which can, in turn, be embedded within the CRM tool to provide the benefits from both efficiency and effectiveness.

In Chapter I, I defined sales automation as "the application of technology to improve efficiency or effectiveness." Since that was written, and reflecting on the entrenchment of CRM in business, I would like to make the suggestion that SFA be more tightly defined, to separate its common element (efficiency) from CRM.

Sales Automation: The enablement of sales effectiveness through the use of technology.

Somehow this has a better ring to it. We've extracted the confusing piece. Efficiencies such as information sharing, electronic processes, single data stores and effortless communication are common to both CRM and SFA, simply because the two technologies got mixed up in the frantic shift toward moving technology into the Front Office.

Once agreement has come on this definition, the importance of the sales method becomes evident. Technology and techniques—computer and sales method, the two are inseparable for tomorrow's trailblazing sales teams. It's worth reflecting on the sales method and fully understanding what it means.

Sales Method

The term *sales method* encompasses just about every kind of idea that suggests a systematic way of selling. Most of the methods followed today delve deeply into the face-to-face interaction with the customer, an area that could come under the general heading of the *relationship*—specifically, the relationship between salesperson and customer during the progression of the sales process (the customer's buying process). Methods outline everything that a salesperson needs to do in their interactions with the customer: how to ask the right questions, how to overcome any objections, how to demonstrate competitive capability, how to judge customer reactions. In short, how to *probe, prove* and *close*. I label most of these methods as *tactical*. They are very important, but they may not be well suited to the computer.

Over two-thirds of *sales automation done right* is devoted to the details of constructing a sales method that comes alive when it works hand-in-hand with a computer, and there is not much in the method about *tactics*. Yes, there is the idea of the fundamentals skills, probe, prove and close. But they are introduced to cover the description of how the sales cycle responds to the evolution of the customer's natural buying process, which follows three fairly distinct sequential stages. Dividing the sales cycle into three corresponding skill-focused stages is a very appropriate way to tune the sales method to the computer. The computer handles all issues of timing within the sales cycle, when interactions should occur, and which skills are necessary, with relative ease. To the salesperson handling many sales capabilities, this functionality is invaluable.

My point is that sales methods designed for computers inevitably come out *different* than those that dwell on well-defined face-to-face tactical planning. If there is one single message that *sales automation done right* has to evangelize, this would be it. The issue can be made clearer by dissecting the major components of the sales method described in this book to show the relationship between the sales method (technique) and the computer (technology). Figure 27-1 shows this.

The sales method and the computer work hand-in-hand to assist the salesperson directly in their sales efforts. This is only possible if the sales method is designed specifically to fit the unique capabilities of the computer.

We said earlier that the method we have developed is not heavy on tactics. The emphasis is on aspects of the sales method that the computer is really good at, such as the analytics surrounding the sales opportunity and the sales cycle. But the book does not neglect tactics completely. It does discuss the skills of selling, but more so in terms of the view from sixty-thousand feet. It talks about the skills of proving, but doesn't explain how to prove—that is for the tactical sales method to discuss. It addresses the relationship focused sales style, but doesn't elaborate on how to become relationship focused or how to improve on existing relationship strengths. In fact, if we consider the 2x2 matrix that is formed from the considerations of relationship versus opportunity focused styles that is explained in Chapter 14, we see that *sales automation done right* is really about how a Quadrant 2 salesperson can move into the coveted Quadrant 4 spot. We don't talk about moving the Quadrant 3 salesperson over to Quadrant 4 because that would require a whole other book on the skills of relationship building.

So, the framework for tactical planning is there, under the general headings of probe, prove and close, but there is no detailed advice on how to use these skills within the interaction. However, any sound tactical sales methodology can be easily layered over the method of *sales automation done right*, which can be considered a sales methodology *platform* for automation. Tactical sales methodology relies heavily on salespeople planning ahead for a customer interaction in a well-structured format, and then analyzing results

TECHNIQUES Sales Method	TECHNOLOGY Computer
Recognize the *actual* sales cycle—defined from the time the sales opportunity is found to the time the deal closes.	Log sales cycle and measure position in sales cycle. Adjust sales cycle as expected close date changes. Advise user how much time has elapsed and how much time is left.
Define the use of fundamental sales skills in response to the natural progression of the customer's buying process.	Calculate the three skill phases of the sales cycle and maintain update on re-estimation of sales cycle. Advise user which phase they are currently in, and the correct blend of skills to used at a particular point in the sales cycle.
Define the probability of winning a sale in terms of two separate issues that affect it—(1) the chance that the sales will go through to completion, and (2), the competitive issues in winning the sale.	Store the user's response to each question as one of three possibilities on a 3x3 matrix, and allocate the point on the matrix to one of six possible percentage values of probability.
Recognize that the value of a sales opportunity is governed by two factors—the probability of winning it, and the position in the sales cycle, specifically, the skill phase of the sales cycle.	Plot a point on a 3x3x3 cube which is determined by the probability of the sale happening and which of three possible skill phases the sale is in. Compare to a lookup table of possible consequences determined by expert sales experience, and report to the user.
Define opportunity focused and relationship focused selling styles and how they should be used in a customer interaction.	Log and classify customer interactions as relationship or opportunity focused. Associate relationship focused with the contact and opportunity focused with the sales opportunity.
Define the opportunity focused interactions occurring within the sales cycle as Critical Interactions.	Display the set of Critical Interactions with the sales opportunity to which they belong, such that the salesperson can easily see their ongoing progress in the sales process.
Define the sales process as a set of Critical Interactions that have been found to be best to win the sale.	Store an ideal sales process in the form of a Critical Interaction set, for comparison to the current interaction history in the sales opportunity.
Define Sales Environment as all issues that affect the outcome of the sale, and show how the fundamental skills are used to discover and influence it.	Quantify current state of Sales Environment through salesperson's answers to a series of questions. Calculate "Will it happen?", and "Will we get it?" and any corresponding changes in probability and priority. Present to salesperson in format of an Intelligent Response.

Figure 27-1: The match between sales method and computer

after the interaction has occurred. This can be done with a pencil and paper, or the paper form can be made electronic within the computer; the result is the same. *Sales automation done right* rigorously defines the Critical Interaction as the major component of the sales process, and it is within the Critical Interaction that the tactical selling occurs—the two sales methods work well together.

Sales Training

If the sales team decides on a sales method, then that method must be trained. The ineffectiveness of sales training gets almost as much attention as the issue of sales effectiveness. Companies will go through the expense of bringing their sales force in from the field for a few days to get intensive training on perfectly good sales methods, only to find that the positive effect of the training is short-lived. The problem is that ongoing, regular reinforcement is prohibitively expensive. The onus is on the salespeople to dust off their three inch-thick sales manuals every month to check if they are following the plan. Inevitably, they don't do it.

There is, however, one sure way to reinforce the sales methodology, and that is to weave it inextricably into the CRM system. Assuming that the CRM software has become the central focus of administration and business process within the sales department, it shouldn't be too difficult to ensure that salespeople get exposed to the sales method whenever they are processing or updating a sales opportunity. The system should be designed such that they cannot do anything but.

What better way to reinforce a capable and sound sales method than to immerse into the CRM software that the salespeople have to use everyday, and get everyone on the same page, with consistent sales processes, consistent forecasting and a consistent image to the customer. The method that the sales team practices in front of the customer has to be the same one that is in the computer. Everyone has to believe in it, and it has to be rigorously adhered to. If this can happen, the wonderful synergies of efficiency and effectiveness can be realized.

New sales methods designed specifically for automation must also be subject to thorough classroom training. The reasons for the method must be understood and respected. But from there on in, reinforcement is much easier as salespeople experience the method every day through their computer. The team has to make the message clear—to work in sales in this company, you must use a computer with this CRM tool and the accompanying sales method.

Conclusion

So there it is, and there is still a long way to go. I hope that *sales automation done right* will act as stimulation for your sales department going forward. Whether you are an executive of a large company with concerns about your sales team, or just a solo salesperson striving to be the best in your field, the material in this book should help immensely. Some ideas will apply directly, some may not, and many can be extracted intact from the methodology and used alone, or modified to fit individual circumstances.

The exercise of making a sales method work with a computer forces a deep investigation in all the mechanisms that make *your* sales process work. This alone often justifies the decision to automate. Perhaps this book has challenged you to do exactly that, if so, good luck along the way. Not only will you have a lot of fun, but your sales team will be a lot more effective when you reach Nirvana.

Keith Thompson
Toronto, 2005

Glossary

There are many definitions scattered throughout *sales automation done right*. This glossary throws in a few more, along with examples that are framed specifically from the point of view of the salesperson. Making a short, all-encompassing description of what a word or few key words should mean is tough to do. As I've learned in my years of designing SFA and CRM solutions, there will be controversial elements in some of these explanations. But then it is up to the reader to look at other reference material to formulate their own ideas. That can only help foster a better understanding of the concepts.

ACCOUNT

An account is a logical grouping of people who work for a common organization and therefore, have shared interests. The account is designated by the Sales Manager to be conveniently targeted by the sales team with a planned sales strategy. Account Management is one of the four core competencies of the management of selling.

Example: "My Sales Manager gave me a new account. It's a new division of Image International Corp, whose Baltimore group have been good customers of ours for years. This new Buffalo division should need at least twenty Industrial Copiers to get started."

See related topics: Contact, Sales Cycle, Territory.

ACTUAL SALES CYCLE

The actual sales cycle is the amount of time that the salesperson has to sell their product to the customer. It is the time between the salesperson discovering the sales opportunity and the time that the customer awards the business to the successful vendor.

Example: "I could kick myself for not visiting Global Diodes more often. I've learned that they want five High Speed Printers, but the competitors have been working on the requirement for over three months. I've only got a month to show them we have a better solution."
See related topics: Average Sales Cycle, Buying Process, Customer's Sales Cycle.

ART OF SELLING

The art of selling is the salesperson's ability to secure a sale through their natural skills at communicating, building relationships and engendering trust.

Example: "I'm in good shape. I get on really well with the purchasing agent at Global Diodes, after working on our relationship for the past year—we are both avid sports fans. I know that he will give me the business if it comes to a tie."
See related topics: Relationship Focused Interaction, Science of Selling.

AVERAGE SALES CYCLE

The average sales cycle is the most probable length of time that it takes for a salesperson to sell a given product or service. The sales team will only be able to derive the average sales cycle through experience of many sales opportunities over a period of time. There will be deviations in the average sales cycle (shorter or longer) because of abnormal influences on the customer's usual buying process.

Example: "It usually takes six months to sell a Type 560 printer, but this customer already has five on the shop floor, and they are pressured by workload. We'll see this one go through in a month."

See related topics: Actual Sales Cycle, Buying Process, Customer's Sales Cycle.

BACK OFFICE

The Back Office is, collectively, the departments or functional groups in the company which are essential to the successful operation of the company, but are not regularly in direct contact with the customer. These could be finance, manufacturing, development, inventory control, shipping/receiving and others.

Example: "I rely upon my manufacturing group to consistently produce a good product. Otherwise, I would find my sales commitment tough to fulfill."

See related topics: Front Office.

BINARY SALES FORECAST

A binary forecast is a prediction of future revenues by the sales team that is determined on a decision of which actual sales opportunities will be sold, rather than taking some form of average or weighted summation over a number of possible sales opportunities.

Example: "I'm including the GDPN deal in my binary forecast for April. Even though the Welland deal could close that month, I'm not sufficiently confident to include it, but it will show up in my weighted forecast."

See related topics: Sales Forecast, Weighted Sales Forecast.

BUYING PROCESS

This is a process that most customers use to purchase a product or service from start to finish. The buying process proceeds in three distinct stages: recognizing the need, evaluating solutions, and negotiating value.

Example: "A customer called for information on our new series of printers. She thinks she will want one for her new production line, and is in the early stages of researching what's available. She'll want to try out her own protocol on a selected few before coming to a final decision."

See related topics: Sales Process.

CLOSE PHASE

The Sales Model defines the Close Phase as the final phase in the three phase sales cycle in which the dominant skill used is closing. In this phase, the salesperson and the customer work together to negotiate a mutually agreeable value proposition that hopefully leads to a successful conclusion for the salesperson. The other two fundamental skills, probing and proving, are used to support the closing effort.

Example: "We've finally shown how our printer will do everything they need. They should have enough information to go ahead. We'd better start finding out if there's any reason for them not to place an order."

See related topics: Close Skill, Probe Phase, Prove Phase.

CLOSE SKILL

The fundamental skill of closing is the ability of the salesperson to uncover any barriers that prevent the customer from placing an order, and to overcome those barriers such that a decision can be made.

Example: "I think all the objections to making a decision have been answered satisfactorily. I overcame their concerns about budget by working out an extended payment plan reaching into their new fiscal year—we should get the order."

See related topics: Close Phase, Probe Skill, Prove Skill.

CONTACT

A contact is a person who could buy your product or who may influence the decision to buy your product. Contact Management is one of the four core competencies of the management of selling.

Example: "Ms. Corning is the one with the immediate need for an Industrial Copier and is directing the sale, but she won't buy without consulting her associate in Baltimore. I also think the purchasing agent will have a say in the matter."

See related topics: Account, Sales Cycle, Territory.

CRITICAL INTERACTION

A Critical Interaction is an opportunity focused interaction that occurs within a sales cycle. Strategies and tactics designed to win the sale are played out in Critical Interactions with the customer. Critical Interactions are most often two-way, but can be one-way.

Example: "I sent the buyer our final offer which showed a 5% discount and an extra year of warranty."

See related topics: Customer Interaction, Non-Essential Interaction, One-Way Interaction, Opportunity Focused Interaction, Relationship Focused Interaction, Two-Way Interaction.

CRM (SEE CUSTOMER RELATIONSHIP MANAGEMENT)

CRM PROCESS

The CRM process is the process that governs the smooth flow of responsibilities between the three Front Office groups of marketing, sales, and
service, in their ongoing efforts to find customers, sell them product or
service, and maintain their level of satisfaction.

*Example: "I'm glad that marketing are still targeting the GDPN organization even though they
are one of our loyal and trusted customers. Every so often a new manager is hired, who has had
no experience of our products, and we need to make sure they get to know who we are quickly."*

*See related topics: Customer Acquisition and Retention Loop, Customer Relationship
Management.*

CUSTOMER ACQUISITION AND RETENTION LOOP

The customer acquisition and retention loop is a closed loop multi-step process diagram that shows how a new customer's transaction is passed between
marketing, sales, and service in a CRM system. In this case, the customer
transaction encompasses everything between learning about a product, to becoming a lifetime user, and potentially a repeat customer (hence the loop).

*Example: "This is the third generation of Industrial Copier that GDPN has purchased. I'm
pleased that Smith's vision of providing lifetime value and service is paying off."*

See related topics: CRM Process, Customer Relationship Management.

CUSTOMER INTERACTION

A customer interaction, or simply, an interaction, is any event in which the
company touches (relates with) the customer, regarding mutual business
relationship.

*Example: "I met with the purchasing agent of Lexington, and they seem set to go ahead with
our offer. I'll enter this into the CRM system so everyone can share the news."*

*See related topics: Critical Interaction, Non-Essential Interaction, One-Way Interaction,
Opportunity Focused Interaction, Relationship Focused Interaction, Two-Way Interaction.*

CUSTOMER KNOWLEDGE STORE

The Customer Knowledge Store is the company's bank of information about all the dealings that have occurred with the customer in the past, good or bad. The Knowledge Store is a historical database of all interactions between the company and the customer.

Example: "I looked back at what had happened with Lexington two years ago when Brad had that account. Brad was very close to the customer, but was suffering from the bad performance history of the old Type 520. I think that stuff is still haunting us."

See related topics: Customer Interaction, Customer Relationship Management.

CUSTOMER RELATIONSHIP MANAGEMENT

Customer Relationship Management, or CRM, is a way of doing business with a focus on creating a long term relationship with the customer, such that the customer is more inclined to offer continued business rather than seeking competitive solutions. As such, this definition does not imply any connection with technology. But the term CRM has grown to mean the computer-based networking and software applications that make the closeness to the customer more easily achievable.

Example: "We've been doing business with Lexington for over ten years, and the efforts we've been putting in with servicing their account and tailoring our product to their specific issues are really paying off. They are very reluctant to try anything from Universal, as the trust just isn't there."

See related topics: Sales Force Automation.

CUSTOMER'S SALES CYCLE

The customer's sales cycle is the time that elapses between the customer initiating the buying process, and the point at which a decision is made on which product to buy. If the salesperson is close to the customer from the very start of the buying process, the actual sales cycle will be equal to the customer's sales cycle.

Example: "Mr. Smith told me that he had been thinking about getting a High Speed Printer, and today his boss said it was a good idea, as funds were available, so he is starting to collect information. I'm glad I'm in at the start of this situation. He said he'll plan to get a unit installed in October, so he will need to make a decision by the first week of September, which is only six months from now."

See related topics: Actual Sales Cycle, Average Sales Cycle, Buying Process, Sales Cycle.

DIRECT BENEFITS OF SALES AUTOMATION

The direct benefits of sales automation enable salespeople to make best use of their selling skills, resulting in an improvement in the ratio of sales won to sales lost. The salesperson becomes more effective.

Example: "I checked my progress in the Global Diode sale with my sales automation system. It suggested that I need to spend more time with the economic decision maker. That is not a bad idea."

See related topics: Indirect Benefits of Sales Automation.

FRONT OFFICE

The Front Office is the collection of departments or functional groups within the company that deal directly with the customer. Typically these are marketing, sales and service.

Example: "I see from my CRM system that the service group was out at Lexington today, and they have discovered that the customer could use another CL-250."

See related topics: Back Office.

FUNDAMENTAL SKILLS

The three fundamental skills of selling are probing, proving and closing. Each of the three skills is dominant in a particular phase of the sales cycle. The fundamental skills are comprised of a set of lower level skills necessary to achieve the primary objective of the parent skill. In any Critical Interaction at least two, and sometimes three of the fundamental skills are used to differing degrees, dependent on the position in the sales cycle.

Example: "It's near the end of the sale and in tomorrow's meeting, my objective is to show the customer that my service can meet all of his expectations, in spite of this being a competitor's account. That's going to take all of the diplomacy (probing), product knowledge (proving), and negotiating (closing) capabilities that I have."

See related topics: Closing Skill, Critical Interaction, Probing Skill, Proving Skill.

IBO (SEE IDENTIFIED BUSINESS OPPORTUNITY)

IBO ESSENTIALS

The IBO Essentials are three pieces of information that the salesperson uses to characterize a sales opportunity. The important parameters of Probability and Priority can be calculated directly from the IBO Essentials. The three pieces of information are "Will it happen?" "Will we get it?" and "When will it happen?"

Example: "This IBO is my best shot at booking something in August ('When will it happen?' is August). The customer is happy with the machines he has already bought from us ('Will we get it?' is High), and the need is very high ('Will it happen?' is also High)

See related topics: "When will it happen?", "Will it happen?", "Will we get it?".

IDENTIFIED BUSINESS OPPORTUNITY

The Identified Business Opportunity is a term used in *sales automation done right* to describe the sales opportunity. Emphasis is on the fact that the salesperson has correctly qualified the opportunity as real. In the sales automation system, IBOs are given unique numbers to distinguish them from each other (i.e. IBO #2020).

Example: "After talking to marketing about their meeting with GDPN at the Print Show, I'm going to open up an IBO for a Type 560 for the GDPN Boston facility."

See related topics: Sales Opportunity.

INDIRECT BENEFITS OF SALES AUTOMATION

The indirect benefits of sales automation enable the salesperson to work more sales opportunities by making administrative, support, and connectivity tasks much easier—in other words, by making the salesperson more efficient.

Example: "Since we implemented sales automation, doing quotations has become a cinch—no more scribbles on pieces of paper that get sent off to Head Office. Now everything flows electronically, and I can see when support has completed the quote and sent it out. It's freeing up more time for me to sell."

See related topics: Direct Benefits of Sales Automation.

INTELLIGENT RESPONSE TECHNOLOGY

Sales automation done right uses Intelligent Response Technology on the computer to compare the salesperson's current performance against a model of the most successful strategies used in the past. If necessary, the computer provides advice to the salesperson on changing strategies to win the sale.

Example: "I entered my best guess on the sale as to whether it would go through and whether we would get it. Then I detailed out my progress—the computer disagreed, and felt that my 'Will it happen?' was not High, but Medium. It suggested that I do more talking with the economic decision maker."

See related topics: Sales Environment, Sales Model.

LEAD

A lead is an expression of interest in your product or service, and represents a potential sales opportunity.

Example: "I got a message from the receptionist this morning. Mr. Smith from Lexington called to request information on the new Industrial Copier."

See related topics: Long Term Lead, Sales Opportunity.

LONG TERM LEAD

A long term lead is one that cannot be qualified immediately to a positive result (an opportunity), or a negative result (close the lead, the customer is not buying anything). Rather, the customer is not buying now, but there is a strong possibility that they will buy in the future. The long term lead is kept open, and the salesperson follows up regularly in order to be ready when the lead turns into an opportunity.

Example: "The service engineer called to tell me that the customer only expected an in-service life of three years, and at that time, would need to buy a larger unit. I will enter this as a long term lead."

See related topics: Lead, Sales Opportunity.

MARKETING DEPARTMENT

The marketing department is the functional group that finds potential customers, qualifies them and hands over positively qualified leads (IBOs) to the sales department. In the customer acquisition and retention loop, the marketing department comes before the sales and service departments.

Example: "I received ten new IBOs from marketing today. They were qualified at the Los Angeles Print Show."

See related topics: Sales Department, Service Department.

NON-ESSENTIAL INTERACTION

A Non-Essential interaction has no real importance in measuring the relationship with the customer or impacting the strategy of winning the sale. As such, it need not be recorded into the CRM system.

Example: "I called the purchasing agent to check into the state of Mr. Smith's requirement, but she was not there, and I did not leave a message."

See related topics: Critical Interaction, Customer Interaction, One-Way Interaction, Opportunity Focused Interaction, Relationship Focused Interaction, Two-Way Interaction.

ONE-WAY INTERACTION

One-way interactions occur when one party contacts the other, but there is no immediate connection or response. A response may never come, if so, the interaction stays one-way. If a response comes later, the interaction becomes two-way.

Example: "I've sent an e-mail to the purchasing agent saying that we will meet Universal's warranty proposition, but I haven't heard back from them. It's been a week already."

See related topics: Critical Interaction, Customer Interaction, Non-Essential Interaction, Opportunity Focused Interaction, Relationship Focused Interaction, Two-Way Interaction.

OPPORTUNITY FOCUSED INTERACTION

In opportunity focused interactions, the salesperson's primary objective is to use true selling skills to win the sale from the competition.

Example: "The final presentation of our proposal went down well with everyone. The President said that we would definitely get the order."

See related topics: Critical Interaction, Customer Interaction, Non-Essential Interaction, One-Way Interaction, Relationship Focused Interaction, Two-Way Interaction.

OPPORTUNITY PORTFOLIO

The Opportunity Portfolio is the list of open sales opportunities that the salesperson is currently working on, and has yet to close.

Example: "Right now my sales automation system tells me I'm working on fifty open opportunities—this time a year ago, I had only thirty."

See related topics: Sales Opportunity.

PRIORITY

The priority assigned to a sales opportunity is a measure of its importance with respect to other opportunities that need to be worked.

Example: "This is a new opportunity that's at the start of the sales cycle. The customer heavily favors the competition, but if I leave it alone, I don't stand a chance. It's tough to prioritize it, as I have a lot of other situations that are about to close in which I am favored vendor. I think I'll deal with those first and then come back to this one."

See related topics: Probability Matrix, Priority Cube, Probability Index.

PRIORITY CUBE

The Priority Cube takes the idea of the Probability Matrix one step further by adding in another three-point possibility, which is skill phase (Probe, Prove or Close). With the Priority Cube, an opportunity has three parameters associated with it: "Will it happen?", "Will we get it?", and skill phase. Each of the parameters has three options, leading to a three-by-three-by-three matrix or cube, with twenty-seven possibilities.

Example: "I'm very confident that this sale will happen ('Will it happen?' is High), but I'm not so sure that I will win it ('Will we get it?' is Medium), which gives me a probability of 60%. I'm in the Probe Phase (skill phase), and I still have time to improve on this situation. I'm going to give it top priority with the hope of moving the 'Will we get it?' to a High."

See related topics: Probability Matrix, Skill Phase, "When will it happen?", "Will it happen?", "Will we get it?".

PROBABILITY

Probability is an expression of the chance that a sale will be won. It is most often expressed as a numerical percentage (i.e. 50%). In *sales automation done right*, the probability is calculated from a matrix constructed from the salesperson's answers to the questions "Will it happen?" and "Will we get it?"

Example: "This sale has a fifty percent chance of us winning in April."

See related topics: Probability Index, Probability Matrix, "Will it happen?", "Will we get it?".

PROBABILITY INDEX

The Probability Index is a unique point on the three-by-three Probability Matrix constructed from the possible answers to "Will it happen?" and "Will we get it?" Each answer can be one of the three possibilities: High, Medium or Low.

Example: ""Will it happen?" is High, but "Will we get it?" is Low." That's position 3 on the Matrix and a probability of 25%."

See related topics: Probability, Probability Matrix, "Will it happen?", "Will we get it?".

PROBABILITY MATRIX

The Probability Matrix is a three-by-three grid constructed from the answers to the questions "Will it happen?" (High, Medium, Low) and "Will we get it?" (High, Medium, Low).

Example: "This customer will definitely buy in June, and I'm sure we'll get the order. 'Will it happen?' is High, and 'Will we get it?' is High. That's position 9 on the Matrix and a probability of 80%."

See related topics: Probability, Probability Index, "Will it happen?", "Will we get it?".

PROBE PHASE

The Probe Phase is the first in a three phase sales cycle in which the primary focus of the salesperson is on the skill of probing. The skill of proving will also be used to a lesser or equal degree in support of probing.

Example: "This is a six-month sales cycle. I should be focusing on probing for the first three months."

See related topics: Close Phase, Probe Skill, Prove Phase.

PROBE SKILL

The fundamental skill of probing is the ability of the salesperson to find out everything about the customer's requirements and to discover all the issues that are behind their decision to purchase a product or service.

Example: "I've got to get to the bottom of how this decision will be made—I have a suspicion that purchasing may try to rein in the budget towards the end of the deal."

See related topics: Close Skill, Probe Phase, Prove Skill.

PROVE PHASE

The Prove Phase is the second in a three phase sales cycle in which the foremost objective for the sales team is to prove. The associated skills of probing and closing will be used with lesser degree to support the proving effort.

Example: "I'm reaching the three-quarter point in the sales cycle. Now is the time to get the customer in front of a machine to test how their application works."

See related topics: Close Phase, Probe Phase, Prove Skill.

PROVE SKILL

The fundamental skill of proving is the ability of the salesperson to provide evidence to the customer and to convince them that the solution that they offer is the best.

Example: "At the factory demonstration today, Ralph proved conclusively that our High Speed Printer could outperform Universal's demonstrator unit on both throughput and color control. He managed to shoot down all the claims that Universal salespeople were making about their demonstrator."

See related topics: Close Skill, Probe Skill, Prove Phase.

QUALIFICATION

Qualification is the process of checking that a lead has the potential to become a sales opportunity. If it is qualified positive, an opportunity has been discovered. If it is qualified negative, there is no sales opportunity, but the record of the lead can be kept for future marketing activity.

Example: "I called Mr. Smith this morning. He is just interested in what's new in the industry and does not need or even use Industrial Copiers. I've qualified the lead as negative."

See related topics: Lead, Long Term Lead, Sales Opportunity.

RELATIONSHIP FOCUSED INTERACTION

In opportunity focused interactions, the salesperson's primary objective is to measure, nourish and build the relationship with the customer.

Example: "It's been six months since the copier was installed. I paid a visit to see if the customer was still happy, and everything seems to be just fine. They would be happy to become a reference site."

See related topics: Art of Selling, Critical Interactions, Customer Interactions, Non-Essential Interactions, One-Way Interactions, Opportunity Focused Interactions, Two-Way Interactions.

SALES AUTOMATION (SEE SALES FORCE AUTOMATION)

SALES CYCLE

Measured in units of time (days, weeks, months, years), it is the lifespan of the sales opportunity. It also represents the only available time to get the selling job done. According to whether you are the customer or the salesperson, the sales cycle may be different. Sales Cycle Management is one of the four core competencies of the management of selling.

Example: "I made one of my routine calls to the Lexington facility to talk to the VP of Production. I showed him the flyer on the new Type 560, and he was thrilled. It has all the features he has been asking for. He checked his budget and he has enough funds to buy one. I think he's serious. This IBO could close in just six weeks."

See related topics: Actual Sales Cycle, Average Sales Cycle, Customer's Sales Cycle, Account, Contact, Territory.

SALES DEPARTMENT

The sales department is the functional group within the company that takes positively qualified leads (IBOs) from the marketing department and attempts to win as many of them as possible. In the customer acquisition and retention loop, the marketing department comes before the sales department, and the service department comes after.

Example: "Over 50% of the leads I've received from marketing in the past year have resulted in won orders. I'm keeping the service group very busy with installations."

See related topics: Marketing Department, Service Department.

SALES ENVIRONMENT

Sales Environment is used to describe everything about the sale that will ultimately determine its outcome.

Example: "I think I've identified all the decision makers, but I'm not sure about the politics of this sale, and who is really driving the purchase."

See related topics: Sales Model.

SALES FORCE AUTOMATION

Sales Force Automation, or Sales Automation, is a way to use technology to improve sales performance, directly or indirectly. Directly, by improving the salesperson's effectiveness, and indirectly, by improving the salesperson's efficiency. *Sales automation done right* suggests that a more appropriate definition is one that leaves efficiency to CRM and effectiveness to SFA.

Example: "Since we've installed a sales automation system, I've found it frees up more time for selling, and the built-in sales method also helps too."

See related topics: Customer Relationship Management.

SALES FORECAST

An estimate of future sales usually provided in terms of booked revenue, but sometimes in terms of product units. A forecast is usually generated by the individual salesperson, and the manager rolls up the total across the entire sales team.

Example: "I don't expect to book much in June, so this quarter won't be too good, but next quarter looks as if it will be a winner."

See related topics: Binary Forecast, Weighted Forecast.

SALES MODEL

The Sales Model is a set of descriptions, understandable by the computer, that attempt to define the ideal performance of the salesperson as they progress through the sales cycle. It is built up from four key components: time, fundamental skills, Critical Interactions, and information.

Example: "I'm about three-quarters of the way through this sale and I should be focusing on proving the benefits of my product. The next time I meet with the customer, I'm going to take my Product Manager to try to see if there are any details of the customer's application I have missed."

See related topics: Customer Interaction, Fundamental Skills.

SALES OPPORTUNITY

The Sales Opportunity is the chance given to a salesperson by a prospective customer, to offer their product or service to fulfill the customer's requirements and needs. In *sales automation done right*, the Sales Opportunity is called the IBO, which stands for Identified Business Opportunity.

Example: "Mr. Parker called to say that the old Universal machine had died, and they have an immediate need for a replacement. They will have to follow the normal tendering routine. I'll enter it into the system as a new IBO that will probably close in September."

See related topics: Identified Business Opportunity.

SALES PROCESS

The sales process is a proven, repeatable and well-established set of Critical Interactions through which the sales team implements their strategies and tactics to win the sale.

Example: "We're about three-quarters through this sales cycle, and I need to think about organizing a demonstration of the Type 560. Seeing the performance of this machine usually puts us ahead."

See related topics: Buying Process, Critical Interaction.

SALES STRATEGY

A strategy is a plan to move from the current situation to a preferred situation in the future. A sales strategy is a predefined plan to win the sale from the competition. Ideally the strategy starts at the beginning of the sales cycle and is enacted through Critical Interactions as the sales progresses. Strategy, tactics and process are intimately linked.

Example: "This is a key sale in a competitor's account. We need to do everything we can to win this one, including offering the best price."

See related topics: Sales Process, Sales Tactics.

SALES TACTICS

Tactics are the actions that are used to put strategies into effect. If tactics are executed successfully, as planned, then the strategy is on the way to happening. Tactics are executed through Critical Interactions and are the "hook" between the strategy and the sales process.

Example: "I know that Roger Smith is central in the politics of the organization. I'll take him to lunch to see if he knows how the decision will be made."

See related topics: Sales Strategy.

SALES TEAM

The sales team is the group of people whose mission is to convince the customer that their solution is better than that of their competitors. The team can comprise of field salespeople, inside salespeople, sales administration, technical support or any other group that supports the sales effort.

Example: "If Ralph from Technical Support had not come with us to the factory, the customer would not have been convinced that the Type 560 could do the job."

See related topics: Sales Department.

SCIENCE OF SELLING

The science of selling is a set of rules that describe how to handle a sale, specifically, where certain skills and strategies should be employed, and to what degree they should be used. These rules have been compiled and refined over many years by sales professionals.

Example: "I'm about halfway through this sale, and still have a lot of proving to do with this customer—I would be stupid to try to close this now."

See related topics: Art of Selling.

SERVICE DEPARTMENT

The group within the company responsible for all aspects of supporting a product or service after a customer has purchased it from the sales department. In the customer acquisition and retention loop, service follows on from sales, but the CRM process flows from service to marketing, because at the end of a product's life cycle, the customer may need a replacement, and marketing must be aware of this new potential for business.

Example: "Bob from service called me to say that GDPN Boston have two of our old Type 90's that will need replacing next year. I'll alert marketing to make sure they meet up with them at next week's Print Show in Los Angeles."

See related topics: Marketing Department, Sales Department.

SFA (SEE SALES FORCE AUTOMATION)

SKILL PHASE

A skill phase is a phase of the sales cycle in which one of the fundamental skills of selling is dominant over the others. There are three skill phases corresponding to the three fundamental skills of probe, prove and close.

Example: "My sales automation system is telling me that I have twelve opportunities that are in the Close Phase. I only have two in Prove Phase and none in Probe. I need to bug marketing for some more leads."

See related topics: Close Phase, Probe Phase, Prove Phase.

TERRITORY

The Territory is the list of accounts over which a salesperson has been given the responsibility to sell their products. Territory Management is one of the four core competencies of the management of selling.

Example: "My territory was expanded today, from everywhere south of Broad Street and west of 67th, to the whole southern half of the city."

See related topics: Territory Group, Account, Contact, Sales Cycle.

TERRITORY GROUP

The Territory Group is the administrative structural organization of the territories belonging to a specific sales team. The territory group concept makes it easier to administer changes in territory responsibilities that happen through company growth or product expansion.

Example: "When Steve leaves, I get his territory, which means that I sell the IC line, and take on the extra geography of the East."

See related topics: Territory.

TWO-WAY INTERACTION

Two-way interactions are willing dialogues between the customer and the salesperson that happen in real time (face-to-face, or on the phone), or quasi real time (e-mail, voice mail, or even fax or letter).

Example: "I sat with the customer for two hours, and we had ample opportunity to discuss how our product could solve a lot of issues in his process."

See related topics: Critical Interaction, Customer Interaction, Non-Essential Interaction, One-Way Interaction, Opportunity Focused Interaction, Relationship Focused Interaction.

WEIGHTED SALES FORECAST

A sales forecast in which the revenue associated with each sales opportunity is multiplied by the percentage probability of winning the order. The results are then summed across all opportunities.

Example: "The Lexington deal is huge; around $1,000,000. But at 10%, our chances are really low. That will still contribute $100,000 to my weighted forecast."

See related topics: Binary Sales Forecast, Sales Forecast.

"WHEN WILL IT HAPPEN?"

The answer to "When will it happen?" is the salesperson's best estimation of when the customer will finally decide which vendor will receive their business and awards an order. "When will it happen?" is one of the three IBO Essentials.

Example: "We've been working at this for nine months. I am sure we will see the order two months from now, at the end of our third quarter."

See related topics: IBO Essentials, "Will it happen?", "Will we get it?".

"WILL IT HAPPEN?"

"Will it happen?" is a question that tests the salesperson's opinion on whether a sales opportunity will go through to completion. The answer to "Will it happen?" can be one of three choices: High, Medium, or Low. "Will it happen?" is one of the three IBO Essentials.

Example: "This customer has budgeted for a Type 560 and is acting like he will get the cash, but he's tried before and has been unsuccessful. I would say that 'Will it happen?' is Medium."

See related topics: IBO Essentials, "Will we get it?", "When will it happen?".

"WILL WE GET IT?"

"Will we get it?" is a question that tests the salesperson's opinion on his or her chances of winning the sale over the competition in the event that the sale goes through to completion. "Will we get it?" can be one of three choices: High, Medium, or Low. "Will we get it?" is one of the three IBO Essentials.

Example: "This division of Lexington has nothing else but Universal Equipment. The customer is happy, and I think for this sales opportunity, 'Will we get it?' is Low."

See related topics: IBO Essentials, "Will it happen?", "When will it happen?".

WORKFLOW

Workflow is the process of getting a task completed by dividing it into discreet chunks, each of which is handled by a different person or group. When complete, the chunk is moved to the next person or group in the process. Workflow works best when it moves electronically, and not using paper.

Example: "The new system for processing orders works well. The salesperson checks the customer's purchase order, and if it's OK, passes it to sales administration to write up. The details then go to order entry for processing."

See related topics: CRM Process.

INDEX

Want to know more?

To view a continuing discussion on the ideas presented in *sales automation done right*, visit the SalesWays Web Site at:

www.salesways.com

- communicate with the author, and the team of creators of the sales methods described in the book
- learn about OPM (Opportunity Portfolio Management) Sales Training programs, that explore these sales methods in more depth
- join the ongoing blog discussion on new ideas and developments in sales methodology, techniques, strategy, and all technological issues that affect sales
- check on the latest CRM and SFA technology products that employ the ideas *of sales automation done right*